4 Days in Eternity

 4 Days in Eternity

4 Days in Eternity

4 Days in Eternity

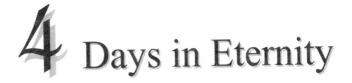 4 Days in Eternity

An Authentic Personal Afterlife Experience

Wayne F.A. Marentette

First Printing, 2001

"There is no greater time than the present. The hidden etheric world of the soul is becoming visible with each passing current event. Only the choice for objectivity remains."
W.M.

ISBN 0-9689985-0-X

Cover illustration by Timothy Phillips

Manufactured in Canada
By White Pines Graphics & Marketing

4 Days in Eternity

Contents

Introduction

This book is dedicated, as am I,
to my beautiful son,
Michael J.J. Marentette.

Introduction

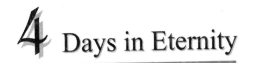# 4 Days in Eternity

Introduction

Before I started writing this evening, I had been imagining the future and what it will be like to hold and embrace our expected son - to see him and to know him as he grows into the world. What kind of a world he will come to know that we are building for him today - and how very important it will be for us, as his parents, to reveal and share the truths and beauty of life itself to him directly. I went on to imagine the millions of other children who would be born in the same month and how these same innocent ones will receive impressions of life from the rich fount of diverse truths of their respective parents. I imagined that within forty years my son's generation will have brought into the manifest world what we, the parents, have inspired in them or denied them as a whole.

My son's world and generation will be shaped by the overall results of humanity's collective dreams that are taking form today, although it will be this newest generation, born at the turn of the 21st century, who will shape today's influences into the profit of the many tomorrow. For I believe that my son's children will profit in wisdom unlike any generation before them, that we are on the brink of a miraculous discovery and that, in spite of any pessimistic or intellectual argument, what has always been innately true yet hidden in the mysterious world of dreams will soon be known to us all. I further believe, and have my own evidence for doing so, that the inventiveness of these next two generations will demonstrate special skills of genius that have been latent in all of us but not within our reach until the birth of the age of technology and artificial intelligence. Of course we will have to let the future bear evidence for itself if my claim is ever to be acknowledged. Even the present condition and instruments of communication used today by humanity, however, bear direct witness to the role that inventive and inspirational dreams will play in the discovery of the spirit within mankind.

For 18 years, since my first experience with near death and dying, I have anxiously laboured to gather every detail that would need to be brought together to prove that the seemingly elusive secrets, mysteries and miracles of life are themselves clearly observable in our dreams and evident to any thinker who might begin to observe the inner world in which the panorama of dreams and impressions takes place. My personal experiences in the afterlife, originally gained over a full four-day period, had led me to a committed study

of my own sensible equipment of mind and consciousness, as well as the psychological history of humanity
and the interactive dream faculty of the masses. I had
studied how it was, and had always been, that the
dreams of one generation of thinkers were the manifest
circumstances endured by all present; how the dreams
of one nature had brought confusion and eventual personal misery to our shared world populations through
manifest expression, while other objective and inventive dreams renewed hope and restored the creative
inventiveness of whole societies; how our common
dreams responsibly raised one civilization to greater
liberty, and yet how unregulated and selfish dreams
had irresponsibly toppled another. In these ways, I
came to understand clearly how it is today that dreams
have become the founding instruments of the enlightened, and yet the imprisoning limitations of the
unaware.

Even then, the evidence discovered along these
lines only amounted to the personal or individual perceptual attainments in the interpretation of the mass
Psyche throughout history. Something much more tangible or realistic, I presumed, such as an event or personal experience that could be confirmed by the
majority with regard to dreams themselves could lead
to the ultimate proof that I sought to reveal. It was
when I realized that only through direct and intimate
personal experience would it be possible for one to
know this great revelation of dreams, that I sought dili-
gently to blend the gains and insights of afterlife experiences with developing the personal skill to communicate these insights. For the first 12 of the last 18
years, I set my sights on finding the way to communi-

cate and instruct an individual directly, so that the event of discovery could occur equally if not uniquely for them. My goal became to demonstrate that the truth of an afterlife could be attained by a thinker before death itself. And that is why this book has taken so long to be written in the present form.

It was not until others had come to verify the experience and evidence of an afterlife for themselves that it could have been possible to have begun to reveal my own experiences in the afterlife in a way that went beyond that of mere suggestion. I knew that the only value in writing about my own experiences of death and life would come about if others could somehow profit from them directly. It had to be that those who would consider the subject and its plausible merits should have the possibility of discovering for themselves that there was much to celebrate about life once it could be known that death was an illusion. I hesitated for great lengths of time feeling I was not ready yet, that the book had to wait, thinking that such a sacred truth deserved the most of what I could possibly offer and there were to be many more experiences beyond the threshold of death that needed to be played out in this life before the whole picture came together as a genuine benefit to others.

On many early occasions throughout these past 18 years, I had often allowed personal friends to know that I had experienced something beyond the moment of death, and that I might even write about this one day. At other times, less invited by myself, it simply became a matter of curiosity for people to ask me questions when they heard that I had been driven over by an automobile and had not been expected to survive.

For many, it was the apparent hoarseness of my salvaged voice that led them from one question to another and always ended with their asking me if I had seen anything or experienced anything like an out-of-body experience. It was very difficult having to explain myself many times over before the full picture became evident to them, at which point I often observed the limits of their speculation of me as an individual. After all, how many thinkers expect to have a conversation with someone who thinks that they have overwhelming evidence in support of the afterlife? I learned the shock that would occur for those who hadn't a clue how to even imagine it to be thus. And so I learned to be private about such things until I could find the medium that would provide answers to the many questions that would naturally occur. For this, and many other reasons that need not be stated here, I am well pleased to have held my patience until now.

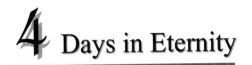

4 Days in Eternity

Part I
No One Dies

The Night that I Died
London, Ontario: 4 May 1979

My father used to say to anyone who would listen, and often without being requested, 'You can't take anything with you when you leave this world, and you'll be lucky to take out what you came in with.' I have only recently come to understand the perception behind his words, though on the night that I was run down by a car, I had spent several hours contemplating these and other sayings of his all alone in a quiet, snoozy hotel restaurant, adjacent to the parking lot where it had all taken place. I had been daydreaming the whole time.

I had moved to London, Ontario only three weeks prior to that night, and had registered to attend the University of Western Ontario once the summer sessions had ended, having accepted a job as a sales rep. in a downtown furniture store where I had expected to earn my way through the next few years. But I wasn't settled with myself. For more than six months previously I had determined to make the move away from my home town to return to school and to quit my job, which ultimately meant breaking a lot of earlier commitments. So many friends and family members were being left behind due to this unexpected decision, and I was struggling most with my conscience over having to separate from my young daughter. Even though I had given every possible consideration to my thought, of the cost that would occur for those I chose to leave in favour of returning to university without their best wishes, and even though I felt it was necessary personally, I couldn't breach the impasse. Was it selfish of me? I wondered at great length. I was unable to rest at heart or in mind.

I would often ignore the facts of my choice and move ahead throughout the day without any serious impediment, though on that night in the restaurant I was determined to settle the matter with my conscience and to bring myself to a final choice. A great deal of dreaming and deduction took place that early evening, including my father's advice, but I could not yet truly decide whether to stay in London or to go back and honour my previous commitments. I told myself that I would think it over again the next day, and with that I was up and ventured into the hotel nightclub if only for a change of pace.

I ordered a drink and stood alongside a raised bar, out of the way of conversation for a time. I was feeling self-contained and reserved that night, and I know that my mood at that time opened my eyes to the events before me in the same light. Being unattached and almost uninterested in the activity that increased over the next two hours, I began to sense the futility that would appear in many of the faces I observed as they turned away from conversation with one another. I seemed to see clearly that night how difficult it was for most to be genuine and unassuming. How pretentious we can all be at times. How easily we cover up our hidden burden of aloneness and uncertainty. It was then that I realized it was time to go home. I was only looking into the same mirror again. 'Have to change my mood', I thought. Generally, I was very friendly and accommodating throughout my early years, and so it wasn't difficult to avoid becoming despondent though complacency sure had set into my stride as I walked towards the exit sign that evening.

Exit

Once I had come to the exit, an overbearing figure leaned heavily into my sight and, without words, I sensed that I was to find another way out. A moment later, this same shadowy figure glanced in another direction and I made my move swiftly beneath his raised arm and out the door almost undetected.

The early spring night air was chilled and misty, which seemed to reflect the tone of the voices I heard echoing off and along the tarred pavement. My attention was turned back towards the exit door where only a moment before I had noticed this same heavy figure leaning. He had a threatening look on his face that I interpreted as verging on hostility, and I thought that his obvious yet voiceless expression might be intended for me when I noticed a couple standing along the side of the building only a few feet from where I had previously been standing. I couldn't help but listen to the argument between this young couple that was becoming more vocal and I decided to linger a while longer, if only to find out the gist of their disagreement. Even then, my curiosity seemed to wane as I sensed the potential for a more violent situation at hand.

I walked a little further towards my parked car though I was still near enough to witness the event as it progressed. Moments later, I was looking in the direction of my car when I heard a convulsive noise. My first impression was that a light bulb had shattered, but as I turned in the direction of the sound I realized that the young woman - who moments earlier had been standing and arguing aloud with her apparent companion - had fallen to the ground. Closer inspection of the scene revealed that the man she was with had broken a beer bottle across her face, and blood was flowing quickly from her facial lacerations. I watched as he continued to strike at the woman and began to wonder somewhat angrily why the figure in the exit door area was not intervening. In fact, he was preventing a growing number of people from exiting into the lot.

It was then that I screamed aloud for him to do something. He responded with a threatening look, as if to say that I should move on and mind my own business. I was overcome by the thought that delivering such an imposing threat to me was of more importance to him than the woman who was helplessly being assaulted right before his eyes.

Shouting and screaming voices issued loudly from the exit door and I watched as a number of individuals broke through to the parking lot and began to encircle the struggling female and her assailant. Without thinking first, I began to run over to the area that was now filling with large numbers of spectators, and tried desperately to get through the huddle of onlookers so as to intervene. Seconds passed before I lunged instinctively towards the man who had continued to strike the female with his fists. We struggled together for a time before he ran out towards the parking area where I observed him feverishly trying to get his key into the door of his car. It was then that I noticed the pain in my jaw and realized that my jaw had been fractured.

I started to walk out into the open area of the parking lot and was assessing my situation as a few men came to enquire what had happened to me and what had occurred earlier. As I turned to point in the direction of the man I had struggled with, the four of us noticed that his car had backed violently into another vehicle close to his own. Seconds later, as I watched him pull away from another parked car, I came to understand that I was still a target for him. I could see him wipe his bloodied suit sleeve across his face as he spun around and accelerated into my exact direction. His facial expression foretold what was about to occur.

I sensed he wanted to just get away quickly from the scene but his apparent embarrassment had given way to selfish neglect. I tried to move out of the range of the approaching vehicle though I was feeling quite faint and one of the men, who had earlier tried to communicate with me, reached out dramatically in an attempt to help me out of the area.

It was too late. I was unable to move away and found myself beginning to fall to the ground. 'Oh my God!' I thought.

Before my knees had hit the ground I was struck by the car. I remember losing my breath suddenly and then my right cheek was forced into the hood of the car just slightly above the front grill. Airborne and helpless, my limbs bounced mercilessly upon the pavement a moment later. It seemed that a frightful silence had seized the night about me. Verging on unconsciousness, I struggled to open my eyes. I was able to see partially, though everything seemed to be spinning and abstract. Fortunately, I noticed that the car had stalled only a few feet in front of me as it was forced to climb an island surrounding the entrance and exit area of the lot. I had thought that the event was over but I was wrong. I heard the roar of the engine and also recognized the sound of the car winding into reverse. Vaguely, I remember turning my head to the left as the rear tires pressed upon and over my chest.

First Impressions after Death

My mind was surging with impressions. There was no sense of pain at the time and for a brief moment, in spite of what was occurring in mind, I sensed that somehow, I would survive. I could hear the crowd about me and I sensed that my hearing was greatly diminished, though I could still recognize the sounds of a number of approaching ambulance or emergency vehicles. Each passing moment seemed like an eternity of its own, yet I couldn't help but notice a humming feeling coming from somewhere within me. It was as if I could hear the feeling itself. This feeling was not only curious but it was a very inviting sound. My attention was drawn to seek the source of this mysteriously soothing rhythm for some time, and I probably would have continued to surrender to this seductive and dreamy influence if it were not for a sudden reminder that I was in trouble.

A young woman who was standing nearby, had leaned over me and attempted to place something behind my neck. Turning my focus away from the former dreamlike impressions, I heard her telling me that she was just trying to help me breathe. As much as I wanted to reach out to her, I was unable to communicate. It was as if an angel of mercy had taken pity on my lifeless body. I wanted so much to embrace her.

This thought kept running through my mind and it seemed to me that the noticeable increase of the humming sound from within had something to do with my overall yearning for her to comfort me. Seemingly detached from any physical connection with my body, yet continuing to experience emotion and sentiment, my attention was absorbed in trying to remain receptive to this growing and seemingly sensitive sound. I felt as if I was being awakened to something never before understood by myself in these first brief illuminating moments. I was conscious of the apparent choice I had as to which way I could direct my focus.

I attempted to open my eyes at one point, wondering if the continued feeling and the apparent sound might itself be coming from outside of myself, and noticed that I was unable to raise my eyelids. No response came to my willed thought, and though it became more clear to me that I might be dying, I remained calm and peaceful. I felt convinced that all would be well.

My breathing had been very stressed since the first moments of impact upon the pavement, though now, as I inspected, I sensed that a refreshingly cool and sensuous source of free flowing oxygen was continuing to make it possible for me to survive, yet I could not tell if my lungs were working. All of my outer physical sensitivity had gone numb to me. I found myself entertaining the thought that, in spite of what seemed to be a disaster, something magnificent was happening. It felt as though an impression was seeking entry into my mind which, I intuited, I needed to resist, knowing that if I were to give in to it I could easily fall unaware into a dreamy sleep. A few moments later, I became aware of a growing and ominous sense of complete loss and doubt. It was as if all was quickly changing and becoming hopeless with regards to my survival, yet I was quietly unmoved emotionally and simply ignored the possibility and the doubts.

The thoughts of a lifetime began to merge in my mind as I wondered more about those who would be influenced personally by the ramifications of the evening that was unfolding. I began to think of those I was closest to, though I couldn't help but feel most captivated by the mystical experience of clearly noting all that had ever passed through my heart and mind over twenty-eight years of living. I felt as if some supersensible form of consciousness had come about in which I was able to understand timelessly so much that was not evident before. It was then that I noticed the familiar hum of the persistent yet gentle rhythm which had actually been responsible for the awakening and activation of a newly elevated sense of awareness.

I wasn't sure whether or not I had chosen to give in to this growing internal symphony, though I did note that the sound was like a voice. A heavenly voice. A voice of utter trust. In a short time I thought I was listening to a familiar harmony of merging voices. There was something strikingly familiar about the experience, and I could not make total sense of it right away, though I was now certain that the background sounds and rhythms were essentially responsible for what was now directly affecting my overall awareness of self. I concluded that my state of heart was allowing me to look into life through a new lens of perception. I surrendered quietly to the processes, thinking I could feel tears within me drop like hot, tiny pearls of wax from a lit candle within and at the door of my very soul. The tears of loss for this world, and for those that I had come to love, welled up from the root of myself. And what then came into my mind caused me to feel great shame in the ensuing separation between life and death.

I had only wished that those I loved could be happy. I felt I had failed them all. I felt as if it were a truth that I would have to face up to personally, and I tried desperately not to cloud the issues presented by feeling any empathy for myself. I felt I was to leave the world with a deepened sense of remorse for what had not been said soon enough, for what had not been done when it could have been done so easily. I felt that my own selfishness had veiled the truth from my eyes. I had been living for me, and my love of others was not genuine enough.

Wishing to accept the full brunt of my own accusation and overview, I became deeply quiet within. It was as if I were waiting for God's judgement and affirmation as I was overcome completely by a newer and more imminent sound that reverberated loudly throughout my emotional body.

A hissing sound in my ears and mind had captured my full consciousness, and it seemed imaginatively as if the very winds of the Earth were gathering together from out of the infinite breath of space itself. It was as if I was about to be snatched from my worldly existence by an all-engulfing breath. Surrealistic impressions and visions poured out very unexpectedly across the screen of my mind, leaving me to feel awed and astonished by the images themselves. It was as if it was intended that I should come to understand something of the agony and ecstasy of personal existence for all who had ever ventured into the world of temporal mortal living. I felt as if I had been guided to uncover some great mystery just beneath the surface of thought itself, that we all come to bear witness to eventually. I believed that I had found a place of relief and release from some great illusion of separateness. A place to rest within the soul of my consciousness itself. A place of illumination and harmony, where the accusations of a lifetime dissolve into greater vision. A place and a state or condition of utter enlightenment and bliss.

I was quite literally overcome by the sense of an invisible presence, yet I was not overly surprised to find that I was about to awake from a long dream of grief, futility, confusion and uncertainty. I gave in totally to the guiding sense of assurance, and in a great dark silence I listened closely to the last few beats of

my heart.
First Reflections after Death

It is quite amazing how fast the processes of thinking, breathing and movement are instinctively reduced to stillness when we are unexpectedly seized by a moment of awe or fright. It is equally amazing to observe the speed at which we recover sensibly from those unexpected near misses we all seem to have at various times during our lives and which, for most of us, thankfully never really occurred. And for a growing number of us in each passing generation, it is even more astonishing to have survived a life-threatening crisis or a near-death experience at the edge of our dreams' limits, where fear is ultimately revealed for the first time as an illusion of the senses.

It's no great secret that we all meditate on the possibility of death and dying many times during our maturing years. As we mature, though, we can perhaps expect more realism from our dreams than we were able to imagine when we were younger. It seems that as we grow older and gain more experience, the quality of our dreams can begin to take on a different dimension in reason, value, appearance and meaning. So too, as the mind likewise expands to accommodate our evolving thought processes, the faculty of mind opens to wider and greater vision. It is often at this later stage of maturity in life that unfounded fears no longer influence both our conscious everyday thinking and our dream life with the same youthful intensity or clumsiness.

The willingness to question everything on perhaps a much more serious and scientific as well as moral level is a common factor and practice for the majority of thinking adults nowadays. And in so many ways almost unimaginable, we have throughout history relentlessly attempted to understand ourselves and our existence through the sensory methodology of inspirational dreams. Yet it rarely occurs to most people that the innate desire for evidence of wisdom, beauty and truth can most easily be found upon the path of intentional dreams, and that lengthy concentration upon the source, environment and makeup of dreams themselves reveals the way. This path reveals the source of attractive dreams to be easily approachable, though it requires the ambition and patience to journey within, and to look more deeply into, our innate selves.

In many ways, the life journey over a period of years is identical in its demands and results to what happens in the first minutes of the death process itself, though we cannot at that point turn or dismiss our attention from the culminating processes. The fact remains that processing information is one of the most fundamental habits of thinking humanity, and when the hour strikes, such processes produce rapid results. What has been gleaned graciously and often painfully through the whole of one's life experience begins to surface in a timeless, culminating way, and the closer the moment of death draws near, the more rapidly our whole life event appears before our observing mind's eye.

Usually people wait for the day of death to arrive as their defining moment, leaving the possibility of experiential realization to chance alone and their unchecked personal habits and tendencies in dreams will feed other desires of the given day instead. Some people, however, attempt through dreams of faith, religion, hope or self betterment to gain some inspiring revelation of contact or communion with the self-appraised host spirit of their belief during their life, as a seeming conscious preparation, and may never consider the function of dreams as the linking bridge of our genius where we pass from wonder to astonishment.

It is only natural for a thinker to dream along the lines of their habitual dreams that were first established in early childhood, and it is rare for someone to think in some new way that has yet to be introduced to them from outside the range of their own personal ideals and dreams. For example, if you had considered yourself to be mortal most of your adult life but had started to wonder about the possibility of an afterlife, you would only have older and less scientific associations with which to begin your contemplation. Most people would not necessarily know that they could deliberately consider the processes of death scientifically as it may occur moment by moment, free of any previous beliefs or limits in education.

What could we possibly consider that would bring about a moment of inspiration and revelation upon which we could be sure of our footing and which would be a fitting start along these lines? What dream could appear in our mind that would reveal the starting point? Could it be that in thinking, we have not yet searched the space or environment within which our dreams appear, and how it is that by detaching from these connective dreams and from unintentional thinking itself, we would have the sure semblance of an afterlife experience then and there? Would we even notice what is left of ourselves, in a formless world of consciousness, where our mind is utterly stilled and calm? How would it be like death, we would have to ask - and how to answer without dreaming into the thought itself? What is it to know and to be as we were in body though without form or imagining? The very thought itself and the possible answers can only come through recognizing and then attempting to assimilate the conditions stated. As it is for many today however, the very thought has yet to be initiated.

Could we learn something about our own use of mind through intentional observation which we did not know before, such as the fact that our mind and dreams are merely instruments and impressions of our innate intelligent self? That the mind serves the realizer, and that the realizer is the source? That the conscious self is doubtlessly known when mind and dreams are harnessed to a quieted state? Many thinkers have approached this line of thought and are defined or viewed in our modern society as scientists and meditative thinkers. The art and act of meditation I have found, is closest to the attempt to assimilate death without having to actually die. Only because of my own afterlife and death experiences have I come to know that the processes of dying, and mediation upon the event itself, is similar in personal experience right up to the moment that we actually leave our body. What occurs thereafter can also be captured through the learned art of meditative practices. However, such individual ambition and scientific scrutiny is a rarity today. Only the most dedicated aspirants to this knowledge can bear evidence to the facts I am stating here today, and the exercise itself comes to these few at the expense of a lifetime of study.

Experience is the key beyond dreams and for those who meditate, though they may not have had an afterlife experience for themselves to help them along, the truth of life and death can be uncovered. There is no need to be unprepared for the greatest challenge our life offers us beyond the threshold of death, though there is a need to understand that we are not so different as we might imagine after we take leave of our bodies, at least in respect to our sense of identity. True, we lose our ignorance and our misgivings give way to clarity, our confusion to certainty, our fears to triumph, our illusory dreams to reality, and our sense of self is fully revealed to be illimitable, yet it is so unfortunate that we suffer much today in the absence of such evidence.

Few today would actually spend much time intentionally wondering what it might be like, even if they found out tomorrow that they have never been less than immortal to begin with. What would your mind produce as a hypothesis, if it were true that we knowingly entered temporarily into form, and then liberated ourselves from form with such an unrecognized ease during our life, just as when we awaken from our sleeping dreams? And what if it were true, that the willingness to let go of the memory of the self that was within the dreams of our evening sleep as we awaken were identical to what will occur when we seemingly leave the form that we utilized for the dream of incarnation?

The hypothesis suggests directly that the awakened sleeper in the end is the soul and that we are, at this moment in form, a living dream of real influence and vital experience projected by the meditating soul within. What if it were true that we only ever truly live just one continuous life, though for a time we have deemed it necessary to experience our existence through the modifications and influences of shapes, forms, personalities and appearances?

Let us assume, as a hypothesis, that as immortal beings we were actually able to define our own expression of intent by exerting some aspect of our will so as to compose an informing impression of communication with others. Would we then understand more of the vital importance to develop experience in our sensory related world? The hypothesis of soul, and the desire for ultimate comprehension of our innate potential, runs not only through the light rays of our soul but through the veins of our own personality motivations in form. We love to exert, to emote, to express and to embrace a measured impression of our invisible experiences. In love, we are moved to action and demonstration of our own central experience, and so too has the spirit in us all been moved to embrace the whole of the eternal revelation.   What if we spent time imagining the possibility instead of ignoring it, or simply maintaining our other dreams upon the subject of death and dying as they are today? Would it make a difference?

I believe the answer is that the fruits of our gained overall realization of self, thus far, may well be known to us more through the medium of our historic dreams. And so it follows that more intentional dreaming, along inspirational lines, would result in greater revelation upon the fact itself.

It seems that our past dreams and interpretations of life are so special to us already that they may take up more of our everyday consciousness than we need to give thought to, thereby disabling us unconsciously from a necessary consideration of other potentials. Being unable to maintain concentration throughout the

day is often due to unfinished dreams and their conditioning attachments, emotionally and mentally. I would
say that the habit of dreaming about past dreams over
and over again may not be so easy to break in order to
get on with new dreams of newer truths. If you are a
frequent dreamer, it may not hurt to spend your dreaming time on something more challenging and potentially valuable.

I had never considered the application along such
lines myself until I was actually confronted with the
reality of imminent death. However, I know that when
our time does come, whatever we have dreamt of in
life, whether vague and imaginary or held to be true,
cannot serve any purpose beyond supposition for what
has yet to be actually experienced. By habit, those who
have yet the time to meet their moment of death consciously, though unenlightened, will only have the
speculative dreamy impressions of the true life to rely
on for comforting until the veil of illusion is lifted once
and for all within the first minutes of actual release
from the physical form. The only other option is to be
prepared by undertaking a serious study of one's true
nature beforehand, where it is very possible to have
experiences that bear true evidence to the fact of a
continuing life beyond the limits of the human form.

The dreams that we weave through every day of our
true experiences in the world will fall away for a time
when we enter into the first stages of actual death, giving way only to the true moments and sentiments of our
unchanged and actualized experiences. It is as if a
moment comes when the need to think or imagine
passes, and the experience at hand begins to dominate
our given attention. What begins in death is a release

from the noises of many unnecessary dreams and a graduating freedom from the innate voices of suggestion and accusation. A new conscious experience in liberty emerges and the quieted soul, free from the fetters of the thinking dreaming world, rests peacefully for a time as an awakened dreamer, absorbing the fruits of a greater revelation of eternity before another stage unfolds in the continuing drama of unending life.

Beyond our imagined perceptions and dreams, free from the impressions of sleep, an awakening occurs to a consciousness of life itself, and the previously unanswered dreams of a lifetime no longer veil the view of reality from our continued vision. Nothing changes for the thinker in the afterlife excepting the loss of all ignorance. Much in the way that we rise from our nightly sleep of dreams to the dawn of a new day in our human life, often elated to know we were only in a dream, we all awaken to ourselves in the living world of eternity to our originating self-consciousness and identity. It is truly amazing how quickly we recover without remorse from the imagined dream of life as a mortal when the final stages of liberty are passed.

How unimaginably beautiful and true is the life we truly live beyond the shadows of uncertain dreams. How very important it is to have remembered ourselves for the first time in eternity. And how ineffably, immeasurably perfect the future venture and glory, once the soul has awakened from the dream of sleep to the dream of life. Imperishability! The truth is imperishable! We are the imperishable truth!

The Afterlife Drama: Stage I

The last few surges and murmurs of my pulse echoed throughout my consciousness, though I was not aroused to respond. I simply allowed myself to participate wholly in the final outcome. It seemed as if several minutes had passed before I came to realize that a heavy, cold feeling had begun to fill my chest cavity. I felt I was losing the former warmth of my body very quickly now. As I continued to observe, I became innately chilled and just as quickly, for some unknown reason, I began to feel my whole body again! Even my hands, feet, and particularly my nose, could be felt again. I was even more astonished when the freezing cold all about me had quietly begun to feel very hot only seconds later. I couldn't understand what was occurring as I was yet unable to move, even though my physical body was alight again. In fact, my body had become so very hot thereafter, that I instinctively attempted to rise up from the ground then and there.

Unable to have any effect upon my form, I felt I was being pressed back further into myself with each repeated attempt to arise. I thought that I had begun to tremble and shake within as an overpowering weight seemed to press upon me more and more with each passing moment, as if to crush me. It felt like a rock had been tossed onto my chest, as if I was being suffocated, when suddenly I sensed I was about to fall consciously, from deeply within myself. The heat in my body became more evident and seemed to increase most dramatically about the chest, throat and head, while I imagined how I might yet take hold of something more tangible.

It was in the following moments, as I began to fall faintly into myself, that a sound reverberated throughout my own inner space. I was plucked as it were, from a vast, empty, inner space, by a sound not unlike a trumpet. It was as if I had attached myself to the only sound of life that remained clear to me. It was the 'hmmm' sound, though this time I noted that it consisted of three basic notes. The sound continued aloud, and I felt I was being elevated back to the surface where my lifeless body lay once more. The weight upon my throat had lifted, though a foul gaseous taste appeared. My first reaction was to clear my throat and to take a deep breath of fresh air. This time, when I made the effort to rise, it seemed effortless. I was stilled in awe, as I found myself eyes open wide and standing directly over my own body.

I took in a breath quickly, though I noticed that there was no limit to the volume I was able to draw upon. I looked around and about myself and noticed that it had become as light as day though I also knew without thinking, that it was mid evening. It all seemed so wonderful. I was filled with utter ecstasy in the realization that I had not died. Something else had occurred though I was unable to think about it. I simply understood all that was now occurring. It was quite normal to leave the body in such a manner, not just for myself but for everyone else. I was now in the afterlife and I knew clearly that much lay ahead, though I was now free and had begun to enter into another stage of consciousness hitherto unimagined. All this and more without the need to think, imagine or wonder, as I had when I was subject to the limiting factors of my human form. I knew then that death was an overwhelming illusion. I knew also that under the illusion of a mortal perception, the satisfaction of life had never been truly appreciated for what it truly is. If only we could have known in our youth that our life is such that no one dies. No one dies.

I knew that I was not yet ultimately free from my form as a conscious sensory connection remained, and that there was time enough to venture further into the drama of the afterlife condition without concern. So I drew away from the scene on the lot and entered into a welcoming light of immeasurable revelation that appeared before me.

Interlude

We can all expect one day that, regardless of what we have imagined possible, our time will come and what was not known before will be seen clearly in the afterlife. What we did not understand this time around will be revealed and understood. How it was that we did not remember, or why it is that we do undertake such a process of life and seeming death, will not be so mysterious to us. It is not as if we learn something new in a human way that aids our understanding when we are liberated from our form. It is more a fact that we remember once again what was overwhelmingly true before we even arrived at our birth. What could never be forgotten returns to our comprehension. It is as if we awaken, not for the first time, but perhaps for the last time, to an ancient yet timeless past - to the remembrance of our true nature, our soul's objective, our eternal journey, and the next step ahead to be taken.

The Afterlife Drama: Stage I *continued*

When I was nearing the first stages of the death process as mentioned above, I was keenly aware that something had changed for me that was directly related to my overall sense of intelligence and consciousness. There had been many brief and fleeting moments during my adolescent years in which I had sensed a momentary elevation of awareness. Sometimes, I had recalled feeling quite intuitive for long periods and cycles throughout my years. Other times, I remember very clearly how it was to feel overcome by something I would have deemed sanctified or holy. I had never given much thought to these moments though I had come to depend on them later in life and would often reflect upon those times when I felt I was able to commune with some aspect of Divinity. I used to suppose it possible to come close to such truths and ideals, such as religion, where through deep reverence or devotion one might be touched or moved by the spirit, though I never consciously understood how truly imminent and natural it was and could have been.

Through the first stages in the afterlife, I had doubtless recalled the familiar rhythm that had been with me throughout my life, though hidden below the threshold of my mind's eye. It was a familiar dream that first appeared before me in the first hours of my afterlife experiences. A dream about the past that never seemed able to break the surface yet somehow managed to gain entry symbolically through my imaginings and dreams in youth. There was a direct link from a more innocent age that had tied a number of memories together in time and which I first recognized as I took the first steps away into a familiar light.

Several thoughts came together all at once in the afterlife experiences and, as the moments passed, I became accustomed to this. It seemed that from one level of focus I could tell what was passing through the minds of those at the site of the incident who were trying to salvage my life. From another level, I realized what was about to take place just a few miles away at the hospital. In other ways, yet simultaneously, I could see and understand the recent past for all who were directly influenced by my accident that evening, including the very man who ran me over. I was somehow able to know that these events and individuals were made up from the same ingredients and collectively amounted to a single experience. There was no real separation other than our bodies and imagined perspectives that evening. All those with whom I came into contact were united not by chance, but by the invisible web of light that now shone ever more brightly about each figure. This state of consciousness that had somehow been naturally implemented or restored, and a visionary sight quite enhanced and unlike that of the human sense of sight, melded multiples of impressions into one cohesive vision and realization for my own digestion at will. I had simply taken it for granted while in a euphoric state that this new sight was and had always been my true sight. Likewise, it was completely taken for granted that the ability to comprehend many things at once was only natural. Through the awakening to greater vision, I had come to realize more fully that there was a practical use of this faculty that went beyond the range of normal or average human thinking.

I had began to turn my vision upon myself, if only to see my own appearance. It seemed the important thing to do, though priorities never seemed to play a role. There was no need for an indication or sense of priority, though there was a slight sense of an urge that became the motive of my enquiry at that time. I understood later how it was that there was an intended structure to the design of the afterlife drama. How it becomes played out to its own ends, though then I only trusted that a greater awakening lay ahead, beyond the impressions that appeared and disappeared before my waiting watchful eye.

When I tried to look at myself, I found that certain physiological traits remained in consciousness, though there was not a body to be found. I had expected legs and arms, hands and fingers, though only the vision of a radiant electric blue light emerged before my sight. I thought of touching my chest and then my face. As I attempted this, I recalled the feeling of my body, though there were only the manifest associations of my expectations to observe. I did indeed have a discrete body. I did remain as an individual in the full sense of self. However, such appearances were largely designed to suit my aspirations and will. I felt very strong yet incredibly gentle. Tall and slim, yet boundless. My hair was long and silky. I could sense a warmth of an atmosphere about me and I could taste sweet water pouring over my soul, revitalizing and cleansing me. I felt I could drink the universe if I chose to. A greater youth and vitality engulfed me then and yet I could even feel the pain of the past sentiments of and for my recently liberated body.

It was shortly thereafter that my attention turned

once again to the familiar sense of my own form as it lay upon the operating table. Instantly, my experience transformed before me. I had not moved into the light before me on the parking lot yet, though I was now present in the hospital and listening to the thoughts and was living the actual experience of the doctors and assistants that were present. I sensed I could experience any other individual's experience. I also knew then that this was how it was for the distinctly informing presence nearby, that had remained invisibly close, yet impersonal throughout this period.

A mood came over me as I drew closer to my own body. I felt as if I were being urged to enter into my body once again and without electing to consider otherwise, with utter trust, I re-entered. My body had a diminishing effect on my sensory capacity for a brief few moments and as I tried to gain some control over the form itself, I felt as if I were instructed to communicate aloud to those attending nearby. I was elated to discover that I was able to raise my arm into the air. One of several surgeons who were present that evening noticed my activity and ran quickly to my side. He was trying to communicate with me and was asking for my name. I could not open my mouth much less speak. I motioned to him with my hand that I wished to write out a message. He put something in my hand, and thinking it to be a pen, I began to write out a phone number. I also felt urged to have him make contact with my family but before I could finish, I held my breath silently and then passed out of my body once more. I watched then as he seemed alarmed to have made contact and now my life signals had stopped once more.

I discovered that the chief surgeon was about to let me alone after they had come to understand the situation at hand. He thought that it would not be of benefit to continue before I had raised my arm in an attempt to communicate. They had determined that I was too unstable and that I would not make it now that I had drowned in my own blood. My lungs had been punctured by ribs breaking through under the pressure of the car tyres when they passed over my chest. My heart has suffered failure three times by then, and a massive contusion to the heart area meant extensive surgical procedures. My spleen had literally blown up inside the abdomen and lacerations had torn my pancreas in half. Problems with kidneys, stomach, intestine and much more were just becoming evident to them, though as the list of injuries was being weighed a new decision to proceed was made.

The telephone number I had given them was an unlisted number and it was established later that same evening that formal contact with my family had been made even though no form of identification had been found previously. I remember noticing at that exact time that the clues to my identity were partly the reason that the surgeons had persisted once I had arrived in emergency. It was thought that I was a police officer and certain officials present were very concerned with the kind of treatment I was getting. It was established later when the phone call had been made to my family that I was not a policeman on the scene that night as they had originally assumed, but the evidence of my identity as the brother of a police officer proved to be a curious thing for all concerned. Whatever they had believed was of no consequence to me at the time, and

I was very much at peace with what was occurring as the decision to proceed with life support systems and extensive surgery had begun.

Transition

Whether I lived or not was not an issue for me any more. My extended life beyond the body was all that interested me and just as quickly as I had returned to my body, I exited once more. Back to the exacting moment on the scene at the lot, I felt as if I had moved through time and was elated. There before me was the radiant light of a portal, an entry of sorts into a new dimension that was beginning to feel so familiar and yet, there on the pavement before me, was my breathless body, not yet attended to!

Somehow I had been moved to the future which would have been no more than one hour later and then returned to the past but with the keen sense that I truly was in the continuing present. Looking away from my body and into the light portal directly in front of me, I sensed the proper method of movement and entry by a conscious commitment to steadying my soul's breath. It was as if I had naturally surrendered all forms of thinking, imagining, vision and mind-use completely, as eventually a welcoming golden silence overcame my very being. It was an elating and vital silence. I felt infinitely alive and at home.

In this same silence I held my breath and the coolness and freshness of a familiar taste returned to my palate. I felt exquisitely quenched of a thirst I had not known to have existed previously. It was my thirst for oneness that was of my soul. It was at this moment that I first took note of a distinction between my continuing sense of self and my soul. My soul's life was becoming more apparent to me as I was immersed into what appeared to be a new outer world, yet I intuitively knew that 'I' as a personality was at the centre of my own psyche, much like being at the centre of my own dream as an onlooker to which I was accustomed when using my mind in body consciousness. I now found my mind to be an environment within my soul, there for the intended uses of my own psyche.

The environment was boundless, without ground, yet it was a place of its own. I also sensed that this experience was not unique and that this drama of the psyche was, and would be, this same way for everyone. It seemed as if days had passed before I realized that this space was a conscious resting ground for the psyche in the initial transformation process of death. It happened that I came to notice my own innate rejuvenation was not a withdrawal into the depths of a blissful sleep filled with dreams and images but rather a release from the hindrance of the limiting body of mortal ideas and previously unresolved impressions. I was expanding without borders and yet remained myself. I could not sense distance, yet movement was the obvious impression that I breathed outwards to. Only when I drew upon an outer breath did I notice the withdrawing of my own sensory nature back towards a central point and a reawakening of my personal consciousness. My breath inwards was the gravity of my sense of place and self. My breath outwards was the release of self restraint into the inclusive nature of the universe in which I lived and moved and had my being.

Surrounding me, and yet within me was the sensitive vehicle of my soul, more evident upon my awakening from this great long moment of rest than I had ever known. I had come to acknowledge my soul as my sheltering intelligent sensory guide in the ethers, and the overshadowing, informing and comforting presence of a Divine source. My soul became my host most vividly from this moment on.

The clarion sound I had followed into the light of this dimension was revealed as the unique sound of my own soul's individuality. That sound rang out vividly one more time and I was collected to myself once more as I was taken by the intentional direction of my soul to the next stages of the afterlife processes.

The form of communication between myself and my own soul was purely intuitive at this stage of the drama. Through the awakening that followed a silent period of rest and rejuvenation, I had learned to initiate responses from my soul to enquiries as they arose. Without ever forming questions in my mind, and without the usual hesitation and wondering that one might be accustomed to when formulating a question, my soul intervened quickly. Visual responses, that would have been part of the natural or functional use of mind while in human form, were countered with real life forms and appearances right before my mind's eye. It was as if a holographic environment would open before me and a drama would be played out which I was not controlling or had not initiated. The impressions in this drama appeared as lifelike as earthly life. Everything that I was used to in my earthly, sense-perceived environment, was included, yet there was more to the visions than I had expected, which led to newer insights into the mechanisms of the nature and environmental conditions in the afterlife.

These appearances were not so much scenarios conceived from my imagination as revelations. As they were played out, the point being made throughout was what I came to call my intuitive understanding, yet it was the means of communication that my soul was employing. It was extremely obvious that there was a tremendous intelligence working much closer to me than I had suspected previously. It was as if I were being inspired by listening to a sweet and pure voice rather than an uncertain human voice of rationality and reason. There was an extreme silence about me and when an impression came upon me, or through me, I understood precisely. It was as if I were the one giving the inspiration as I learned that I was indeed sharing the consciousness of my soul with myself. This duality registered easily in my mind and I suppose I accepted the fact that I was less informed and all the while the truth was within me and had not come to the surface before. I reckoned I was awakening to a certainty that was mine in another time. For all it mattered to me then, the whole drama could have ended and being left within the company of this great and wise companion of consciousness, I would gladly have surrendered. It was bliss indeed to know there were others and that the great ones were nearby.

Aside from the images of incomprehensibly beautiful spheres of life and the exacting quality of intelligence that transferred the truth of the light before my open eyes, there was so little I had come to realize, and more was all that I desired.

I was concentrating upon the picture of the Earth

below my feet and the many lights and movements that were passing in and out of view in the upper atmosphere of our planet and without second thought I found myself moving back to the world and entering into my own psyche again. I felt as if I were becoming healthier as the events proceeded. Each new revelation, such as the movement of souls coming and going in our world though invisible to the human eye, was an unexpected surprise. I was able to observe the themes of this inner world that was sadly undetected by the masses as the many intervening intelligence of our humanity went about the business of the moment.

The growing sense of inner strength and conviction renewed, allowed me to understand the ramifications of the fleeting yet cumulative responses of souls to their incarnate shadows. With each new revelation a stream of questions arose within me and was imperceptibly succeeded by a new series of direct impressions. It was as if the whole picture was revealed when only a partial curiosity arose in me. I had a feeling of jubilance as I ventured further into the process and surrendered to the return to my mind's environment. The outer world disappeared from sight as this inner world was re-entered and, along with the sense of endless awakening, wisdom and peace, I felt a heightened sensibility in my responses. It was as if I had become a supersensitive body of impressionability.

I was being allowed to observe the outer and inner appearances of a sentient body that belonged to advanced souls and to identify how it is that our human senses are merely the extensions of a greater sensibility belonging to the soul. I learned quickly that the mechanisms of the soul were responsible for the appearances of the human form and all its ability to foster and dissect information. Through feeling alone, a world of events was easily comprehended. There was no confusion and from this point onwards the revelations had a growing sense of infallibility. I had not expected to obtain infallible intelligence but I recognized that I was being given direct insight into events as my soul perceived them. In this way I came to further understand that I was also being instructed. As I surrendered to instruction, the events took on a more specific theme.

Slowly we release ourselves from the hindrances of the human form and it all seems so automatic and all becomes quite wonderful and miraculous. It is at this time that the inner work and the stage of reckoning begins. For any soul who has managed to maintain and build a sense of self accountability during human incarnation, the process ensues with greater clarity, and a sense of purpose and conviction impels us to embrace the afterlife processes for what they are. It is as if some souls know they have come along a certain way, while others who have arrived in the same hour of release from form may remain tied to the emotional body of their form. A magnetic resistance that we might call the 'instinctive urge' persists just as it did habitually while upholding the habitable body. Whereas we would expect to find a commonality to the afterlife drama, each drama is of its own choosing! As we were in life, we often are at first in eternity.

The stages and dramas that most describe my own process had shed some light on the fact that I was overjoyed and wholly accepting, while others I had noticed had tended to shy from early communication with the soul. I found that while some die in their sleep, a grad-ual awakening according to their sense of reality then and there produces the effects desired or required by them until a transition towards the revelation of their departure from the body has culminated naturally. We can only hope to accept what comes unexpectedly, and with gratitude, as we enter naively into the hands of that which is our causation. However, in as much as all things are original and true, there was a lessening hes-itancy on my own part and by my own allowance of speed through the continuing processes and exposures to come, I was certain then, as now, that inspiration occurs as one advances their attention and will.

As much as we breathe to some degree at our own pace in the human form and with as much trumpery as we like, so too do we pass through the in-between worlds of the afterlife and into the true life once more at that pace which is perfectly suited to us. This means that many may never get past the first stages of the blissful release from the form and the awakening to the beauty and bliss of Divinity before the sleep of incar-nation occurs once more. They may choose to lavish the moment for aeons of seeming time, yet nothing would be wasted. Others still not yet able to complete the first objectives of personality development in this world are not able to manage the mind related transi-tions and can generally retreat to gather poise in the deep sleep of the soul. These may awaken slowly and eventually they discover that the ease of the sentient nature is attained. It is as if we are encouraged to be calm and accept but the resistance is also a necessary aspect of the evolving personality as the soul finds the most suitable condition that will bring about the needed desire for reacquaintance with the eternal truth.

So in many cases there are those that eventually pass through all of the varied stages and processes that necessitate the transfigured enlightened conscious-ness, with the understanding that the moment of utter triumph is uniquely driven by the innate will of the individuality within. There are also some who have no need to consider the process of succession through the varied stages of the afterlife as they have done so while living in human form before the moment of release and have learned the great truths much earlier.

In all cases of transition in the afterlife worlds and environmental spheres of activities, regardless of per-sonality development, the task and goal is to succeed in the fusion of personality, psyche and soul into a sin-gle unit of Divine consciousness. It is not so different from the general theme of graduating classes and grades that we find in our own incarnate world of development, as the soul has as its greater task the union of soul and spirit much later on. We could con-sider grade school to represent the stage of personali-ty development required by the soul to enter higher education. From the first days of high school to its ends, we could say the main preoccupation of the soul is effectively to bring about conscious rapport with the personality and to begin to manifest that particular consciousness of the mechanism and nature of the soul itself. University would be akin to developing the greater cumulative consciousness of a liberated soul that has succeeded in liberation from the unintention-al use of power and attribute expression. A doctorate in our world would be like having attained final liber-ation from the need for form and incarnate experiences of individuality. Individualization and mastery of the powers of the indwelling spirit are the overall motivating tendencies of the soul.

The first stage in the afterlife is the restoration of our former wisdom and mastery through the revealing, or as I first recalled it, the judgement phase.

Judgement Phase

Once I had become accustomed to managing the speed of the inspirational visions and impressions taking place before my eyes and flowing through me like feelings in a warm current of life-giving strength, I was led to see and hear the thoughts and impressions as well as the outcomes of many of my earthly contacts and influences that were not possible for me to have known about in my own little sphere of activity while in earthly form. It was during this period of adjustment and gracious exposure that I came to engage in an ineffable trust for my soul as well as the continuing process that now seemed to have a structure and a format that was divinely profitable.

The very first scenes that appeared before me while still being held within the environment of my soul's body and rhythm were of my childhood. In this first scene I was able to relive, and yet maintain at an observer's distance, a particular summer day when I was four years old. My mother had been watering the front yard and my brother who was seven came running into the yard in his bathing suit. A few of the neighbours' children were cheering him on to run through the spray of the hose. My mother turned to him and sprayed him as he dashed away. I was sitting and watching from the bottom step of our wooden front porch and had been sprayed with water as he ran by the first time. It was then that I decided to join in on the fun. So I ran up the steps into the house to find a bathing suit for myself.

As that memory was recurring visually, my attention was redirected and adjusted to a second scene that took place without my previously being there to have witnessed it. My mother had chased the other children away by yelling at them while suggesting that she did not want to have her lawn ruined that afternoon by them. Her face showed impatience, complaint and a threatening frustration as she turned to raise her hand in a warning to my brother to stop encouraging her to continue to interact. He was crying as I watched myself run out the front door then, and onto the lawn in my underwear. As I turned to look at my brother, having wondering why he had been crying then, I slipped upon the wet grass and actually began to slide for a few feet. In doing so, I had inadvertently carved a gash in the lawn with my heel. I thought it was great fun but as I began to stand up, I found my mother had rushed over and slapped me forcefully from behind on the back of the head. She was yelling aloud then and as I observed the shocking and unnecessary punishing effect that this event had upon me, the visual environment was suddenly brought to a stop by my soul.

A feeling seemed to rise from the core of my psyche and I noticed the light of the past memory change. Suddenly, a variety of wavelike shocks of energy moved through myself and then into the stilled vision, until a hue of brilliant green light entered the top of my head as I stared in amazement. The scene was set in motion again the next moment. Within seconds, my mother had rushed over like a tempest and held the forced spray of the hose in my face. As much as I cared to get away, I was unable to. I struggled with her for several minutes until she came to realize herself what she had done. The children standing nearby looked astonished and bewildered as my soul revealed what had previously been hidden from me.

In the next moment, my soul showed me how this event had affected the observers present that day. Undeniable events of the future that were seemingly connected to my mother's influence that day appeared as intuitive visions. I learned through this exposure of cause and effect how three of the children were greatly influenced and had suffered much anxiety over this hidden event for many years to come. As for myself, I observed how this first of many similar incidents of childhood abuse and humiliation had ultimately influenced a whole life decision I had made prior to coming into the world only four years earlier. It was to be my goal then to integrate the necessary stage of consciousness that would best suit the intended study and outcome that was generally planned.

My soul then took me into the next vision that connected a series of lifelong experiences. By having brought about this former memory, and by vitalizing my psyche with the particular hue of green vibration, I was able to recall completely the exacting mental and emotional impacts as they were during that stage of my young life. My soul had taught me how the impact of certain experiences had directly affected my psyche and the overall development of my consciousness, by means of clear intuitive vision. It was like seeing things as the soul does. The intention was to have me understand clearly how experiences themselves were either limiting or liberating in the course of one's life. I sensed further, and it was evident much later in the afterlife experiences to follow, that my soul had a particular reason for initiating this vision and accommodating me with direct insight into matters previously unsuspected by myself. I was receiving instructions on the nature of the soul and its mechanism, not only of and for myself but also of others. It was through this technique that I saw deep into the heart and soul of my mother and how it was that she had suffered the conditioning of her own lifetime. No judgements followed on my part with regards to her or anyone else's behaviour after my soul had revealed that particular truth, and a growing sense of compassion was giving me a greater sense of conviction as the drama proceeded.

These lessons had a synthetic quality to them and it was as if each memory revisited was part of a chain of events that would all come together for me in due course. I was anxious for the next lessons and memories of my lifetime. I knew that whatever I had not known before was now to be revealed, and yet I also sensed that there were regrets ahead.

Revisiting Childhood

I recalled that I had been sitting in the grass out of the view of my mother and had been crying in embarrassment over the incident with the hose, when I asked myself a question aloud and in anger. 'Why? Why was my mom so mean?' The same vision of green light began to swell around the outer edges of my body as I continued to observe the experience of my childhood. I also took note of a soft indigo-coloured flame as it seemed to grow out of the green hue. This was an indication to me that I was able to observe my mother's thoughts and I was also shown her soul. It also served to answer the question I had often wondered in childhood. In spite of the demeaning, humiliating and often painful punishments imposed upon me by my mother throughout the early years of childhood, I had always seemed to understand that there was something wrong with her. I had often attempted to find a solution for her though I was not informed enough to explain that I felt she was taking on too much in her life and I could see how she was always stressed and anxious. This was my way of accounting for her abusive behaviour, although I had often felt as a young child that I had already somehow understood it. Sometimes I had wondered if I was the only one that knew and even that thought seemed to be more than I could have gained from my environmental education then. It was this green hue, that seemed to represent the inspirational and balancing influences of my soul that had watched over me as a child, that had helped me at that time to see the truth.

Indeed I did remember being directly influenced, even to the point where my feelings would change and I was left dwelling in a sort of dreamy and comfortable state. I never felt alone throughout my childhood, though had it not been for the intervention of my own soul in an effort to maintain the intended integrity of my personality, I suppose I would have fallen victim somehow to the experiences of punishment on a daily basis. I was relieved to understand how my soul really was there on multiple occasions to see me through and most of all when I was quietly pondering the truth of my own life.

After some time of experiencing my own mother's psyche and her young history, I understood how we are all a part of a great unfolding drama. How it is that we are all souls in a process of conscious evolution and how it is that our experiences though apparently unique and different, result in the same measure of identification with the overall truth. The light vision faded again and I felt at peace in respect to my earliest childhood frustrations for the first time, and this was due mostly to having gained a soul's insights into the whole of another's life, not unlike that of any other in our shared world experience.

The next instant I was back to the scene in the front yard where I had been wondering why my mother had been the way she was. Once more I was consciously immersed in this past memory. My mood had changed dramatically from a deepened sadness to joy as an inspiring impression came to the fore of my young mind. It was as if I had received an answer similar to a voice within saying, 'I exist!' I exclaimed this aloud several times over and felt uplifted and awed each time I did so. I noticed then, in this afterlife revisitation, how my soul had intervened to comfort me and to break the thought-form of abandonment and anger that had been passed to me by my assimilation of my mother earlier in the day. I was relieved of the trauma of that incident and given full recognition of a former dawning that began a series of experiences in consciousness, motivated by the impulse to regain that same moment of inspiration again. It was the feeling of that particular dawning and its overall effect upon my mind that I remembered most.

Throughout my remaining life period and until the accident of 4 May 1979, I had recalled on several occasions how it was that I had begun to seek out the mystery of existence for myself. The particular moment this had occurred had served to show me the means by which inspiration could be attained. I had come to cherish this first experience, though until the afterlife drama, I had not recognized the essential truth that I was indeed attempting to assimilate a measure of receptivity within myself with that of my own soul. It was in the intervening vision of personal existence, accompanied by an inspired rhythm of rapture that filled my heart that same day, that was largely responsible for the line of enquiry and study that followed in my later years. For me, it was as if I had spoken to God and I had somehow been given a great vision of self exclusivity! I was also reminded by my soul then in the afterlife drama how natural it was to expect others to have been motivated by the love of life and personal existence itself.

It was due to a premature use of this sense of the commonality of our existence that many mistakes and errors of judgement came to pass as well. I saw how this one connecting experience caused me to believe that others were inspired by the fact that they too existed and how wonderful it was to have realized that same fact. Only later in life did I realize that not all whom I met had been so inspired as to find life itself the principle motivation to love, fair play, morality, equality and especially of gratitude to God.

Revisiting Arizona

I

My soul took me through many experiences of synonymous euphoric aspirations and contemplations in my youth which I considered to be experiences of inspiration. When all had been revealed, I came to realize how it was that the first endeavour to contact the Divine in nature and in man had begun. It was this theme of personal endeavour to reveal the invisible attributes of a seemingly hidden Divine cause in life that generated the many hours of remembering in the afterlife.

The visions began to take on an instructional tone and as each memory was revisited, I sensed an expansion of my own psyche. It was as if I had come to be very still in the light of an immeasurable truth. I was no longer anticipating the next moment and I had become quite used to realizing that I was catching up with my own lost sense of history. It was as if the past and the present began to meld into one unit of time. I had begun to feel consciously matured. The sense of frailty, fear and vulnerability that had gripped my mind in the first moments of actual death had begun to vanish altogether in the certainty of my return to the ethereal home of my soul.

It was during one particular memory that I began to recognize that I was different and yet I was still myself. I was more mature and experienced and yet I had not lost any sense of my incarnate history. I had come to experience the fact that I had always been as mature, though having to work in this world through the vehicle of the personality, I had lost the sense of my own gains. Suddenly it came to me that I was no longer the frail personality that had left his body nervously on the tarred pavement only hours before. Now it became clear that the soul and my consciousness of self had begun to merge. I was becoming my soul. I sensed then how the separation and the seeming illusion of such a separation was not only necessary but just how valuable an asset it was in the development of the soul itself.

That particular experience was of a series of days that I had once spent in a small and isolated part of the Arizona desert at the age of fifteen. Of all the visions, experiences, memories and expansions that had taken place in the first twelve hours of the afterlife experience, the memory of San Simon was the culminating event. My soul had drawn upon specific memories of my youth beginning at the age of four and onwards until this one period of time with a most specific purpose.

I had come to a crossroads in my life. It was due to my own intentions, actions and innate calling here in this place and time that my future sojourn in this world had begun to take shape more concretely.

I was eleven years old the first time I left home thinking that I would be doing my brothers and sister a favour by leaving, as the beatings might stop for them. My childhood had become quite a strain on all of the family members and we shared a deeply wounding lifestyle of continued punishment. Regardless of our complaints to the authorities at school and church, nothing had occurred excepting more punishment and threats to make our home life public. My mother's embarrassment with my willingness to expose her was becoming quite dangerous. And so by the time I had turned eleven, I was prevented from doing my regular homework at night, maintaining friends, being allowed to go outside after dark, and for every need that sprang up during these years my mother would find an excuse to prevent us from attaining our necessary goals. As it turned out, a friend phoned my home in my absence and told my family where I could be found.

Again at fifteen, when my mother had gone to great lengths to prevent me from attending high school, I knew I had to become independent quickly. It was time for me to begin the life I was most interested in and I decided to put my education off for a time. I travelled through the United States looking for jobs where I could and hoped to find a high school where I could finish my necessary education away from home. Although I found this most difficult, I was eventually led to a small town in southern Arizona.

I had arrived in San Simon in the middle of the night some three days before Christmas. I had hitched a ride into Arizona from a man travelling from Texas to Phoenix. For some unknown reason this same man wanted to let me out on the side of the highway in the middle of the night. I only remember him laughing aloud as he sped off into the night while I stood quietly in the utter darkness. I noticed a light in the near distance though it was not near any connecting road that I could see and it certainly was not from any car on the interstate highway. The air was frigid and I could only think of finding a shelter for a time, so I ran along the road's edge hoping to find a turnoff ahead.

It seemed as if I had run for hours and I was getting very cold when I heard the scampering of a coyote in the brush nearby. I stood very still, making certain that my breath was silent, and trained my sight along the roadway as if to search out the movements in the night ahead. A few minutes had passed and though not a sound could be heard, I did watch intently as a distant light began to close on me. At first, I thought it was a car that was on the other side of the highway, but then I noticed this same light become still then diminished almost back to its source. It was a very dim light indeed but a few moments later I saw it only a few hundred feet off to my right.

I caught a brief glimpse of what seemed to be the aluminium door of a trailer or maybe a mobile home that had reflected the light of someone who had been passing by in the darkness. Someone had been returning from the outside of the trailer and had quickly turned the light on to the steps of this old relic of a mobile home. It was enough for me to realize that there must be other homes about. 'Perhaps there'll be a place to stay for the night or maybe a gas bar somewhere over the horizon that I hadn't noticed earlier,' I thought. I believe it was my fear of the dark and the possibility of being pursued by the coyote that caused me to run quickly towards what I could now see was an aged mobile home.

II

The closer I came to the old trailer the more I realized I had come to some type of temporary campsite or trailer park. There were no stores or gas stations to be found. The ruins of an old brick building a few hundred feet away from the dirt road that I was standing on only served to disappoint me further. Upon closer inspection I could see that there had been an attempt some years earlier to develop a park or rest stop, but that it had been abandoned. The five or six trailers I could identify in the darkness were all that was left, and these were very old indeed. I wondered if I had possibly come upon a commune of some sort.

If it were not for the frigid air that evening, I suppose I would have wandered back to the highway and waited for another ride. I turned my attention back to the trailer that I knew was occupied, and began to debate with myself whether I should knock on the door. I was certainly thirsty enough to, though I was very prepared to run for it if necessary. I tapped on the door lightly, especially after realizing how frail the door itself was - it had begun to shake wildly at the first knock.

Soon I heard the sound of muffled voices from inside the trailer and then I noticed a ragged old curtain being drawn away from a window next to the door itself. The next moment I heard a fumbling sound, and then a flashlight aimed downwards upon the floor of the trailer appeared while the inside screen door was being pulled open. Someone was standing back at arms' length from the door and then I heard her voice. It sounded like that of an elderly woman. I was immediately concerned that I had frightened her and began to apologize for having disturbed her. I moved away from the door myself as I spoke, if only to let her know that I meant no harm, and I believe the only reason I continued to talk was because I felt she deserved an explanation.

I knew from the look on her frail, aged face that if she did not understand why I had knocked on her door before leaving, she would have been even more alarmed for the rest of the night. She couldn't hear me at first and so I repeated myself several times. I was very surprised when I heard a child's voice from inside the trailer attempting to explain what I had said at the door. To end the confusion quickly I said, 'I'm very sorry, ma'am. I was hiking through the area and I was left on the side of the highway just a while ago and I was thirsty. No cars were coming as it is late now, but when I saw a light come from this trailer I thought to ask for a glass of water. I am so sorry. I should have realized how late it was. I didn't mean to scare you. I will just leave.'

'Oh! Wait a minute young man,' came the reply. 'We have milk. Will that do?'

I was amazed and astonished by what happened next. She invited me in to her trailer and to be polite, I stood by the door and was thanking her, when the first impressions of the inner world of her trailer had come to meet my eye. She was a very elderly woman, in her late eighties I suspected. There were two very young identical twin girls around the age of five, huddled in a blanket in the rear of the trailer with their eyes fixed on me in deep curiosity.

I discovered that the woman had been left to care for the children by her granddaughter some three years earlier, when she had abandoned all three of them here in the desert alongside the highway. The trailer was no more than 14 feet long and maybe 6 feet wide. The grandmother was using a single burner Coleman outdoor stove-top as a heater and to cook. The small fridge under a sink that was not plumbed was used to store eggs that the grandmother got weekly from an elderly neighbour. For food, there were three large plastic bags of puffed rice, one bag of rice, and a large container of powdered milk. Water had been kept outside in a covered barrel at the back of the trailer. By opening the back window of the trailer she could reach the water and save the trip outside. An old plastic bucket with a wooden cover was used as a toilet, also to be found behind the trailer.

When she finally mixed the milk I had began to weep but desperately tried to hide the fact. I was so overcome by her sweetness, her generosity, the children's predicament and the lifestyle forced upon them. My mind was racing with a fever I had never known before in my life. I quickly excused myself and exited the trailer. I sat down alongside the trailer and made certain that she knew I would stay nearby for the night. She came to the door with one of the two blankets that I had noticed the children cuddled in earlier, and I almost died of embarrassment and shame. I cried deeply and for a long period that night. Unlike any time before, I had never suffered such a continuing grievous moment. I could barely breathe for an hour afterwards from the swelling in my throat. In just a few moments of time, and as many words, I had come to bear witness to the whole of reality right before my eyes. I knew that night what was meant by a picture being worth a million words.

It was around five in the morning and I just could not pull myself away from the side of that trailer. I felt as if I should just stay put until they were all safe and secure and only when the old woman's lifestyle changed. Somehow, I felt connected to the people and events that took place that night in a surreal way.

Even as the event was re-enacted for me by my soul

in the afterlife drama, I could not stop weeping one more time. I had breathed inwards only once and my weeping flowed out more deeply than I had ever thought possible. I experienced a grief in the afterlife from having loved, that I had touched on but not understood so clearly the first time around. I can only tell you that I felt my soul's heart had been broken into pieces that night. My life had suddenly become completely unimportant. I wanted simply to forget that I even existed yet I wanted to survive if only to intervene on behalf of this abandoned family.

I came to know the shame of humanity that night and my soul took me further to show me more. I experienced sorrow unheard of, inexplicable compassion, unbounded grief. I found the heart of God that night in the light of compassion and in the strength of the grief that led me into greater revelation. I found that grief had been the power that the grandmother and the twins had lived on. I found their good-natured and sensible acceptance of their lot to be my humbling. I found their love in the deepest of isolation to be the reward of existence itself. I saw deep into the soul of the grandmother with my own soul's help and was reminded of why I had sensed a great shame come over me before I had exited her trailer home. She had compassion for me. She had truly worried for me. She was more concerned with my plight than her own. I did not know it that night but I had understood how it was that these three souls were my own guiding light. If it were possible then for me to have died for them in exchange for a period of comforting and a greater opportunity for the young girls, I would gladly have given all.

I stayed with this family during the Christmas holidays that year before moving on to Tucson where I went to work immediately. I made certain that I returned shortly thereafter to the same trailer and these three precious souls. I had saved enough to have them move into Tucson which was only a few hours' drive away. I understood that this would be enough to get them some real help. I had never fully recovered from the experience itself until the drama of the afterlife had come about and it was this moment that began a whole new series of events that were to follow.

I sensed with some relief that I had understood how it was that I had been guided through my own choices in youth by my soul. I began to perceive the necessity of the overall process of revisiting certain impacting moments of the past though I had no idea of what I was about to discover next. As the memory of the grandmother and the twins began to fade away, a faint but persistent feeling of shame deep within my consciousness began to arise. Without warning, I sensed I had been left alone for a time in my own mind. My soul was not responding as it had throughout the afterlife experiences moments earlier. I felt as if I were beginning to shrink and was somewhat unprepared for the next moment as I came back to body consciousness in the operating room of the hospital.

III

It had seemed so offensive to me that I was returning. I was beginning to taste my body again and could not escape it. I was shrinking inside of it, I thought. I called out to my soul once more in an attempt to be relieved but the burden of the loss of sensitivity came upon me for a time, that I suspected might just last too long. I wanted to finish the drama. I had no desire to stay or to return to my body. The surgeons were successful and now I lay inside a body that I could not escape or make use of either. I began to feel the foulness of the body upon and through my senses once again. Though I could not control the body outwardly, I could smell and see and sense inwardly. It was as if a fog and a swampy smell followed by a terribly repulsive taste of gas was upon my breath. I had been placed in the intensive care unit of the hospital and only when I had finally began to surrender to the inevitable did I notice a means of retreat from my body. I attempted to recall the last memory of the time spent in the desert in Arizona and when I touched on the former grief and the revelation of the compassion of the soul, I was able to exit the body. Once again I began to experience the last thoughts of the evening at hand. The sensible rhythm of shame directed me into the light of the afterlife then but for a time it seemed that everything had changed and now it was all downhill from where I was. I was somewhat frozen in shock as the unconscious memories of the past began to rise in abstract, sequential periods. I was moving through a seeming fluid light sphere of impressions that seemed to have an effect upon me that I would have never imagined in a million years.

As this tunnel of images and visions surrounded me I felt that I was moving, though not in any particular direction. If I focused on the wall of light that was filled with impressions of the outer world to the left, I only seemed to draw nearer to the wall, yet there was no limit itself. This sphere contained the sounds of many voices over historic time and I also heard the wailing and shrieking pleas of animals and beings submerged in deepest pain. I had not heard such sounds before and the cries of many caught my deepest attention. I began to feel frightened as I was still unable to enquire of my soul directly, or at least it seemed that way to me then.

In reality, I was facing my unconscious consciousness. All that had ever occurred for me historically was now before me, though in seeming disorder. Not only was I to find that I was entering into my own innate world of instinctual fears but I was about to face the visions, fears and dreams of humanity past in this same environment. Before me in motion, were the memories of all that had transpired in the history of humanity for more than millions of years of time. There truly was no need to fear at all, but I did not know that until I finally arrived at my own shame, regret and remorse captured in the annals of historic time.

The shame and regret of a lifetime as well as all of the innate visual symbols which organized, generated or copied from impressions gathered out of many lifetimes were now before me. And much like in a dream that one might term a nightmare, I found myself being hauled down a winding staircase deep into the bowels of the darkest instinctive corner of the universe. I heard screams below that sent shivers and streams of shocking energy though my psyche as well as the body I seemed to have picked up along the way. The memory of sensory and bodily perceptions came to life in this particular corner of my psyche and it wasn't until I came to be shown that these symbolic experiences were the remnants of ancient instincts and thought forms that I was able to rest once more. It truly was a shock to my psyche, though these seemingly lucid and real impressions did have a liberating effect once they had been played out to their end. Most of these incidental and seemingly horrible portrayals of my deepest hidden fears had been born out of other lifetimes where death in a variety of ways had occurred previously.

Sometimes I would be subject to events in history that seemed to have nothing to do with my life and yet I was able to witness my evolving self in another body, experiencing such things as grief, terror and fear. All of the darker instinctual and animal base passions of the body were to be found here along with the memory of others I had observed to have died over time. The ignorance and shame of humanity was the theme, and the memories of shame from my little life dissipated into my disinterestedness thereafter. When the whole of the history of suffering humanity is brought to light, we will all be grateful that our soul will be up to the task of understanding the whole picture of reality and not just the part. It was due to holding on to certain painful parts of my own history that I had missed so much of the value that was invisible until then.

It was after these experiences into the depths of doubt and uncertainty that the limitless experiences of the soul began and the light of the agony and ecstasy of life began to blend into one cohesive vision of perfection. I rediscovered that my greatest attribute before my present incarnation was compassion and love. The quality of these attributes had formerly become personally painful and grievous to my evolving psyche in many incarnations and the shame I had felt in the last moments before leaving my body amounted to the desire for death itself. I had wanted to die to life. As a soul freed from the fetters of the human form, I desired death and sought a means by which I might surrender all for the sake of those I chose to love. What I had not realized was that certain ancient instincts were playing upon the attributes of love and compassion, and that the urge to union, through love of the Divine, had taken on a passion for self-sacrifice beyond the needed experience that my soul had gained.

In other words, I was experiencing a male or spiritual attribute of sacrifice and purpose within my soul but had not connected the spirit to the events of grief in the world of appearances. Formerly, I had perceived self-sacrifice to be a means to an ends for others' suffering. The truth is that the suffering of others in the isolation of individualized incarnations is not the whole truth of the limitless spirit within these same vehicles. During the incarnation, I was unable to identify the eternal spirit having a longing for the gains of an incarnate and often painful life. Instead, I had sympathized with the human personality as a means of communion with the Divine.

The experiences such as the one mentioned in Arizona with the grandmother and the children were a means for connecting me to Divinity and to the Divine in us all. It was the plan of my Divine guide to lead me to liberation from the confusion of mortality and Divinity, as they embrace the moment here in the spheres of attainment. Until then, I had grieved over the illusion of loss in both worlds. Continuing onwards into the depths of the afterlife experience, I had come to moments in my life history that had stood out to be highly important affairs and issues that had never been resolved, such as those experiences involving my son.

I remember having had the feeling that I was somehow sitting in judgement of myself, and it was a matter of conscience for me that the many hours and months of previous concentration on my relationship with my son had remained unfinished.

Revisiting My Children

I

I was seventeen when my son was conceived in the summer of 1969, and was then serving a five-year educational agreement and contract in the armed forces. I had only recently come out of basic training and ended up on a training base located in Victoria on Vancouver Island. It had been almost five months before I was granted leave and allowed to leave the base daily. On one particular night in the early summer of that year, I was invited by my new associates to go to the downtown area of the city where we were going to explore our new base and home.

I was reminded how it was that I went out of my way to speak to a young woman who was driving by with her girlfriend that night, and had asked for the chance to get a tour of the city. We had no transportation of our own and after some initial conversation, two of us were invited to take the back seat of the Rambler and cruise the speedway. It was common in the late 1960s for people to go cruising at night and at one end of the city there was a drive-in restaurant that seemed to be the focal point for the main groups who were doing likewise. This particular fast food drive-in restaurant was also the turn-around point of a four-mile stretch of road where on any given night, one had the opportunity to converse with two or three hundred people within my own age group. I had established a closer relationship with this particular young woman that evening and for several weeks, or whenever I was able to get leave, we met together with her girlfriend and began to develop new friends together.

I was reminded by my soul of these moments and of when I had begun to feel close to this young woman and I sensed and remembered the heartache I had endured when she told me that she was already engaged and would be getting married in the fall of that same year. I was reawakened to the events that took place over a two-week period, where out of heartache alone, I had left the base illegally one night just to find a means and a way to interfere, if not intervene, in the relationship she had finally exposed when she let go of our exceptionally close and growing relationship. That same evening I had managed to contact her and asked her to meet me downtown on a familiar street corner but to no avail - she made it clear to me that she felt she had to go through with the marriage. Having listened and learnt from her that she was not quite as happy with her male friend then, after having spent many weeks with me, I appealed to her once more in an attempt to clarify my feelings and I persisted in getting her to allow me to see her once more. The next time we met secretly, away from the downtown area, as her boyfriend had become aware of my presence in her life, that we sat together alone in a car along the ocean front. That evening we shared ourselves intimately for the first time.

A week later I was due to leave Victoria for a training exercise at sea, which was going to take six weeks.

I assured her that I would seek her out on my return and then spent the next six weeks dreading the possibility that she would change her mind and still want to get married as planned. On my return I was jubilant to find she was anxious to see me again and had been fretting over me for the whole time I was away.

My soul then took me intentionally to the night when I found out that she was pregnant. I was reminded of how much I was afraid then. How confused and disorientated I had become, knowing there was little chance of being able to afford to assist her, much less share a lifestyle with her and our child that she was carrying. I was reminded of statements I had made that evening as I went for a walk alone and sat in the park along the ocean's edge.

Over a period of three days I had found myself analysing the events of my life and how one moment had led to another, to the point where I had found myself at seventeen years of age becoming a father. I had reckoned I was unfit and unable to provide for a family and that I had no true idea of how to even begin, and on top of that, I was blaming myself for following through on my emotions and interfering with her life. I remember feeling totally selfishly responsible, for having swept her away from a secure and comfortable relationship with her fiancé and friends, and not being able to assume full responsibility for her then. I had concluded that it was in her best interest that I find the way and means to support her and to continue our relationship into the future, but even then I was not granted permission from my superior officers to get married. I was at an all-time low and was ashamed to have destroyed this innocent girl's life.

II

My soul was beginning to interact with me as the events unfolded as they had in true time, and I remember feeling that I was now to be judged for my former ignorance but all I could do was cry. I remember crying aloud so much that there seemed to be no end to the breath being released in this environment when suddenly I was taken into a room where I somehow felt that the context was changing.

The room was not familiar to me and I was curious to see what it had to do with the immediate experience where I had only wanted to die or disappear. I was informed intuitively then by my soul that this was the present-day life of my son. He was only nine years old then and as I glanced about the room, I took note of the toys and posters in the room. In the next instant I saw my son coming into the room to go to bed. I stood there for what seemed like hours as I watched him lying in bed with eyes closed. I recall how relieved I was in those minutes to see that he was generally happy and that his life was spiritually healthy. I then began to wander through the apartment where I came upon his mother who was entertaining a male at the time and was told to take notes on the spiritual tone of her and this other individual's souls. In the next moment I was viewing her continued history without me, as we had separated after only two years and she was about to be married again.

I was shown how all intrusions in or on a soul in their incarnation by other souls who were just as unaware or naive were managed in the overall scheme of their life's objective. It was here that I began to understand the workings of justice and the means to the ends by which originality and free will are able to act on a blueprint for success in every soul's life history. I understood well then how we are here to attain our future glory, our triumph over ignorance, and not to please ourselves in sensory ways alone. Becoming wise is the objective goal of all souls presently in or out of incarnation. Feeling somewhat relieved but still feeling that my judgement had not yet occurred, I was whisked away by the clear intent to see my young daughter.

It was in this moment that I discerned quickly where I was in time, and how although I was still in the afterlife experience, I was also able to relive the past, and visit the present ongoing events in the natural world. I am sure that I would have liked to have pondered the situation for a longer period but as the impression of my daughter came to mind, I was once more in the past history of my and her life. The environment broke out before me in a cold and soundless room. I was struck somehow for a moment as I watched my own former self standing in the delivery room on the day that she was born. The sounds of earthly life were once again negotiable and I was locked into the sight of myself only three years earlier.

III

I was astounded to recall how I had begun to pray innately aloud in the delivery room that day, as it was the thought that the complications occurring then might well lead to the collapse of her and her mother's life. She was trapped inside the birth canal for several hours as she was upside down and the doctors were experiencing great difficulty in their attempts to turn her around. It was too late for a Caesarean and only a few minutes were left on the clock before the blood loss and culminating events would lead to a choice to save one of them.

I remember swearing and vowing myself to a life of utter righteousness and spiritual purity if only then, an intervening hand could come into play for both of them. And I remember exclaiming to God that I had been an immature and selfish parent previously who was living in denial over my son, and that when I had felt it was reasonable for me to accept the full responsibilities of fatherhood, I could do nothing more than watch as others fell victim to their chance experiences with myself. I recall feeling expectant then as I had gone further within my own prayer for salvation of my wife and our daughter and had urged the universal hand of intervention to take the time remaining in my own life and to give it to these two souls who were much more deserving and innocent.

A moment later, I was reminded how I had forgotten that day overall, and how little I had come to realize as my daughter and wife were whisked out of the hands of death. The issue then was the shame that was the root reason for the reminiscences of the past and present that I had managed to carry with me every day of my continuing unresolved life.

Restoration

By this time in the afterlife experience I had come to know that there was really no accountability that would ever be deemed as a judgement or that would lead to accusations which in turn would lead to punishment of any kind. Every time I had come to be reminded of my own sense of regret and shame, I was returned to the hall of records historically and reminded of the basic laws of the incarnate life of humanity. I saw the visual presentations of history where I had come to feel the shame of my own given selfishness, only to be shown how it had never been clear to me that there never was an accusation followed by direct spiritual punishment of anyone in the past.

I was shown how life after life we tend to work out our misgivings or shortcomings and, under the guise of a new personality, we are given the freedom from the historic past to proceed with a sense of purity and cleansing. It was as if we are all automatically understood to be unenlightened and that it is expected that we deny, hide, fear and want to escape our seemingly unchangeable expressions in time and space.

I was shown clearly by my soul that a serious effort to be self-accountable had subtly persisted throughout my life even though I could not comprehend the governing premise of the incarnation itself. Each time I was relieved to find I was understood, and much more than that, I was shown how everyone has and will always be understood for their regrets and shortcomings as a forgetful and uncertain individualized entity. It is only on the day of certainty and union with our souls that one is relieved of human ignorance.
Whether we are accused by our fellow humankind of participating in the terrible acts of the early crusades, or of being unconscionable in any time period, we are given life anew and begin where we left off. In these

experiences dealing with the entire history of my personal relationship with humanity at large, individually, and with my own innate sense of conscience, I came to realize that the first stages of the afterlife, for those who are unaware of the truth itself, is a restorative one. It is the equivalent evaluation of a personality against the soul's objective that takes place in the first days of the afterlife experience and as I had come to be settled with my own merits and had come to peace of mind and heart over the history of my own ignorance, I was prepared for whatever was to be afterwards.

I learned ultimately to trust the process of the Divine. It was understanding how our guides and the presence of divinity in us all connect so uniquely in forecasting and bringing about intervention through outer experiences in our incarnate lives that allowed me to have direct insight into the workings of the whole universe and the nature of the Divine therein. I knew at this stage that any further judgement would only increase the quality of wisdom and joy that I was now remembering to have expressed, long before my own incarnation. I began to understand how all things are in order throughout the universe, that we human beings are on the verge of accomplishing our conscious objectives as souls, and that the basic plan for the remaining aspects of manifesting our Divine attributes lies ahead.

I came to understand that each of us in incarnation is observed by the Divine with one single intention, which is to enable us to achieve our goals. As I was being hosted by my soul and seemed to become more like my own soul than my previous personality, I was able to marvel in the notion that we are all seen as

Masters in the making, regardless of our apparently limited expressions while in physical form.

By the time I had finished with what I had anticipated as the horrors of judgement and punishment, along with dealing with old pain - which is misunderstood as being consigned to hell - I had come to see how the layers of human ignorance are stripped away slowly and graciously in the afterlife from the evolving psyche. I also saw how it is that the adventure in incarnation itself is considered as the prelude to our own Divine manifestation. It is as if we begin to remember at a specific point in the afterlife, that we have been around this cycle and wheel of events many a time before. It is like attending school in the heavens by attending the daily class of incarnate life until the final degree is attained.

Life on Earth is a school for young evolving souls destined towards self-mastery of the spirit. A life on Earth of eighty years is like an hour's dream for a soul in sleep or in full waking consciousness. I discovered that our level of maturity as souls in the afterlife is what determines our need for further experiences and for many cycles of time. Once one was able to concentrate as a soul upon their own incarnation, they were then free from the need of an afterlife drama such as I had experienced.

To awaken fully to the Divine within us all, into the true life experience as a manifest soul in this world, is indeed the actual present goal of all souls. I can tell you that there are souls so advanced that their opportunities to enter into multiple historical periods of time in many spheres, dimensions, and throughout the whole of time and space at will, are unlimited and they have no need for the limiting shapes and forms found in the manifest worlds of incarnation.

The privilege of utilizing time by the limits of a manifest form in incarnation and to experience history, as the history of the Divine Dynastic Drama of Love, is exactly what an advanced soul is doing when they enter into the incarnate form called the human body itself. It was the next series of experiences that began to touch on these stated themes that gave me the insights suggested.

The unconscious memories formulated by thinkers in the world throughout history, as well as the symbolic visions of the unenlightened and frightened souls of time and space, were being dismissed from my vision as I came to know how such conclusions were the creation of our imaginations when we are most vulnerable and unidentified with a secure universe of intent. I was once again intuitively aware that images and impressions by the mind of an advancing soul in human form were powerful enough to attract us back to the source of their manifestation in time and space. When we are free from the illusion of mortality, and under the guidance of our spirit alone, all our former manifestations in unenlightened times could be called back out of manifestation. As much as we would wish to take back our thoughts at times, in eternity we can and do! The images of our minds do not last forever and have no life of their own outside our continued desire and attachment to them. In this way, I began to recall how it was that we actually and intentionally generate our own appearance as a personality in time.

These revelations began as a word that was voiced aloud by my soul as I was stilled within the shell of my own developed psyche. A shattering and rending of that shell began in the later stages of the first phase of the afterlife experience. The very perimeters of my sense of self began to give way and only when I surrendered to the liberation of my memories as a personality was I able to unite with my soul once more. It then became clear that through the vehicle of the physical form and by utilizing the brain and mind, I had generated a living impression of myself. I had deduced my self existence from the seeming reality of every moment's experience as a human thinker. The sense of 'I', which is often the only sense of self we manage to attain in any one life, is actually thought of and invented out of our remembering the order of events in seeming time, which is then captured by our psyche. Our soul consciousness is unregistered in our psyche most of this period, or at least until the final stages of the actual development of the psyche has taken place overall. Only then are we ready to awaken to our soul, or to be awakened by the soul itself, to the transition in consciousness preceding or following death which brings the entire impression of this to bear for the psyche itself.

It is true that we part one day from the maintenance of and need for the historic memories of the developing personality that we so loved and cherished and so too do the memories of those personalities we loved dissipate at the right moment. That is when the whole of the processes and development of spiritual attributes comes into play, after the residing personality has been liberated from uncertainty.

What is remembered of our existence in every incarnation stands to remain in our true and lasting consciousness, though the illusions, delusions and misunderstandings of the personality give way to the faculty of the soul consciousness itself. It comes to be known one day, when evolution has met the critical stage, that the soul seeks union with the developed psyche and the personality. We do not lose our sense of self but, for the first time in eternity, we begin to take pleasure in the triumphant realization that this is in fact our last life in suffering and forgetfulness!

From that day onwards, with soul and personality united, we never forget again. Likewise, we begin to take joy in understanding that we have awoken for the first time in our eternal history, and that from such a point of attainment, the rule of forgetfulness that exists between the incarnate opportunities is over. This is and will be the most liberating moment of our gestation as spiritual offspring and signals the birthing or resurrection stages in our future development. It is very like saying we have yet to establish ourselves as a continuing persona in eternity and on the day that we are truly born anew as the first personality to be salvaged in eternity, we actually begin to assume our illimitable powers of association, intelligence and doingness.

Through this dramatic stage of liberation from the thoughts of the one life, and the uniting of the soul with the consciousness gained of the little self, the need for separation from our past memory and experience in the long-lived universe is forever left behind. Some billion years of time from now, when we have long advanced even beyond the kingdom of souls, a faint memory of our origins of individuality will be anchored in the present day and life here, on our little blue watery sphere.

Conscience

As I look back upon the moments spent being subjected to a measure of fright and fear of ancient instinctual origins, not then aware of the need for such a sudden change in the format of experience in the afterworld, or of the differences between psyche and soul consciousness, I am reminded of a great truth discovered there. In every true moment of history, a single element of the soul and the influence of the soul upon any personality in time stood out before my watchful eye with stunning impact. I could see what many have come to call the conscience of humanity. I was never so awed to realize how the soul of each individual, regardless of their particular quality of personality expression for good or for evil, remained steadfast and sure in support of the individual psyche and the right to evolve as personalities. I understood how the law of the soul prevents direct intervention or action upon the psyche of any one personality when the choices made for personal expression are done so without the foreknowledge of the soul itself. This was the natural evolution of the psyche through personality development with only the innate sense of conscience striking a semblance of a recognizable chord once in a while.

The soul itself maintains a steadfast meditation upon the awakening personality throughout, in any one life incarnation, while the activity and objective of the soul itself may be greatly enhanced or utterly unnoticeable. Only in the lives where the aspiration of the psyche to know itself comes into fruition in sincere ways, and only after outliving the ideals and desires for form existence itself, does the soul become known or sensed to exist as a reality.

Though the actions of many in history are generally unseen and unrecognized, when one considers the influence upon them of an elusive and informing source such as the soul itself, it is nevertheless true that the sensible soul is justly responsible for the actual evolution of the psyche of these same individuals. The conscience within each psyche, serving as a germ of truth itself, is largely responsible for the present sensibility and civilization of humanity, truly defining man as that special something other than animal. When such a sensible yet elusive and all informing attractiveness towards right is developed and only when the personality perceives the need to refrain from living outside the range of a resolved conscience, does the active soul begin to have the right to intervene and impose according to law.

I learned clearly, that the seemingly elusive sense of conscience in us all serves as a medium of contact between the evolving psyche and consciousness of the soul itself. It is when the sensible aspect of conscience is awakened in the personality and registered in the heart as a finger of truth itself that one begins to take the first steps away from the wheel and cycle of pain through human incarnation forevermore. This then is a recognized activity upon the mental levels of consciousness.

When my sense of disgust for certain personalities during my life was revisited in the afterlife drama, I came to know that all that the personality holds to be true and dear in life is greatly influenced by the innate sense and appreciation for beauty and illumination, and further, that whatever the personality had found to dislike in life regarding the choices of action in others was directly influenced by a recognition of another being's departure from matters of conscience itself.

If we look again at the figures of our recognized history on Earth, bearing in mind the effect that their conscience had upon their daily decisions, we would find that those who lived outside the range of an elusive yet all-informing sense of conscience were most responsible for the corruption, horrors, pains, and decay of our humanity and its living institutions of the day. In this light human history could be understood to be a testing of the conscience of the leaders of our world and their ultimate effect upon the consciousness of the masses.

On further inspection we could determine that those who did indeed speak through their conscience, did indeed add to the determination of the modern civilizations of today. In all, the two polarities of those who live in and outside the range of their own innate sense of conscience have brought us all to the determined and strikingly familiar values of justice and social goodwill towards one another.

Many times in youth and adolescence I had come upon my conscience and found myself admitting to myself just how insincere, selfish, or pretentious I had been. Only when I reached the root of such truths did I ever feel free from the usual regret, guilt or shame. I remember feeling that I should never go too far away from my conscience in thinking, though I never developed the habit of looking to my conscience before deciding on premeditative actions. It was due to this overall neglect or forgetfulness of the value of such a wise and elusive council within myself that I had not discovered that there is no such thing as a troubled conscience.

Only through the afterlife experiences was I able to see clearly that though people say that they have a problem with their conscience, it is only the personality that is troubled in the light of conscience. Trying to deny the voice of conscience only causes more of the grief and restlessness of most personalities. I discovered then that the stress of everyday life and its attendant anxieties were only indications from my soul that I needed to resolve myself to such issues. It is for the sake of wisdom alone that the intervening voice of silence calls us at all to the issues at hand. Again, there is no punishment for unenlightenment though there is continued discomfort that leads to many psychological difficulties over time from avoidance of these issues which are, in fact, matters of conscience. It is as if we need only be truthful to ourselves and search out the truth of our misgivings to discover greater wisdom, insight and liberation from all forms of human ignorance.

I remember suggesting to myself at one point in the afterlife judgement experiences that, if we only knew that everything was a matter of conscience and if we could only have been told or shown that, we would all be free from the ills that blight our overall health and vitality. Not only our health becomes restored by living under the light of conscience but rapport between the soul and personality actually begins in this way.

When one is receptive enough to the still quiet voice of conscience, there can be no mistaking the revelations and inspirations that follow. Living outside our own sense of wise council suffocates the sound of the voice of conscience along with our creativeness, turning us into subjective fault finders. That is when the accusatory, complaining and punishing aspects of our personalities begin to take hold. Only when we face our conscience do we find relief from such syndromes. The universe does not punish and neither should we, but when we choose to do so, we only punish ourselves by cutting off our vital sense of pleasure and true satisfaction in our incarnate life.

Past Experiences of Conscience

Of all the experiences within the first stages of the afterlife, the most revealing impression was of this fact, that the innate sense of wise council in man called conscience, historically and presently, is a great regulator of justice and harmony in the incarnate worlds.

In one clear example that was an actual event in the afterlife experience I came to understand my former blindness and unenlightenment. I was in Grade 4 and had just run out to the schoolyard when I heard the recess bell. I ran quickly over to a nearby ditch alongside a farmer's field that bordered the school ground. I was searching for snakes, crayfish or anything similar that I thought might make an impression upon the girls in my class. Somehow, I had unconsciously accepted the fact that if one is not afraid to hold creepy-crawly or slimy critters, girls would find you attractive and even worthy of affection and trust.

I was just beginning to make my move with a garden snake I had found slithering alongside the muddied edge of the ditch, and as I turned to show the girls

my quick and fearless skills, a larger boy took the
snake from my hand and used it to scare the girls away.
Although I was unmoved by his actions, when he
turned and tried to push the snake into my face I
rebelled and wanted to get even with him for my own
sense of humiliation.

Within moments, I found myself being tossed
upside down and he was pressing his knees into my
arms that were flat on the ground. He then pulled down
the seat of my pants and shoved the snake into my
underwear. I was terrified as I was completely over-
powered and unable to escape from his clutch, though
I did manage to pull my arms underneath my chest and
reach into my clothes to search for the snake. I heard
a number of children and classmates laughing aloud
and, when I was finally released, I became very embarrassed to notice that a girl I particularly liked was having a roaring, gut-wrenching good time laughing at my
expense.

I couldn't find any humour in the situation and
remembered wishing I could humiliate him just as he
had done to me. I felt that I had lost my integrity as a
male and that it was unrecoverable. From that day I
swore to get even. But even though for several months
the feeling stayed with me, I never did have my
revenge on him.

On another day some fourteen years later, when I
was working as a supervisor for the Ford Motor Corp.,
it so happened that this same fellow was one of the
adults working in my area, under my foremanship.
Although I was reminded of that time, and of my previous desire to get even, I simply ignored the fact, pay-
ing little attention to the man himself. In fact, what was

revealing was my disinterestedness which, in itself, demonstrated a quality of arrogance and disgust within my personality that had a conditioning effect upon my own perception of people and of life at that time.

Yet I was really feeling distinctly alienated from him and even have to admit to a certain dislike for him. Moreover, I was unable to feel free in relation to my own sense of conscience as I still had not let go of the memory. Many of the other men that worked under my supervision greatly approved, - and were even fond - of him, but I could not feel that way myself, regardless of how he now behaved. I could only look at him as if I were seeing right through him, attempting all the while to ignore what might lie behind the desire to hide behind my eyes.

I was personally troubled by this and had spent many hours wondering why I could not let go of such a petty and immature perception, though only when the experience was relived in the afterlife did I come to understand it clearly. For it was then that I discovered that my choices to like or dislike individuals were directly linked to an unconscious recognition of their shortcomings in relation to their own innate sense of conscience.

I had actually charged this person unknowingly with lacking conscience in the original act and had left the memory unchanged. I was very surprised and equally awed to learn that each of us has the ability to recognize to some degree that particular measure of conscientiousness, ethics, morality, or principle, and such is determined sentiently. It is a matter of evolving instinctive development that this innate detection of another's spiritual well-being can be identified. Depending upon how much direct attention one pays to the subject, clarity and focus can enhance this innate attribute of the soul itself.

These early conclusions regarding my feelings towards certain people often made me realize how unlike myself it would be for me to act against my own conscience by maintaining my dislikes. It was my discord with my own conscience that was responsible for the continued memory of self-conditioning and this eventually led to my freedom once I realized how to resolve such issues and how to live with my own conscience. Later I discovered that everything we do, every aspect of our expression, appearance and sense of worth throughout life depends on how true to ourselves we are when making conclusions in the light of conscience. It does not matter whether one is conscious of this fact or not, the effect remains similar. A greater appreciation for justice and the laws of life itself can be gleaned as well as truth of one's own essential purpose through progress as a soul in incarnation.

We acquire wisdom by recognizing that our actions and influences are a matter of conscience; the evolving personality gains insights and wisdom through true compassion for those who have yet to know they are of Divine origins. I found that at specific times when I myself had humiliated others, much of the satisfaction for life was lost over time by not having resolved the unrest in my overall view of myself. My very love of life had diminished due to my not having resolved innate issues of conscience over even the slightest, most subtle actions. Having freed myself by seeking to resolve old experiences with my conscience, it was akin to communicating directly with the soul. A mode of opportunity for scrutiny and a seemingly wise sense of inner council and guidance emerges. I never suspected that my main problem in life was that I did not notice the infallibility of such a sense.

At another stage in the process I also learned that every excuse I had for losing interest or affection for others came by having noticed something in them that seemed to verify they had lacked conscience. It had not occurred to me, though, that while my judgements were partially correct, it was my personal opinion and subjective conclusions of others which lacked conscience. Much was gained in this way by understanding the means and ways of others in the world who as yet do not perceive their own truth. My own revelation came about as my soul showed me how my conscience was resolved prior to my appearance in this lifetime and that it is the same for everyone.

Though I witnessed the absence of conscience in others historically while in the revelatory light of the sprit, these memories have also been long resolved by the attendant actors within their own sphere of life and contact. The lesson of this lifetime, however, was more about the condition that has come to be known as personality syndrome. In the afterlife drama I saw that conditioning takes place in youth that is directly related to a syndrome that is relative to the instinctive qualities of the human brain and that the evidence of another lacking conscience while correct in context may not be seen for the truth at the root of the material form we inhabit.

I was shown how the tendency to complain, criticize and punish others has become a world problem and that few thinkers in our time have yet been liberated from this syndrome. It was not until much later in the afterlife process that this was understood clearly, so for now I will only mention it and will bring this revelation to light preceding the second stages of the actual afterlife experiences (see page 203).

As to the fact of one's experiences being a matter of conscience, my soul demonstrated the thought process to be a methodology of experience and challenge to the awakening individual, and that through the recognition of certain principles arising out of the watchfulness of one's conscience, the whole of history could be easily observed and understood. As I was given the opportunity to do so, it came to me that, as souls in progress, everyone who might now be recognized in our world as a historic figure and even our present world leaders could be reconsidered in the light of their own personal association with their innate sense of conscience, observable through speech, conduct or policy.

An example of this occurred as I selected certain individuals who were a part of my own life experiences. I learned to see all historic figures in this same revelatory light afterwards. The insight that I sought to utilize was as follows; 'Those who have an awakened sense of conscience in their lives are apt to be leaders of integrity and their influence in their time would and should be seen to be objective, uplifting, or positive, at least as far as the masses were concerned. Those who did not have this awakened sense or who did, but did not listen or care to follow such innate guidance, would and should likewise be seen for their fruit.'

Upon close inspection of these individuals as well as many historical figures, it became very clear how we are all spiritually perceived in our day. It was true that those who have lived in the light of conscience had added great invention, literature and revelation in positive and lasting ways. Indeed, the present free world is the result of those who sensed that all was a matter of conscientious freedom. Those who did demonstrate a negative or reserved sense of conscience proved to be most influential in confusing, separating, abstracting and suppressing the masses, generating the great sea of blood and sacrifice over their unchecked selfish motives. When I recognized that people are known for their expression in the light of their conscience, I began to see how little the personalities of these historic figures mattered. It was through this that the insight into the world of historic periods came to light and later, how my own acquaintances and experiences in life proved the measure of my own light.

I came to know what it was to realize the challenge of daily life in the world of human incarnation. I understood that every thought and every action weighed upon the mind and psyche was a challenge, to be able to live and learn to live in the light of conscience or to suffer the ramifications for having not perceived as much. It was not as if there were some form of punishment generally, or some kind of karma for being unenlightened in our incarnate lives and so it was that the challenge to live in the light of conscience was not a general rule to be followed and kept. There was no hell or endless pain for the awakened soul; however, there is conditioning of the personality and of the psyche through ill intent and selfish aspiration. Only in the choice to hang on to selfish desire does it work out that a soul is prevented from aiding the psyche in any one life from attaining the liberated goal of enlightenment. I say this to establish the fact that the reason for our challenge to recognize our potential is not easily comprehended by those who have little insight into the matter of the innate conscience in man. These experiences of testing are truly only a prelude to the eventual use of one's own potential power to shape and influence life in general.

A principled control of these powers is subjectively maintained through the vehicle of the form and the organs of the body by the soul so as to insulate one from one's own unenlightened wishes manifesting objectively. The law of life as a soul is to not impose on another. The freedom to do is a fundamental reality for us all though a need to comprehend the doingness of our nature is the temporal objective here. Only in the denser sphere of shapes and appearances can the evolving ego gain the necessary gift of identification, or in particular; the sense of self! As light beings, unaware of our own Divine nature as yet, and likewise unaware of our self-generated manifestations, we are immersed into a world of appearances created by ourselves. It is not as if we have not ultimately decided on this venture in incarnation.

I should suggest here that prior to our earthly incarnate stages of development, and long before the sensitive vehicle called the soul is manifest, our nature is Divine and therefore our power to manifest is likewise. It is our Spiritual intent for individuality rather than our soul's intent that leads us all to the seemingly sacrificial life of a struggling personality, unaware of the possible communion with our soul through the still small voice of conscience.

Our soul, having evolved sentiently through many shapes and forms over manifest time, follows the innate instructions of the Divine Spirit within. These instructions and activities of the soul are subjectively manifested in our personality aspirations along with our sensory instruments. It is through the sense perceptions that the personality gains vital information from both inner and outer worlds, though only when the sensory equipment of the soul is discovered as the precursor of these can the understanding of power, limitation and liberation be discovered. I should also say that only through the right use of the soul's senses and their employment in this world can liberation from form be attained. It is as if the soul and the personality must unite while living in the light of conscience shed by the innate Divine spirit within, before the understanding and the sight of immortality and eternity can be revealed personally.

With regards to power, and the sense equipment of the soul, I was shown how we are all materially bound (as personalities) to draw conclusions of events and experiences many hundreds of times per hour through self-talk and visualization. This of course was now with the understanding that we do so with or without the utility of, or intentional use of, our own sense of conscience. It is a primary function of the body to be an information processor working on our behalf that we use in our incarnations to develop thoughts into forms. To think with intention and to wrap our thoughts up in feelings, and then to empower the memory of such conclusions, were revealed as the very means used for all things manifest in the universe. Even the billions of parts of the human appearance are composed of intelligent and attractive forms that aid us in our developed wishes of life manifestation, for as long as we are willing to maintain the vitality of their combined units of life. When the soul departs the form, taking with it the vital will and energy of its own doing, the lesser units of life return to the natural resources of the involutionary worlds for further progress as souls themselves.

It is no error to perceive all apparent units of life as generative souls with a yearning for self-consciousness as much as we ourselves have today. Nor is it a mistake to consider that the conscience of particles in physics conforms to this unified law. Every aspect of our visible universe is in the process of developing that same consciousness that we innately long for when we say we seek the truth of ourselves. And so it is that desire, feelings, emotions and empathy represent to a certain degree the quality of will that one senses upon the progressive road to illuminative consciousness in eternity. I am not saying that love, compassion and benevolence or even grief is a lower grade of desire or will in man, but that the way one uses these attributes of the soul in a feeling way such as to produce empathic rapport or to desire to possess and to preserve, or even in self-defence, is the experience that registers most for us when the soul is not known. Once we know ourselves to be souls, we find that our manifestations in time and space under the direction of an agreement with one's sense of conscience, tend to uplift the individual and those relative to the invention or predilection.

Love is a conscientious power as is the polarity of love in the expression that we call grief. Love is that aspect of our nature that draws us to shape and produce form by desire for union in all kingdoms. Grief is that particular power of love that releases the bonds of our creations in this world of which we so longed for. I found that as much as many personalities were given to living outside the range of their own conscience throughout history, and that as they produced the effect of harm and injury through affliction of other souls, the need for grief becomes understandable. It is that single aspect of love that prevents the further alienation from the truth of most victims in the world, bearing in mind that the unenlightened masses are largely the victims of a former ignorant society that was effectively manifesting evil upon the world stage due to the misrepresentation of conscience.

Our present and past grief is the relief of the desired attachments that caused the original increase in evil. Selfishness is diminished by true grief. False pride comes to dissipate and an awakening of the Divine in man takes precedence in the heart in such cases. By the affliction of the soul, we serve all the generations of souls to come who will ever inhabit our sphere of education in form. By our own past and present tolerance and expression of grief, our character is developed to a true conviction of, and for, perfect justice. By understanding one's conscience through the experience in grief, the soul arrives at the goal selflessly and not alone. Through grief, the nature of the power latent in man comes to be known as the liberation of all. So it is that shame, regret and remorse are the liberating elements of a thought construct within the consciousness of incarnate humanity brought over from ancient times. In our own way today, we serve the masses of the past, present and future. This vision is an uplifting experience for the soul on its own plane and may not be readily understood by the reader as yet. However, it is only by desire for the good that one can ever know the triumph of a lifetime to have been the selfless gesture of good will to all.

The Dream of Life

It is true that many of our earthly thoughts and loves are presently held as dreams and impressions made out of the desire of our own thinking, but it is not clear to most that thoughts are living things; that thoughts are living influences that reach further than our spoken word, and are the origins of much of what we see and identify that is built out of our environment. The term man-made is merely the very surface of a given truth regarding thought-generative manifestation.

Most people will be very surprised in their afterlife to discover that dreams and the feelings that hold the dreams together as thoughts are like possessions that we unconsciously wish to have and remember forever. They will be surprised even more perhaps when it is perceived that what occurs in our natural field of experience is largely due to what one thinks. Think hard and long enough about any one thing and such a thing appears. Even our unfinished reactionary thoughts of anger, frustration - or, as in my case, 'humiliation' with the boy at school - hold very special meanings to us all.

In very much the same way that a thinker will use the field of vision that we call the 'mind' during sleep periods to speculate and generate hypothetical propositions out of curiosity, the world environment offers a field of greater experience in sensibility and challenge for the thoughts that swing out of our dreams and through our actions into the world at large. Premeditating through dreams with the guidance of one's conscience is what perfects the overall manifestations of our living societies. Premeditation and skill, implemented to bring about the manifestation of any one thing without the guidance of conscience, accordingly often demonstrates itself as a devilish invention. It would be like imagining that there are many levels of dreaming in which one may feel completely detached and safe, and yet another stage of dreams that offer greater challenges where we are convinced temporarily that we are in fact living within such dreams. Most of us have had dreams that we are more than happy to awaken from, having remembered the illusory effect that the drama had upon us. In a similar manner, the soul of the individual enters the dream of life and partakes of a world temporarily that appears to be very real and one in which the illusory effect is sufficient to gain the intended outcome of the originating desire or intent of the dream. Our outer world is a field of opportunity and contact for our soul and yet we are that soul, though unlike the thinker involved deeply within a self-generated dream, the challenge to a soul is to awaken within the dream and resolve the experiences before departing.

I should also mention that while I am using this model for comparison and example, the soul is very much aware before the dream of life begins that other souls will be involved within the identical field and the interaction and challenges that face us all are a highly desired value. The facts of one's conscience are forgotten in each incarnation and if people look closely at their own dreams they may be surprised to find that they are always dealing with matters of conscience whether they know it or not. Every dream is a comparison or evaluation of character and how one manages against those with or without a keen sense of conscience. The child who fears that someone is chasing them in a dream is truly afraid of individuals who act out of conscience though the child may never understand this.

Only when we realize that there is no such thing as death will it be possible for advanced thinkers to make use of their thoughts in productive ways, and this due mostly to a sense of the burden of mortality manifesting from the unresolve of one's conscience that lies just beneath the surface of our everyday feelings. I learned that many things make up a momentary experience and that these are our inspirations hidden in the light of memory. Often, we take our memory for granted not realizing that upon inspection it is possible to recognize our former intuitions hidden beyond our first judgements in any given experience.

In the case of my humiliation with the boy in the school yard, for instance, my soul aided my sight by allowing me to see all the other recognitions that I had ignored for the sake of focusing on only one aspect of that memory. There before me were the manifestations of my own thoughts. I had not sensed that I had experienced a momentary analysis of my own self in that self-denied state of humiliation. In that light, I saw nothing and felt only that first impression of embarrassment. I had actually darkened my mind to any vision in that instant. I ignored the impressions and intuitions that were pouring into my mind. I had ultimately shut out the light.

Convinced as I was in my youth that I knew myself, I was gravely unaware of even the basic function of my own senses let alone my mind or consciousness. Due to this rather static negative state and condition, I was deep within the dream of life and had actually shut out the potential to look into those matters that were meaningful to me. The ability to identify or to account for the way in which I used my mind during this experience was unknown to me. I learned quickly how the masses of thinkers present in the world then and now make use of the instrument of mind but have never learned to use it intentionally with or without the aid of their conscience.

Our great problem in youth, in our very real living dream, is that we are left to raise ourselves and the particulars of our sensory instruments and mind are negated. We may have taken many lessons in life to heart though rarely did we ever hear the instructions on how a mind might be used in general to reveal the mysteries of the universe. Even today the habit of unintentional mind use is the most obvious problem for the developing psyche along with conditioning impressions brought about to these minds by unaware adult societies.

Thousands of times every day we talk ourselves into and out of conclusions, beliefs, conditions, situations and dramas while utilizing our minds to ponder the possibilities without ever knowing that we rarely ever do use our mind intentionally. People may say that they use their mind today to think of tomorrow's events as a method of preparation but, upon close inspection, it becomes clear that the moment of the choice to use the mind for such an experience was not intentional. We are often lured into the next stage of mind use by conditioning that is an unconscious influence in our lives. There are few today in the world who can actually decide what they will use their mind for before they actually put their mind to use.

It was this illusion of self-accountability that is most responsible for the illusory and dreamy effects upon the psyche during most of, if not all, the life of an individual. Only in the afterlife drama have the many come to realize the dream of life and then it is a little too late. As stated previously, the goal is to awaken to the fact that we are immersed in this environment and have the ability to sharpen and intentionally use the instruments of perception at which time it would be opportune to awaken to the facts of our choice for such an immersion. To remember is the first and foundational goal. Then to gain wisdom with regards the nature and workings of our potential in the world of impression and being. To be prevented and suffocated by false ideas, concepts, illusions and interpretations of self by an uncertain world happens to be the condition at present though it was not the intended outcome. The suppression of ideas over historic cycles has always been the agent of ignorance responsible for the shortcomings of humanity's free-will choices.

What is at the root of man is the desire for the continued happiness of the many. What the thinker must return to is this same vision of the world that he was led further away from in former times. The end of the selfish, unconscionable aspirations, dreams and thoughts of the many would - and will - lead to the restoration of the field of experience truly desired by the soul in which death will cease to be an earthly experience. What the souls of humanity wish to manifest in our present world through continued choices for reincarnation into the forgetfulness of our sphere temporarily is an ending to the dense material objectives and appearances themselves. Materialism has had its day. The psyche and the personalities of this world are sufficiently prepared and may now enter into the next stage of development and creativeness where it will be possible for a transition to occur, beginning within the very heart of present-day dreamers among humanity. I will return to this later as there is still much to reveal about the afterlife drama.

The Psyche as Mechanism and Creation of the Soul

I

I would now like to clarify what has been stated so far about the afterlife drama.

The first stages of my afterlife drama was an actual revisitation of my entire life experience, though it was upon and within the environment of my own psyche that these primary and foundational experiences occurred. I was free from my physical body and had no actual personal sense of an appearance of my psyche so to speak, though I was the observer and I was also the experience. I was as much a part of my psyche experience as I am even now in relationship to my seeming outer environmental experiences in and through the sensible human form.

I had senses though they were greatly enhanced

and found that my human senses were merely the out-
growth of my own psyche and soul. I could see though
there was no actual receptacle for an eye or eyes,
though it was equally understood that sight originates
upon and within the psyche itself. This sense of sight
was what I called 'identified', meaning, that in all that
I saw, I was the producer and therefore the object
being observed.

When I recognized my personal worldly acquaintances here in this environment, seemingly trapped in
time with me, they were there as a complete representation of themselves. The full impression of their own
innate nature, comprehension, and even their very
soul, inhabited this environment. This was something
of a mystery to me as I knew that only I was out of
incarnation at these times yet I did discover much of
how it was possible for the soul of another to be in
many places at once and to have left a working record
of its nature in our memories themselves.

I should point out that all I have stated so far was
generally taken for granted and I never found it confusing at all. I say this mostly to aid the reader in
understanding that the entire process is very natural
and one simply goes with it all, as if it were something
we are used to. It is a very alluring and gentle experience of awakening that we can all come to depend on
and utterly trust.

The usual notion of time and space which causes
the average thinker to see things, events and personages as fixed in time and space was clearly revealed to
me, though only after the separation from my own psyche as an actual experience had occurred. Until that
particular separation had occurred, hence affording

the first outer view of my own psyche, I had assumed that there was nothing at all outside this innate environment. At the time, this would have been simply wonderful and would have fulfilled any hopes or dreams I could ever have imagined. If the experience had ended with the psyche itself, I would have been very satisfied, and so it was very astonishing and I felt quite elated to have been privy to such an event overall.

It seemed that from being within my psyche it was borderless and, when looking at the psyche itself, it became apparent that the field of experience desired is itself actually the outcome of many millennia of preferred choices born out of our mass collective innate desires. The perfection of such impressions and environment of the psyche were beyond my range of comprehension in these moments, though it was the flow of pure intuition from the soul that made it possible for me to organize my psyche in such a way as to become aware of the workings of the psyche itself. This was for me a new lesson in a new science altogether. I had learned in my youth that space was made up of less than one per cent matter and the remainder was a void. Here in the afterworld, I came to see that matter itself is not a fact at all. The spark of life that we would call a conscious individual, in the light of the science of being as I came to call it, was a willed action involving electromagnetic (or willed) impulses.

All appearances in the world have developed out of a blueprint of the potential for light to spiral and spin into the seeming appearances of matter itself. In this view, the very molecules and particles that most scientists perceive as the fundamental platform of substance and existence in our world are in effect nothing more than vortexes of light energy travelling within a spin or spiral, thereby creating the sensory illusion of time and space itself. I came to know a world of light in which the soul, through deep concentration, could impel light in such a way as to take the shape of the idea or impressions being communicated.

From that moment on I had come to know that the cause or root of all appearances was itself impressions from an evolved source called the spirit. In this same way, a man may imagine his invention using his mind, and then proceed to make up a blueprint of the imagined prototype before attempting to bring the idea to an observable or working condition in view for all to see, touch and utilize. Another way of looking at this may be considered by asking yourself how many times you imagined a response and then set out to make your point through speech as a means to pass on your gains of insights.

In this manner, the psyche mirrors the activity of the soul, though the presented idea brought about by the world thinker may not be perceived as having a quality of impulsion to it that goes well beyond the spoken words. Nor would one normally perceive the spoken words of our thoughts to have a life of their own beyond the intended influence of being heard. The effect and influence that speech has on a thinker is not yet understood scientifically and so it is not abnormal to think that thought is a disposable and uninteresting influence. Only the influence that the speaker desires to have upon others tends to be the driving force of speech itself.

Rarely will you find someone who treasures thoughts as personal creations responsible for shaping the world at large. Not perceiving this, one may find that life is about something other than the inventiveness of our thinking itself. One might also think of mental impressions and dreams as non-essentials, or as having value only when sufficing to provide the ends of the desired nature. Many think only to suffice the needs of the day while always in the back of their minds the desire for repeated pleasures of the form and the hope for long life tend to be the prime motivators of life itself. For those who do not understand the nature of their own power to impress and to bring objective results into manifestation through speech, their dreams may be merely a form and source of self-entertainment.

In the afterlife kingdom of the soul and of consciousness, however, the objective of manipulating and taming light through the willed conscious act to motive, to invention, to exploration and to discovery, is the basis of the justification and meaning for self-existence. To not know that you can make and shape your life and your future through thinking is perceived as an almost intolerable experience in suffering according to the soul. To live in the world of light, where there is no time, no limit and no fear of death, is as natural as breathing is to the average thinker of our world. In fact, we have and will spend more of our life existence out of form than we will ever find ourselves experimenting in and with the limitations of form itself. The limitations of form are temporal and only justify the ends when considered from the angle of the evolving soul. The psyche that I observed as having been my own was only a mystery to me for a short time in the afterlife experience. Within moments I noticed the patterns of the psyche and how it was that there were many working integrating parts. Just like the various parts of the human body and brain, so too the psyche has various specialized parts that act as a whole under the influence of the consciousness of the soul. It is the soul itself that conducts this arrangement of parts and I discovered that the soul was also the generative agent of the spirit.

In the same way that the central nervous system provides for a purposeful network of communication and integration of all the essential parts of a human body, the life energy of the spirit that I have called soul consciousness can be seen to provide an analogous integrity of the psyche. I was shown how through desire for form experience, the soul manages to generate the blueprint of the psyche within the scope of its own vision, and upon the decision for form in our world as a human, a vehicle is found that will suit the plans. In this I saw how the genetics of a conceived cell were the result of many experiments of long periods of time in our sphere, where the blueprints of the universe were replicated in diverse orders to become the foundation for the substance aspect of the body of appearance called man.

Similarly a genetic psyche drawn out of electromagnetic impulses, appearing in size and relative sight as that of a grain of sand and swept into activity by the concentrating soul, begins to spin and spiral and move according to the whims of its originator. Gathering the necessary atomic material, or as I saw it then, as light assimilative energy, the spirit makes its presence within the life sphere of the soul of the parent to be. As in other kingdoms of our world, this same blueprint lies beneath RNA and DNA and is the doorway for the intended light to flow into the form. A soul inhabits the conceived cell which is the blending itself of many souls considering the egg and the sperm themselves very near the moment of conception itself.

The light of the soul remains in the true sphere of existence and takes form through direct concentration on the manifested psyche producing theatre, the quality of the personality to be upon the embryo all the way up to the moment when the first breath is taken outside the womb. Following the intake of breath by the infant, the objective of the life is then played out by the maturing ego in the body, though the soul often intervenes at certain specific times. Once the personality is developed, however, even the soul that is the focus of that life must not interfere until the conditions of the law have been seen to be fruitful and ripen.

II

Allow me to expand further on the influence of the soul upon its own invention. A connection between the soul and the brain is established though loosely in the region of the pineal gland in the brain, and a second thread of light emanating from the root of the soul enters into the thymus gland right next to the human heart. Through the blending of impression and of light entering into the heart and into the bloodstream, a sensible and intelligent activity begins to foster the body unto maturity. The blood carries the vitality of the continued aspiration of the soul that eventually merges within the brain of the individual until a more appropriate time and opportunity for contact can be made with the brain in maturity.

As the personality is assimilated throughout the form, the given historic and genetic impressions of the soul of the mother and of the father unite with the soul of the indwelling presence and then a second merging of the psyche begins around the age of 14. By the time one has reached the age of 28, and this is true for most today, the intuition is beginning to make itself known and the place of its origin within the head becomes a growing concern to the individual. In these ways, the soul is able to gather impressions and engage in a rare form of communication with other sentient beings who share a common privilege and opportunity to expand upon their own conscious abilities. The gains of one life are the gains of the soul forever and in this way I have come to understand the act of incarnation as an educational adventure in eternity where the potential of our own nature has yet to be touched upon to any degree.

III

Getting back now to the idea that the psyche is a mechanism and creation of the soul, I would like to say that the psyche itself is a microscopic replica of the universal blueprint itself. This means that the whole of the universe is capable of recognition by the soul. It suggests that the soul has the distinct opportunity to discover the who, what , when, where, and why of everything. In fact, everything that is, has been and will be has been given to the soul as a gifted opportunity and as a map through the eternity of the One great life. Every moment and every event is recorded within the psyche of the universe itself and access to this record is possible for the soul that has come to know the workings of this blueprint. It also means that we are made in the image of the One great life.

Even as we are the conscious extension of our souls' aspiration in this world, the soul itself is an image of that great One life as well. In this mysterious and miraculous way, it can be known that when we are dealing with a parenting soul, we are actually dealing with a representative of the originating universal entity that I regard as God. I should also state that one particular benefit of generating the psyche and personality aspects within the confines of an incarnation of great limitation and pain is that a specific uniqueness and originality becomes our individualized gift. I am suggesting here that the prime import according to this scheme of education upon the material plane is to provide the gains for individuality!

I will return to this subject later in the recounting of the afterlife drama.

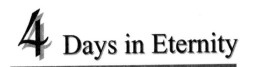

4 Days in Eternity

Part II
The Second Step

The Afterlife Drama: Stage II

It had been some eight hours or so before the attending doctors, surgeons, and specialists had completed their task of stabilizing my body before they moved me into the ICU.During this same time period, I had returned to the hospital scene on two distinct occasions and was able to capture the notion that my chances of surviving physically were against the odds. I was not troubled by this news and a certain disinterestedness regarding these facts allowed me to free myself from any further concern. It was not as if I did not care that my body was being maintained on life-support systems that first night, or that I was not going to live, though I was curious as to how the link between my liberated self and the physical body was being maintained. My greater interest and choice was to continue further into the drama of the afterlife and release all other interests for the time being.

For the short time that I had returned to the scene and had actually entered back into my body, I had noted that there was little I could do to aid in the healing processes, though I was given insight into the fact that on the second time I had returned, my host rhythm had subtly changed and was sufficient to organize a balanced condition within the body. I had been informed that I had actually influenced my own body chemistry by simply transferring my natural sensory condition back to my body while being elsewhere.

I soon came to understand how my regained sense of joy in life, along with the dramatic influences of the afterlife experience, were enough to inform my brain and its active information network. The message received and acted upon by my brain was one of vitality and excitement. A measure of strength and conviction had also brought about a direct influence over the healing processes.

I was shown how the effect of one specific rhythm when influenced by another host rhythm, tends to communicate their stateliness and how it is that one tends to adopt another's likeness. In practical terms, it would be like being in a very despondent mood while not feeling very well, and then feeling suddenly uplifted by another person's presence in the room which thereby has and acts as a direct effect on our body chemistry.

The effect that we all have on each other at any given moment is not necessarily comprehended so well by the average thinker of our world at large, though even the slightest change of mood or attitude by one thinker upon another is an easy matter to relate to. It is simply another means of direct communication used by all of us at all times, though little time or study of this great assimilative quality is known by many. In my case, there was tremendous stress on my body, especially during these first eight hours of surgery and trauma, and even though I was not participating consciously, my own mood and state in the afterlife scenario was trickling back to my body along a silvery thread responsible for connecting the two as one. It was my soul's restorative influence, being of a greater purity and vitality, that was nurturing me by its presence, and was likewise automatically managing to aid in the work of salvaging my body that evening.

This process of transference through contact I had come to understand was also a form of communication for all of the informing intelligence to be found in the less dense worlds and spheres beyond the material one in which we live out our human lifetime.

It was when I stepped out and away from myself in the very beginning of the drama that first night, towards a tremendously informing light of understanding, and away from my body that had been left on the paved lot, that I found myself being informed subtly by the environmental conditions about me.

I had not known then that the means of communication, other than through the seeming channels of intuitive inspiration from my soul, had been largely environmental. The source of inspiration I had understood then was from my soul's ability supersensibly to inform me through visual, mental and feeling influences. Only much later, following the first stages of accountability for my personal incarnate actions in the afterlife processes, did I start to become aware of the method and approach to shaping my own impressions as a means to respond to my soul.

It had never occurred to me early on that I had no sense or desire to speak aloud as with a voice, and it seemed quite natural to me that communication with my soul was as it was. I would simply feel what I wanted to say or know and it came about from that single intention to pass on an impression. This sensible action is identical to what occurs moments before we usually open our mouths and begin to speak aloud in normal cases. The want or desire to inform, shape and influence is what brings our thoughts to life directly. Though there is a working system of communication throughout the entire universe in all its diversity, that can be understood if studied directly, I simply took it for granted then and for the greater period of time in the first stages of the afterlife drama.

Knowing that I could ignore the conditions and situations that were taking place at the hospital scene safely, I ventured onwards into the continued processes of revelation and liberation from my former ignorance.

The Parallel World

When the liberation of my psyche from the thought forms of my human career had come to an end, I had already spent a great deal of time capturing the workings and merits of the environment and activities of this in-between world. I watched for what seemed like several days as the activities surrounding the world's daily events were revealed.

Where I was at the time seemed to me to be a parallel world. The Earth was within my view and yet I was somehow privy to the sounds of many voices belonging to the numbers of liberated souls. I was utterly silent and it seemed to me that I was in a deep meditative act of concentration. I had become curious as to what might occur next for me though my attention shifted to a larger group of individual entities that were gathered together near a city of tremendous light and beauty.

A moment later I found myself instantly transferred to the place I had taken notice of. Once again I felt the presence of an informing presence though when I had arrived at the location suggested, I took note of the fact that I was generally free for a time to follow my curiosity. It felt then to me as if I had a personal guardian, and I remember feeling quite young as I proceeded to listen in on a conversation that was occurring within the larger group.

Within seconds, I found myself at the centre of the conversation though I was not imposing or attempting to communicate personally. I was following the conversation when I took note of the fact that a series of impressions began to merge in my sight and then I realized that these particular entities were quite adept at sharing multiple impressions with each other that began to paint a final picture for me. I was beginning to see how they worked together and what they were planning to do though I was unsure of their particular roles here in the sphere or world that I had entered into.

I recall how my attention was shifting again towards the city of light that appeared only a short distance away. The individual entities that were in conference when I had arrived were leaving the city and were going back to what I thought to be another system from which they had come.

My curiosity ablaze, I began to question every impression I had gleaned. As I turned slowly towards the city before me now, I recall listening to my soul. I was informed that there were many millions of advanced souls who have already passed through the human conditions of incarnation at one time or another and in other systems than our own. These advanced souls and spiritual adepts were described as active members of an organized fraternity, having their own particular skills and objectives, who at one time or another had taken on the temporal decision and commitment to work with advancing organizations and groups.

I was surprised to find that we were part of a system within our local universe consisting of many levels and varying interests that had been organized for aeons of time. These particular ones that I was observing and listening in on were not from a planet within our own solar system but they rather were located as a fraternity and a dynasty well beyond the environment of our local galaxy. Their present home was described as a place in space rather than a home of origin or of a planet.

I found myself wanting to ask more and more and learned that within our own world there were large organizations and fraternities present upon many levels: some close to our planet, some within a relative dimension where the Earth remained visible such as the one I was now in, and more still on physical levels as well as spiritual. I took it to mean that the community at large here on Earth numbered some 60 billion in all. Of the six billion inhabiting the planet there were many who live and work among us who are already beyond the transitional stages. Each group or family as I came to know them who were maintaining form and appearances as we do in our human career, although strikingly rarified and beautiful, had dedicated themselves to a particular phase of development according to their skills and it was of major import that I was informed of how, through sacrifice alone, the order remained.

I was made aware of certain facts regarding the long histories of these dynastic members who serve the direct interests of humanity which caused me to feel a common denominator with them. I was able to sense the quality and stage of development that some had already attained, and in doing so I also found that these particular individuals were not interested, at least for the time being, in gaining a greater freedom from service to the human worlds of material evolution. Their main interest was to see the system and its numerous developing souls to their desired ends, and I found that some have been here for many hundreds of thousands of years relative to our sense of time. As I was becoming more aware of those surrounding me and going about their business, I began to feel that I had returned home for some unknown reason. I began to realize how much sense it was making and also sensed that a decision was imminent.

At one point I remembered having been here before, a feeling of déjà-vu. Some parts of the city of lights, stretching out before me for miles and miles in length and breadth, were very familiar. I recalled the sense of space I had once encountered when entering a French cathedral. Another, even more auspicious occasion was when I visited the US Enterprise while touring an American base. I was unable to gather my memories together but I sensed that I knew the way through this city and had begun to feel that I may have even known some people here.

I was trying to recall how that could be when I had a sudden flashback of going to school here. I could almost remember the rooms and the people involved. As quickly as I put my concentration into trying to recall having been there, I was moving effortlessly through the air towards a section of the inner city. As I passed the entrances to the inner city I recalled a former sense of youthful enterprise. I was now nearing an area where one could say the residents of the city would have their home or their own place and family. I had discovered that there were families here! In fact, I was informed that many of the present groups of souls that were at present on Earth had at one time or another lived here for lengthy periods prior to the globalization of our races. It was a long distant past that I recalled, and a general sense of this period began to come to the fore of my consciousness. I went next into an area where the permanent student residents were located.

Here, I was informed, the younger souls were being instructed in the sentiency of their nature and specialized courses were taught in similar subjects such as physics and literature along with many other subjects that seemed appropriate though almost unimaginable. I remember feeling that by simple observation, I was able to tell at what stage of conscious development and maturity I was in comparison to others here. The younger individuals, though the look of age was not present, seemed almost naive as I observed them eagerly wanting to discover what was taking place as I was escorted through the city.

Perhaps I had perceived them as naïve because their sweetness and unchanging glances were so angelic and compelling and because there was no semblance in them of egotism or instability. However, I was also able to identify the wiser and more purposeful nature among most of them that demonstrated tremendous conviction and control. In every case, I felt as if I were understood clearly by all, and that I too was able to see a comparable difference. Not unlike incarnation on Earth, the faces of the many I had come to observe were as unique and varied as their demeanours. They were as interactive and humorous as young adults and children on Earth are, and it seemed that common systems and processes were replicated here.

In time, I was shown how we on Earth have carried forward our remembrances of this city of cities through inspired works, dreams, visions and concentrated efforts. The architectural designs were somewhat similar to that on Earth as was the plant life, and the lifestyles of the many were almost identical with regard to study, family and sports-related entertainment. There were no televisions as we have on Earth, though there were holographs available of newscasts and educational themes.

Magnetic walls made of a very thin organic material served to initiate these broadcasts that were not limited to news in their sphere, but it was quite normal to gather information on other systems beyond our world as well. Their technology was built within the framework of the entire city and each of its structures, though no noticeable electricity or energy outlets were to be found. I was becoming anxious to discover more about how this could be possible and questioned why earthly life seemed to play so little part in this great and significant reality that was so near and so perfect. I didn't have to imagine what a difference it would make to us on Earth if we only knew, I thought, but as I enquired in this manner, I was instructed to enter into another region of this marvellous city.

Doing so, I found myself able to see myself for the first time. In front of me there were three highly evolved male figures.

The Expansion and Evolution of Consciousness

I was informed by them at once that they were spiritual representatives who were awaiting my arrival. Until that moment I had only identified the radiant effect from my seeming light body and had not thought to question it. It seemed so natural and familiar that I felt I had already become accustomed to the afterlife continuum here. I had taken it for granted that my appearance was similar to those with whom I had come to identify. Other than the colour of the outer skin being more of an indigo white and sometimes gold, I never thought to look for a mirror.

However, here in front of three very alert and obviously intentional figures, I saw myself in their com-

bined thoughts. There was a unique form of communication with these three than what I had come to adjust
myself to thus far. Up until that moment I had perceived myself to be communing through some sort of
empathic quality and intent alone, but now I was experiencing the actual impressions that these three spiritual beings were sharing simultaneously on conscious
levels. It was as if we had exchanged consciousness.
My consciousness was theirs and theirs was mine!

Within moments of meeting them, I began to feel
somewhat sluggish and devitalized. My immediate
impression was that I was being called back to my
body and just as quickly, I was visualizing my body in
the early morning hours of the second day at the hospital. In the next instant I was being shown a process
that I was expected to participate in that reminded me
of the hospital itself. They were about to perform some
sort of surgical process that was not about the body but
about the separation of my lingering secondary
thoughts from my consciousness.

I was told that an expansion of the attributes and
qualities of consciousness itself was about to be established in order that I could pass on to another stage in
the afterlife processes. Little did I realize that I was
about to experience the full range of memories over the
historic past. Though I had revisited the past and was
able to identify the true visual memory of the history of
humanity, I had not expected to awaken to all of the memories that were mine preceding coming into incarnation.

They explained to me through direct telepathic
communion that I would feel out of sorts for a time but
that was only due to the exchange and restoration of a
quality of energy unlike anything I had ever sensed in

the incarnate world or even in the city that I was now in. I was given impressions of others who had also come to understand this procedure and as I was observing the impressions of these others I found myself succumbing to a sleepy unconsciousness. In what seemed like only a few minutes, but would have actually lasted more than a good hour of time as I had understood it, the outcome had been achieved.

It was then that I remembered having lived there for several periods of time over a longer period of no less than 300,000 years of Earth time. I recalled how it was that I had come to our world with many others in order to participate in an experiment that was about to begin here on our little planet. Our homes, lifestyles and even our original families were already used to living in an immortal sphere of our own, and so coming to Earth then was just another part of the ongoing experiment with life in shapes and forms. I first recalled standing on the surface of our world and observing the rise of the Sun to a new day. My actual place of residence then was upon a spherelike station in the upper orbits of our planet. There were others doing likewise and the sky was filled with our presence like so many stars in the night.

I then recalled how experiments that we would call 'scientific' were the first stages of our habitation here. In fact, many of the smaller creatures we find on Earth today were originated by these groups of researchers and the science of light that enabled us to tame and make use of light itself was the standard. There were many other thousands of participants that came from very advanced and distant worlds of our universe as well, and their focus was on the other planets and systems in this localized universe. These beings were not only immortal but had varied shapes according to their will, and often a gaseous state was the most suitable for hundreds of millions of them.

Not all of the arriving participants were able to shape change and much of their reason for coming was to participate in the opportunity to do just that though the experiment was intended to last for several thousands of years. These less advanced but equally important groups were not generally aware of the science-based knowledge that was being used freely and openly upon our world, though there was no law to limit their access either. In fact, the only law outside the bounds of the continuum that existed were related to the simple gesture of imposition. It was not allowed that one could impose their condition or state upon anyone else, and, regarding the creatures that were being experimented on, there was to be no misuse by sentient imposition upon them whatsoever. Only those who were able to understand that they existed at all were subject to these laws and the officiating members were also the hierarchal order of the world from which I had come and where the transference, or upgrading of consciousness itself, had not been allowed to occur. With this in mind, the host of billions eventually arrived and began to settle in our local solar system for the great experiment. I recalled how very important this one law was and before the day was out, I had come to remember the reason for it.

In ancient times, long before our world even existed, advanced groups of spiritual entities, who were responsible for maintaining and protecting the advancing systems that were then only just maturing and gaining consciousness, had come to impose upon specific groups whose interests in consciousness and its pliability were being exemplified by using beings from these same systems without consort or agreement. In simple terms, the practice of cloning and advancing consciousness directly in the material worlds of evolution was being applied, and these incidents presented a new and unexpected situation for us all. A great deal of damage to the less advanced creatures within these same systems had occurred.

It would be like hearing tomorrow in the news that a scientist had come to learn how to transfer intelligence from one being to another, and in doing so he demonstrated the fact by making a dog equal to ourselves in intelligence. Though the dog could not talk, it was certainly able to understand that it was now a victim of its own instincts and, to a larger degree, becoming aware that its short life was all that it would ever get unless the scientist was to make sure the same intelligence was transferred sooner than at the time of death.

The ability to transfer consciousness from one form to another was not a new scientific discovery and the improper use of this technology had long been prohibited. The temptation to use this technology by most of the unified order had, until those moments, never been challenged.

Consider that our consciousness is transferred slowly into the very form we inhabit as humankind. Then consider that we also have a continued opportunity to take other forms though not like the scientific methods mentioned above. The idea here is that consciousness is all that is evolving in the universe, while all other things adapt or interact, and the temptation to find a suitable form from which it would be possible to advance for long periods without having to transfer to another body might be easily understood. However, it is not necessary or correct to transfer one's consciousness into forms that we prefer at the expense of the creature life that would be utilized, and further, the ramifications automatically exclude the natural processes that have been predestined by Divine intent.

In short, I was able to recall how certain groups that had come into being through the natural direction of the originating and perfected influences of our universe were unable to control the temptation to advance as other worlds had. These groups wanted to upgrade most unnaturally to the most advanced stages of consciousness and identification to be found within the limits of the material worlds of appearances themselves. It should be understood that in as much as there are more than 700 trillion inhabited spheres not to mention the cities in space, or multidimensional worlds themselves, our particular evolution along sense-related lines was not always the same. In other words, we might imagine having twenty more senses in our human incarnation that we don't have now, or everyone changing to a specific look and body type. At first we might think how wonderful it would be but the diversity of life in its eventuated task of gaining a range of conscious lifestyles would bring an end to diversity itself. Or, if one wants to really go out on the limb, imagine that there was a limit to evolution! Well, without understanding the full ramifications, which was impossible to comprehend by these specific groups at that time, this indeed was a fact that was occurring at great expense to the societies where it was taking place.

This scenario I have just mentioned has come to be known today as the Great Fall by most of the institutional organizations surrounding religious studies today.

There are huge societies of entities differing in shapes and appearances and sensibility of consciousness, even now in our local universe that have continued to suffer along with humankind because of the earliest incidents mentioned, though the effects and transitions that remain today are soon to diminish altogether.

Although there is and remains to be some measure of distance or disagreement that persists among certain groups of entities, the ramifications have come to be understood fully by these same. Even still, these groups have themselves suffered as they have lost the sense for spirit that is so true and alive to all others except them. Pursuing, and attaining to some degree, their original experimental goals has ultimately prevented the natural sentient condition for evolution of their own consciousness among their races. When one of these entities suffers the loss of a limb or damage of the bodies they inhabit, they are restored through highly advanced cloning techniques, and that is the most of their experiential gains with spiritual matters that they have attained. Even though they could allow themselves to die as we do on Earth through release of the form, the sensibility of the spirit within has been lost for them. It is for these reasons that there remains today a number of protective fraternities whose task it is to uphold the laws and to prevent these same entities from free play with our societies. I will speak more about this in later chapters.

As I came to feel complete once more in the presence of these three spiritual authorities, I remembered the original purpose of my own recent incarnation and it was in that moment that I began to prepare myself for the return home. The cities of light that stand ever so slightly above the present cities of our material world are home to millions of spiritually advancing groups from many other worlds though many of the original incarnates have either returned home and gone on to greater things, have advanced to higher levels of the limitless paradise worlds, completed their tasks in the formless worlds of supreme formless individualities, or are the advanced souls from out of the generative societies and races of our own little watery planet.

Within these groups are some of the aforementioned great ones who have returned or have continued to this day as authorities of the world races and who manage the evolution of consciousness itself. Still others remain at very advanced stages of development spiritually, as informing sources or empowered influences over our societies themselves. There are also a large number of formless spiritual guides, adjusters and messengers whose task it is to intervene impersonally in world affairs. Of the last group, there are great personages who instruct and reveal the nature of the will of the unified universal order and who oversee the millions of world servants.

In my case, I came back to our world on numerous occasions throughout my own career, as a means of maintaining conscious integrity with the masses as they have graduated from one expansion of consciousness to another. It was my own chosen objective to understand the whole of the appearance of individualities and the advancing consciousness of Deity as it works out in the limited though originating material worlds.

A Career in Eternity

I guess one could say that I am something of a behavioural specialist who has chosen to observe the entire process from one end to the other. I say this at this point only to shed some light perhaps on the idea that as it is in heaven, so it is utterly similar on Earth thus far. Our motivations, opportunities, privileges, systems, careers, and of course our own sensibility for uniqueness among the many, are so very similar. The one difference perhaps is that there is a bridging of consciousness that we can expect to observe in humanity that is slowly emerging and surfacing today which will bring the next major expansion of consciousness to all the inhabitants of our sphere and system whereas there is already a working collective consciousness of all the inhabitants in our sphere.

That being said, there is only a short time remaining before the two worlds are united. Within a very short period of time (a reason for my own appearance today) the kingdom of the soul will soon be revealed and the worlds that I have spoken of thus far will be identified likewise. Aside from the fact that such a stage of development just happens to be the most impressionable and liberating experience for the souls of our particular world, I had chosen to experience the loss of consciousness in returning through birth in order that I might glean the very impact that will occur for the many who must pass through the transition from individuality to group consciousness. I felt personally that if one could understand the world previously, and then be enabled to participate as others would have to do in the collective, that the event would represent special opportunities for the longer goal ahead.

Allow me to suggest here that one is always subject to choices with regard to a career in eternity. The choice made by myself and many others for active service to humanity through to the end of ignorance ever more, and the development of associative sentient skills for such a continuing task would also serve to promote and advance such skills to a point where it would be possible to linger for a time with the whole of humanity in the paradise worlds of the formless spheres.

Much like having to choose to specialize in certain educational standards in our world, one seeks the ultimate goal that is knowable and then finds oneself living the lifestyle necessary not only to attain the outcome but to be elevated by the particular stages of progress along the way. In just such a way, we have all chosen whether we know it now or not, to be and to express that which is innately possible.

I know that many who have considered the continuity of life beyond the human kingdom have likewise allowed themselves to accept the premise that there is a paradise awaiting, though I am likewise aware of the fact that few are ready for the paradise of 'eventuated attainment'.

It is only natural for a thinker in our time to want to

be released from the illusion of mortality, pain and suffering, while also hoping that work and learning also come to an end. The idea of feeling or being incomplete doesn't usually rest well with the rational mind though it is also a truth worth knowing well. It is a fact that we shall not come to the unfathomable, ineffable, immutable and infallible end of our journey following the release of our human forms, but rather we shall feel complete in union with the Divine long before such a time or rest occurs.

It is best to get used to knowing that the meaning of life is not found in its ends but rather in its Divine livingness as we pass through one stage of uncertainty to another, and on to the heights of the infinite. It is a complete truth that we are incomplete though this does not mean that we are incomplete intelligence. We are what we are, though the unfolding and wilful emulation of our innate and Divine nature is a progressive one. Such is the commonality of a master and an aspirant.

Though the most advanced are best informed, when it comes to understanding and being like the universal intelligence, there is no barrier or limitation between the least and these, when in the company of each other. One speaks intimately with the Divine though the Divine are not aloof or unable to share in our likeness at any time. This can be one of the many very special surprises on the day that we come to commune with the Divinely well attained. Each of us has the ability to commune with the highest of the highest even though our transition in consciousness and identification may take until the ends of time and space. In this, there is liberty and further evidence of our godliness to come.

The Journey

Going further now into the next stages of the afterlife, I was concentrating on balancing out the vital energy influences that had come upon me through the revelation of my former self. In this unified condition I was still able to feel that I was also subject to the limits of the human brain and as I was about to ponder the decision to live or to leave the body permanently, I found myself being surrounded by a larger group of spiritual authorities within the same area of the city.

There was so much more I wanted to do and to see and, likewise, there were other former earthly relationships that I wanted to seek out, but time was growing short for me before the decision was to be made and I was told that we were going back to my most recent home outside our local solar system. As I felt our moving together, as if bound by our unified wills, I discovered that we were being transported from out of this world and I watched as we fell away from the face of the Earth while swiftly moving towards the Sun. It seemed to me that we were advancing away from our planetary sphere though my sight of the Earth from this position persisted as the feeling of falling backwards and outwards, this sensation was unexpected.

As we approached the region of our extremely radiant Sun, I was awed and astonished to discover a most angelic host numbering in the hundreds of thousands that were coming and going from the Sun and throughout our system. Their appearance was of an electrifying gold, blue and white, and I was informed that these were specific groups of willed angelic hosts, and it was their objective to act upon the immediate instructions of that particular authority I had referred to as the 'Light of the World'.

They gave the impression of being very wise, complex and determined. It seemed through observation alone that a great deal of insight into the workings and activities of the entire sphere was clearly known to them. I couldn't help but interpret the impressions to mean that these specialists had a continuing and perhaps unimpeded contact with the greatest of our local authorities in the spiritual spheres.

My journey continued beyond and through the Sun itself and within moments our solar system fell completely out of view. Though it seemed that we were making great speed, it likewise felt that there was little motion as we proceeded to our determined destination. My impressions of the Sun, and the numbers of highly advanced workers, were becoming more expansive as the thoughts of the authorities present had mingled their impressions with me in a single-minded way.

I was shown how the Sun was home to these advanced and empowered authorities, both visible and formless, since its original culminating moments of activity. Many of the individuals within these groups were themselves following the direct impressions of the residing authorities while also attending to the matters of our entire solar system. They were the protectors and initiators of many earthly events and were most responsible for the overall integrity of the evolving systems. A certain class of these individuals were working more closely with the evolution of the planetary deities than with the populations of souls and it was then that I was introduced to another aspect of the resident spiritual authorities.

It was to be known that certain of these highly developed and almost unfathomable dynastic authorities had originated within the highest realms and spheres of the universal order. It was the objective of some of the creator deities to furnish themselves as if with a gown of light in the material worlds through the eventuation of a planetary system. Once they had appropriated the body of a working system, their objective was to bring about the outcome of an even greater authority not to be found or known in the material worlds at all.

Their primary objective was to be of service to their own respective authorities by building and maintaining their focus within the system they were manifestly responsible for. Following the initial stages, they were expected to persist in the preoccupation of eventuated life. In some cases this could mean that several billions of years or more would be spent concentrating every moment on the outcome desired. In our particular case, the Sun represents the authority of the solar deity that was utterly responsible for our swinging, spinning and wobbly little planet along with all of the life that has appeared in the system itself.

It is as if these authorities and creator-like entities were the originating sources of all life to be found in the universe, and their obvious task was in eventuating individualized life and diverse forms best suited for the intent of establishing a response through conscious development. In each case, the unique dynamics of these most advanced parenting authorities were manifest in and through the populations of souls that appeared through their system until the cumulative ends of the goal itself. As such, the variable qualities and nature of the One Great Life were diversified and manifest in the character expressions of all those who have ever been eventuated.

It would be like saying that the differences between our mass characteristics and attributes as earthly beings would become noticeably different than those of other systems, even though the identical nature of the one life was evident in all. In saying as much, one could imagine that the innate qualities of one's parents are most often responsible for each sibling's appearance and, to some degree, their overall demeanour. Just as one chooses relationship with another in our world, so it follows in the highest of all spheres.

I believe that the common denominator that stood out most for me then was the simple fact that the diversity of one's nature comes about through the activity of relationships within the whole of our universe. In any given situation, there is a commonality between all spiritual beings. We all belong to one original dynastic family. In following this impression one could easily understand how it would be possible to perceptually discover, appreciate and understand the nature to be discovered in each other. If I noticed a certain quality in one entity, I was able to identify this same quality in myself even though it had remained unrecognized earlier. In other words, the longer one associates more directly with the most advanced ones, the greater the opportunity for discovering a likeness that is commonly innate. In this same way I was able to understand how the sense of conscience most noted in the human spheres of activity was also a sensibility present in all others.

As for the most advanced, I came to understand

how one aspect of our nature that is evolving along with our conscious condition at any one moment comes to be a power at another time. As in the aforementioned case about conscience, I was able to identify the condition of the will to be similar. The will of the angelic hosts found in the locale of our own Sun was a most immovable quality of a perfected sense of conscience along with a steadfast sense of righteousness. The companions with whom I merged demonstrated a tremendous expression of attributes on the spiritual levels such as benevolence and compassion which had, at one time or another, been developed through participation in a human career as we do now.

I am attempting here to indicate some relative truth that we are all of the same family and that we are all born of the likeness of the originating source of life everywhere to be found in existence. Knowing this, even though I was in constant awe, I felt overwhelmingly comfortable being looked upon by these same beings. I knew that whatever they might see in me that I had not yet understood was indeed completely understood. I felt there could be no surprises on their part and I learned to depend on this as a trusted revelation. I was also informed that the least important issue for the advancing souls of our spheres, as well as others, was the human personality. Very little importance is ever given to the misunderstandings or ignorance expressed by faltering personalities whose objectives were not yet integrated enough to aid them directly.

I was assured that the main themes of work between the undeveloped ones and the resident spiritual authorities were only of a spiritual nature and that the musings, dreams and complaints of the thinkers of our world had little to do with the attentiveness of the waiting hierarchy of servants bestowed to our keeping. In having noted this, I was reminded of the illusion of mortality that continues to be the main plight of humanity. I was relieved to know that the petty ramblings of those who would discriminate or judge others with such harsh criticism in incarnate situations, especially over religious issues, were largely ignored. It was in moments such as these that I had begun to aspire to reconsider the needs of humanity even though I was passing on to greater truths and realities with each impression.

As we continued in our journey through time and space, I was reminded of the residence of the Great Ones on the Sun and I was stunned to recall that I became innately anxious and felt very small in those moments. It was in thinking this that I found myself merging with one of my companions. I was moved to remain very still and calm as his consciousness fused with mine and I captured the awakened vision of the one called 'The Light of the World'. I remembered looking, or at least observing, certain aspects of the many who were present at these moments, though I had avoided direct contact for some unknown reason. Going further, I was shown how many feel compelled to look away from such purity and power; advised as to the normality of this moment, however, I was being urged to take this vision and allow myself to feel the full impact of being recognized by this great authority. In doing so, I had succumbed to a despairing grief that almost dominated my entire consciousness.

A moment of doubt entered my vision and I noticed how I wanted to avoid being noticed as I felt very unworthy of such a contact. It seems I felt I was at a loss to allow myself to be exposed and, in remembering this, I was further compelled to investigate the doubt itself. As it turned out, I was continuing to carry a greater sense of shame over failure on my part to awaken earlier to this great light even though I had certain experiences of a very true effort within my incarnate life. Even though I had come to know the truth to some degree about an innate spiritual contact, I had largely ignored the opportunity for contact. I knew from what followed that certain experiences, even at this lofty position of privilege, had remained unchecked and I was assured that the remnants of the shame I felt were due to the gradation of my own transition in the afterlife. Because I was still connected to my body which lay in coma in the hospital, I was continuing to be influenced to some degree by the unconscious temperament of the brain and its working organs of perception. Until the decision to stay or to return was made, I could expect some interference even now and further into the continuing drama.

I settled for the explanation as I was given to see the whole of it clearly and returned to the vision with greater conviction. When I looked into the eye of this great spirit that I had felt deeply within my own soul throughout the years spent in incarnation, I came to see and notice qualities of such rarity and beauty that I asked for forgiveness for my continued ignorance overall. I felt as if I fell into myself and wanted to die to this great truth and that was when I understood the true sacrificial nature of this being that had found its way into my life through the passionate aspirations to love and to be loved.

There was an even greater truth at the tip of my consciousness that I was barely able to touch on then, but I persisted in attempting to magnify this recognized causal condition. In the moment following I heard the sounds of so many voices singing great words of manifest praise and I felt I was beginning to understand true joy and the grandeur of a perfected heart. It was of a selflessness that was beyond my reach and I was unable to match its emulative quality, but it did cause me to want to embrace the whole of the universe within my still pulsating heart. I was reminded of times when I had met someone who surprised me with their humanity and who had such a tremendous effect on the way I chose to live on Earth, when I realized the word was humanity itself. Our humanity, I thought, gave way to our collective sanctified love.

I had identified the sense and feeling of a true humanity just below the surface of many in my lifetime and in history itself, though through the continued sounds of these heavenly voices I came to reproduce the quality of the one I came to call the Christ Spirit.

The City in the Sky

We were nearing our destination and there before me was what appeared to be a tremendous civilization, beyond the limits of any system or planet. An emerald green hue permeated the space about us as would the Sun on a given summer day, though only a distant constellation could be seen in the background. This was a city in space. Larger than three Jupiters in size, a radiant appearance and multilevel, multidimensional sight. Here, one could see the unveiled truth every-

where. It was as if this location served as a foundational platform for every form of intelligence to be
found within our universe. But I couldn't make out how
this community of a trillion or more individualities
could be accessed: there didn't seem to be any doors
or walls yet one could see the mobility of many in the
transport upon this sphere.

Within moments I remembered having been here
before though my first impression was that we had
approached a constellational resort. A place for relief,
or rest, away from the usual activities and responsibilities of our spiritual selves while active in the material worlds.

I was observing our approach and I felt that I was
awakening once more to a brighter and more vital sensibility though I was informed that the environment of
this scheme was alive and intended to influence. In
short, it was to be known and understood that as one
entered the various levels, their consciousness was
interactive with the core environment and this was to
provide for a collective consciousness for all others
while here.

The starship, as I had come to term it, was made of
an organic material that was able to maintain a rhythmic connection. As I thought to ponder what might be
found upon another level than the one we were on, I
found that the form of communication I had recently
been experiencing with my three hosts was identical in
nature. I was given to feel that I was absorbed within
this environment rather than having entered, and I felt
as if I were utilizing the consciousness of millions. I
could see everyone at once and began to understand
everything that was occurring everywhere at once. As

we moved through a section of the upper levels, I took note that against the open space there was no glass, structure or walls and that it seemed that the boundaries were themselves consciousness. I discovered that they were of a light substance and that indeed I was correct to assume that a highly advanced form of consciousness did provide the structural integrity of the entire vessel.

As to the similarity of the city of lights found in the Earth's atmosphere, this vessel offered similar accommodations and opportunities for its residents, though the residents were of an order and appearance unknown and unrecognized by myself. I became introspective and the sensibility range of the masses found here had an expansive effect upon me overall. I could feel that there were scientific endeavours such as experiments and such going on here and that shared technologies were being investigated and taught.

I found myself ignoring the communications that were occurring within their own combined rhythms for the three companions who had brought me here, though within moments I was being asked certain questions by another intelligence that had us join his company. I took it to mean that he was applying some sort of humour to what he was asking though I was not familiar with the inferences and I was left to listen and participate for the time being. This was the first time I was asked to sit down and soon after there followed a drink that was to be shared by all of us.

My first thought was that I had not even considered the thought beforehand though I was quick to try this out. As I reached out to a glass placed before me I noticed that my appearance had become more obvious here and it was then that I was myself from every angle. I appeared to be about 7 feet tall, slender, ash blond to golden hair. An orange hue was about my head and an indigo colour was radiating out from my forehead as well as throat. It was as if speck-sized lights were barely moving though they did move uniformly every time I gestured or intended to communicate.

While speaking even then without a voice, streams of light issued from my throat and surrounded those present. When I stopped, these lights seemed only to settle back into my aura. As I observed my companions and the newly introduced authority I could not discern any reaction, though when they spoke or gestured it was quite different than my own expression. The table was surrounded with light of varying colours and a natural harmony of movement within the expressive light streams seemed to articulate symbols. These symbols changed only slightly as each continued their communication and then, as I began to understand what was being implied, I saw that they were explaining what it was that I had been brought back here to do for a time. I was about to be left to the company of this one spiritual authority, like a child being dropped of to school by parental guardians, and was to remain here until their return - although when that would be I had no idea.

I was taken to a room within the inner core of the vessel and found that I was able to continue to pursue any idea or invention within my consciousness here in a very private way. I was informed before I was left to myself that I was to be prepared for dinner which would be within a few hours and that there were clothes in the room that I should put on. When I looked at the clothes next to another vessel of fluid left for me to drink, I was astonished to find it had a living feeling to it. As light as air, and as radiant as the energy flow that was observed in the earlier conversations, the red and gold coloured material was also intelligent. I remember looking intensely at the liquid left in the clear vessel like glass and wondering what it was, although as I drank it down, I became very light and drowsy. I had not slept before and I had not sensed the need for sleep but I did lie down next to where my clothes had been left and fell into a deeply rejuvenating and blissful sleep.

Revelation and Return

I

The time had come and I was up and dressed within a moment following the innate call to join the dinner table of special guests. I followed the instructions and found myself entering a room on the upper levels of the vessel where some 200 others in similar attire were already assembled. Soon after sitting down and remaining quite still and comfortable, a voice echoed in the room and the lights were altered simultaneously.

It was as if everyone was one big family, and had known each other for eternity. I simply gave way to concentrating on the voice and noticed that this was the first time there had been words spoken aloud. The sound of the words being stated was unbelievably profound and I felt the whole group of unified participants were being elevated by what seemed like a continuous prayer. I was attending an honorarium for several unknown spiritual hosts who were well identified by the visual impressions I was collecting to myself.

It was as if a celebration of sorts was occurring here while at some other location, millions upon millions of others were also in attendance through telepathic rapport. I felt very privileged to hear about the passage of a couple who were recently united and who had been selected for service as ambassadors to another sphere mostly unknown or heard of in this region of the universe.

A great light appeared and then a voice unlike any other was heard and the semblance of a face appeared overhead as everyone seemed to unite with this same speaker. I gave in as did they to find that I was within the consciousness of a great being most responsible for the organization of the diverse intelligences throughout the entire galaxy and beyond. This, I supposed, was the equivalent of the Cosmic Christ but as I was drawn to listen I came to realize that this entity was of a formless sphere where the originating activities of our universe had been founded. Godlike! was all that I could think then. This must be what God is like!

The conversation and adulation had come to an end though I was overwhelmed by the excitement of having met a being that was so close to the God of my dreams.

I was instructed to return to this same room later and to wear the clothes selected for me by those who were caring for me. I suspect three or four hours had passed and in that time I felt as if I were being prepared to stay here, and that perhaps tomorrow the futile struggle of my body back in the hospital bed would end. With that in my consciousness, I returned to the sleep that I had experienced previously. I remember concentrating upon the possibility of staying here from this point on and I suspect that is why I found myself back on Earth standing before my body for the third time in three days.

II

It was in the early morning of the third day when I returned to the hospital almost instantly, and without any direct evidence of having travelled as I had with my earlier companions, so I wasn't sure if I was just projecting myself or not. I listened to the nurses as they approached the other patients during their rounds and I realized that a major decision had been made earlier that morning as to my future stay at the hospital. When they approached my body, I remember hearing them talk about my relatives who had been staying in London for the past two days. It seemed that my parents had come to visit along with my wife two days earlier and that my parents were going to return late in the afternoon of this particular day. My wife had found a place to stay in the nurses' residence as was usual for out-of-town family visitors who needed to remain nearby.

After comments on my health, they implied that I might not make it past this morning unless they could get a sign from me that they could interpret as a turn in the right direction.

I remained for a time if only to observe my own body at length and found myself attempting to communicate with the others who were in ICU then. Moments later, I found myself speaking to my family though I am sure it was in their dreams. It was suggested that they were going to travel to London to say goodbye to me as they had chosen to think it was in my best interest to be released from the life-support system at the doctor's suggestion. My mother was more insistent that they should do so, though my wife was having great difficulty in accepting the fact that she would have to sign for such a procedure to end my life. She wanted to hesitate but felt the pressure too much to bear since she was unable to understand how this could have happened and was even more uncertain as she discovered I had not paid the life insurance when it was due for the past three months.

I had moved to London and I was not sure if I could afford the insurance policies any longer, so I requested they be cancelled at the time, and now that I was about to be taken off the life-support system, she would have no other means of support. Going back to work as a widow of 28 years of age was of no consolation to her. I tried to comfort her, but in her dream she thought she had somehow contacted me and wanted me to remedy the outcome. She was seeking my agreement to be relieved of the responsibility for the impending decision when I dismissed myself from her presence. I was deeply saddened for her that this was about to occur as I was not yet prepared to make such a decision in the light of what was happening to me in the afterlife. I felt I needed more time than that which was circumstantially allowed.

I pondered the situation for a time and I was able to gather that I had become somewhat aloof from having to consider whether or not I would want to survive my body, or to continue on with the processes that were obviously rewarding and liberating to say the least. I did sense that there was a greater dullness and limitation in staying and finishing my human career, along with the uncertainty of how long the suffering or disabling conditions might interfere with such a choice. I wondered what good it would do, or of what value it would offer to anyone if I did choose to return, and I felt pressed to make a more informed decision.

Unlike the first moments of release from my body - when I was free to proceed without guidance to choose, and with the situation in mind I chose to exit the building where my body was being prepared for a final exit likewise - knowing I would not have to leave in the earlier way and with a greatly enhanced sense of truth and reason, I flung myself out to the skies above.

The Divine Dynasties

Capturing the first glimpse of a new day, I found myself holding my place above the city of London, and watched as the Sun rose above the Earth's edge of time and space. Turning my direction immediately following this event, I thought of returning to my place on the space-based platform. Within moments I was moving through the well-lit sky and out towards my place in the heavens. It was just like awakening from a sleep in the morning while on Earth, as I awoke to the room where I was soon expecting to be met by my new host and guardian.

I was continuing to deal with the evening's revelation and wanted to speak to my new host before the scheduled meeting; however, within a few minutes I found myself entering the great hall where spiritual tributes, praise, and jubilant honours had occurred earlier. This time fewer than 30 individuals attended. Most of them were blessed with tremendous beauty and an air of distinction, and I was awed once again by a sense of Divinity in each of them. The females that were present had captured my attention a little more than the males who were present as they seemed so heavenly and I remember feeling I was absolutely in love. There was such a strong urge from within that impelled me to enter into conscious union with these few though I managed to maintain my integrity.

My impressions were ignored at best and I felt I was childlike to them though there was a moment when one did communicate with me and I felt uplifted and renewed. It was as if she gave me the strength to ignore the sensitivity I had not expected during this time. A moment later, I was privileged to experience a great vision as my host guardian spoke aloud. I was given the impression of a highly glorified couple who were responsible for the dynasties and powers as well as all of the intelligence that had come to be a part of their system. We were consciously united in our vision as the words continued to paint the picture of our relationship to this couple, and it was as if we were giving ourselves over to a commitment to uphold the laws and relationships that were the founding statements of whole societies.

When the spoken word had come to an end, I felt as if I had come to see the history of this particular region of the universe and it appeared that there were dynasties like this same one to be found elsewhere throughout the established kingdom. It was much like honouring a king and queen who themselves were a part of a larger dynasty. I assumed from the impressions that these incredible entities were from another group of individualities of a distant past. I was also informed and assured thereafter that a great sacrifice had been made by this couple originally and that this had set the precedent for the establishment of their order throughout the material dimensions of time and space.

They had come from another world unknown to any at the time our local universe was coming into order and their history was measured in billions of years. I was shown how they, not unlike the thinkers of our world, having invention and creative talents along with a highly advanced sentient control of their environment, were penetrating our dimension and establishing aspects of their worlds within ours. Their intention was to bring about an acceptable integration, through inspired revelation, of the existing systems from which they themselves had evolved in the earliest of times. Many of the worlds where they first appeared had been known to these spiritual authorities in the earliest days of our universe's appearance and though they had completed their first tasks billions of years ago, they had continued to oversee our evolutionary development and from time to time, they were the intervening principalities most responsible for our discovery of each other until our day.

I witnessed an unimaginable scene in which I was able to see the dynastic families in all their glory. I presumed that the authorities mentioned earlier who were being given great respect as a couple were from what I thought to be paradise. Somehow, in my earthly career, I had managed to capture a similar vision that I took to be a creation in my mind of my own liking, and it was this vision that I had held to be the visual response to paradise. Now that my vision was confirmed, I felt able to understand more of the origins of our universe and how the idea of greater glory could not have entered safely into the human psyche earlier.

I was in utter awe and astonishment thereafter and observed how comfortable I was becoming as the moments passed while knowing not only that I had survived my own incarnate life, but that now I was somehow immune to any sense of heavenly judgement. I felt I was finally free and that from this moment on I could begin to integrate the impressions of a larger puzzle that would create the true picture and history of the heavenly Divine Dynasties. What might occur didn't matter to me now as I was like a young boy who was prepared to venture out into the unlimited worlds of imperishability.

Eager to see what was to occur next, I felt I would ask what would be expected of me in the day ahead. Before I could raise my question, my curiosity was vanquished. I listened as a decision was made and I was informed that I would be escorted from this room and would be taken to certain areas of this deep space vehicle in an effort to reacquaint me with information and activities that I had come to understand so long ago in my career as an evolving son of light.

When I was referred to as a son of light, I was not surprised but I did feel an acceptance on an intimate and personal level which raised my heart to the fore of my consciousness. I felt I was on fire and in the brilliance and flush of the moment, I offered my love and adoration to the group present. I felt tears in my heart similar to those I had experienced in the first moments of my death on the parking lot which reminded me of my earliest objectives which were to love and to serve.

I was escorted from the room moments later and a

feeling of elation brightened the way for me. I was moving through a corridor that pulsated with light though the light itself was not distracting. It was as if the movement towards a specific section of this rather large vessel was identified by the interactive quality of the environment within the transparent walls themselves.

I was with just one of my hosts and out of curiosity had asked whether there was any kind of recreation. Instantly we began to change our direction. There was no interference from my escort and within minutes we were sped along to an open deck area that seemed unpopulated. Here, it was explained, was where certain games would occur between various challengers drawn from the whole of our local universe.

I was shown former sportslike activities where hundreds of players had come to participate in something similar to our Olympic games on Earth. The differences here were that it was quite possible for serious harm to come to many of the players who were similarly limited due to their physical bodies. I was shown how, in competitive sports where one could put their greatest effort forwards though bound to fleshly bodies, there was a potential for damage. I was likewise advised as to how these same players were not fearful of participation because care and treatments by physicians was instantly available.

Before one could participate, one would undergo a process similar to diagnostic assessments and information and samples were taken in advance. It was not unusual for those in limiting bodies and forms to have registered samples and data registrations to aid the medical authorities in case such injuries did occur and, on many occasions, there were notable athletes from various worlds who were known for their ability to pursue their goals in these games without hesitation even when serious injury did occur.

I was amazed at how so many worlds had integrated so naturally without any sense of comparable envy. Even though there were societies of a widely diverse intelligence and consciousness, the seeming limitations, differences in strength and evolution were simply not an issue. Each species, race and group of participants had come to depend on each other while their stages of development were nurtured and supported as their own special uniqueness. It was not as if anyone was in a hurry to transcend the norm, regardless of their conscious attributes. I was shown more about the actual resort areas following a slight discourse on the constitutional realities of these inhabited worlds and their relationship to each other and it was when I came upon a lake-sized body of water that I was captured in a moment of sheer amazement.

An emerald green lake that seemed to flow out into the universe, with no sense of an edge or retaining wall, was being used by those on retreat here, and even the spiritually advanced with less dense bodies of light were at play in these waters. I was told that their special healing qualities made the waters attractive to many, though the sentient reaction to water by those with bodies such as mine was a peculiarly physical pleasure that was not available to all. It seemed that such large bodies of water were not to be found in our earthly world, and were of little importance or sentimental value as we had found it to be. I was surprised to discover that the water when I entered had dulled my sense of consciousness and it was as if I were entering a microscopic copy of the entire universe. Here in the waters, I felt I was being inverted or transported to a world of musical delight while being made to feel that I was in an inner dimension of light.

There were intelligent forces at work in the water and as I moved away, I felt I wanted to return. It was as if a very special ability to synthesize all that was known to me had come about, even in the short time I had experienced this world. I made a note to return to these waters later on and without thinking further, I was once again escorted to what seemed to me to be the helm of the ship itself.

It was like walking into an underground secret government base with holographic communications appearing in the foreground, and beneath us were instruments similar to what one might expect to find in a great science fiction book. I remember smiling while imagining how similar the symbols on the panels in work areas seemed to be to those often portrayed in some of the better special effects movies on Earth. Though I was standing on a platform overseeing the entire area, I felt somehow rather large in size and was attempting to understand how this was possible when my escort stepped forward and transported us to the central hub area of this workplace. Much to my surprise, I noted that the assembled workers here were of a synthetic body type and that their skin appeared to shine like plastic. They were able to stretch their limbs and hands effortlessly in any direction though they only appeared to be about four feet tall.

All of these workers had dark, shining hair that seemed to reshape their appearances each time I observed them. It was as if they never looked the same at any time. Their countenance, or appearance, was always in transition, though I was told that while in this particular area we were involved in an energy grid that was constantly in transition, thereby giving the appearance of speed and movement unlike the normal continuity of time.

Somehow, there was a magnetic field that was interacting with these individuals and, when I had adjusted my conscious vision, I was able to step into the entire group's consciousness and could then see them as they were at normal speeds. To the human eye, it would have looked like they were blinking in and out of time at incredible speeds. I was likewise informed that due to their pliability, they were best suited for such environments. It was explained to me that we were travelling through general space at an average speed of about 70 per cent of the speed of light. Though this was normal, there were many occasions where this vessel could travel through other dimensions and appear in time and space precisely where they chose to. I found that speed had a great deal to do with the objectives and preoccupations of many of the attending entities and societies and, likewise, this vessel was only one of a number within our locale. I was informed that several fleets of this type of vessel were used as transportation through and within the general systems of our Milky Way and that they were used much in the same way we would use ferry systems on our planet.

I found that a great deal of time would be spent here observing the methods used to attain such sophisticated goals and that I was beginning to see another aspect of our connectiveness as defendants of these earlier races of heavenly beings. With that in mind, I joined in the collective consciousness of all who were present and working in this particular part of the vessel as a means of pure discovery.

The Development and Expansion of the Universe

Being most interested in the beginnings of these united societies, and wanting to quench my thirst for more information on the history of our material worlds of evolution, I found myself witnessing a program that identified such data from the records kept onboard. I discovered that there were libraries of records regarding historic time much like those I had found myself experiencing in the first stages of the afterlife.

The differences here were that I was now an observer whereas earlier I had been unable to detach from the actual historic experiences. These visual and consciously related information programs did not appear outside the observing eye of an individual but rather within the consciousness and it seemed that the creators of these historic archives had allowed for a detached capacity on behalf of the viewers to be the actual choice of any who would choose to adjust to them.

If one wanted full immersion into the past, it would allow for one's overall sentiency to engage as such and it was possible then to live the standard of the time just as if one had lived that life oneself. In short, I found that I could enter into any phase of history and at any location in the material worlds, or I could choose to expose any one moment of history and to immerse myself totally as a seeming participant. It was also used to discover the life of any one individual in history where it was possible to integrate with that single thinker to discover their thoughts and reactions at any given time to the events and impressions to which they had been subject. There was never a sense of limitation in the use of such records and, as usual, it all seemed natural and trustworthy.

Following through on my curiosity of the past with regard to the eventual development of these transport vessels, I was awed to see that the universe had long been almost uninhabitable until a time when direct intervention from an unimaginable race of heavenly beings had initiated their plans. The plan in the beginning was observed and understood as an intentional experiment in the manifestation and development of those systems capable of producing individualized offspring.

It was not generally understood by the advancing races that came into being under the direct influence of these great ones whether or not the intent was a means of externalization of their own kind or whether the diverse forms that could be found were ends in themselves.

In the first third of time where the appropriate seed life was being initiated in the sub-atomic worlds, an interaction and exchange of information between single units of life had begun to set the stage for eventual recognition of one another.

In human terms, I would suggest that the material dimension of time and space was a predetermined experiment itself. Once a specific stage of expansion and opportunity had arrived through long periods of time, another stage of development in the atomic spheres was initiated where it was possible for our present systems to coagulate or gather together through their own developed condition of consciousness.

It should be born in mind here that every particle or sub-particle to be found in our universe has the individual ingredient of intelligence which allowed for a behavioural transition over time in each. As an electron would eventually find itself returning to our dimension, though active as an atom in its reappearance, so too were the lives of the microscopic world able to relate intelligently to each other.

We could even say today that it could be known that atoms, electrons and photons actually learn to act, emulate and appear in exact copies of each other. While the microscopic worlds were gathering momentum and developing families of their own through sentient association, the basis and foundation for sense relationships had been founded, thereby allowing for another stage of development.

The second phase of development came as the destined microscopic families of light particles began to gather into magnetic grids, patterns and spirals which were actually brought into being through influences from without. That is when the appearance of the dynastic and Divine families ushered in the worlds of appearances. As the microscopic world began to identify with a new form of energy called 'consciousness', a newer pattern of behaviour was most responsible for the shaping of magnetic fields and eventually the distribution of light.

What we now call radioactive material was and has continued to be the primary food of the members of the sub-atomic worlds. The patterns mentioned were themselves an attempt on the part of the atoms and particles to shape and flow together in patterns of sound-influenced light, just as the initiator had desired. The design or motive of the attending Deity was itself the result of a developed response to the sound or tone of the actual entity responsible by the adjusting atomic individualities. In these ways, our material spheres began to take shape for another very long period of time.

In short, it appeared that an intelligent act of will had brought the systems of our manifest universe into being though the uniqueness of our universe was safe-guarded by the activity of innumerable creator-like beings.

I was quite aware then that there were no two beings or things such as units of life that were truly identical. The only identical realities of our material worlds were the basic impulse and blueprint which generated the laws of intelligent association in order to persist in generating individuality throughout every space. The key ingredients within the motivation of the originating intelligence, it was understood, were origi-nality and individuality.

With such foundations, all the lives of the one life within our universe could eventually identify the whole of the universe and it was further recognized that there was to be a day when, through the attainment of such wisdom, a continued transition was possible through assimilation and emulation of the more unique beings and existences. In other words, it was intended that the primary intelligence of a life would eventuate con-sciousness, and that this consciousness would eventu-ally demonstrate how to be like another thing or being.

It was understood by me then that this meant that there were those of many grades of development to be found within our universe, and that through contact we would be able to attain their exacting attributes, abilities and wisdom.

With this in mind, I had come to understand some of the basic principles of the continuing universe and saw how we are all of an ageless past. Working our way through evolution and knowing that assimilation was the basic key to development, I came to know some of what would be later known as the true motive of God.

Again, I will try to translate what I was learning. I observed one of the founding principles which was retention and the ability to process information. In this, I found that every unit of life had the ability to sense and identify impacts or impressions from other active lives within the space surrounding a single life, as well as from a generally cumulative impression from the universe at large. This I came to understand to be sentiency. It was this primary ability to remember, to make a record of, to retain as it were any information that was not generally initiated by the unit of life itself. Although every impression and action upon another being was recorded innately within the unit of life, the workings of the actual life were likewise recorded. In much the same way as we receive impressions from the outer world of appearances as humans, along with those impressions that well up within us all, a greater sense of history and of self is established.

We need only think about our memories and how important they are to us and then think about the many impressions we are subject to every day. Not only do we deal with the obvious impressions that we know as self-talk, mental visualization, and reason, but like-wise we are subject to developing responses to impressions from our bodies within and without. Another person's influences has a direct influence on our whole life, and we take all of this mostly for granted as well. What we can learn from this is that every second that we pass through time, millions of impressions are digested and acted upon by our brain and its working parts. In saying so, it could be inferred at least that we are, in physical terms, information processors!

It was through the principle active law of information processing that the very ability to respond intelligently had come to be developed. In saying as much, one could understand how it was intended that we are all expected naturally to gain eventually enough impacts and impressions from life that we can evolve beyond the very vehicles we make use of in material time.

Allow me to suggest that upon close inspection of the human body, we could scientifically discover that we are, in appearances only, an organization of multiple intelligent lives. Perhaps we consist of trillions of individual parts whose interaction and previous development through time has been gathered together like a supercomputer and, acting within the laws of physics and of life, we may find that these trillion or so lives actually aid us in our intent to identify our exacting innate nature.

Behind the seeming spaces of our atomic form there is an intelligent life acting as the cohesive attribute of the many trillions of individualized parts. In this way we can see how the whole of every kingdom in life has been gathered together in the formulation and final appearance of a human being. In these same ways, all other beings and systems have a common association. Looking further into the general theme of eventuated life, I was able to see that the blueprint for life preceding the activity and interaction of the infinite numbers of individualized lives was an exacting copy of all the lives and gestures attained to those first moments by the inventing Dynastic hosts. This meant that the outcome was to establish a sphere of consciousness whereby these Dynasties could eventuate their own offspring. In this way I came to understand that our universe was a place and a stage for the eventual birth of Heavenly beings!

We live in what can easily be seen as a Divine womb. In saying so, I was able to witness the majesty and miracle of supernatural existence.

Still further into the records of history, I observed the co-ordinated efforts of many unbegotten beings who themselves seemed to have never been subject to the very identifiable standards and limitations to which we are. In my own way I thought to compare the workings of the female appearances and, attributing the quality of birthing in human life as was discovered in the Divine life, I found that the main preoccupation of the male hosts was to some degree similar to ourselves. Though these corresponding assumptions were verified for me I continue to find it difficult to reconcile such within the limits of my own language. Even so, I was able to comprehend that there are exacting processes in each sphere of consciousness, and that the prime directive of service to the female aspiration towards birth was the present condition of our choices and expressions while living the Divine life.

Since the female was being shown to be the main preoccupation, I continued to observe the stages of development that eventually led to the prepared environment and opportunity for human birth. Much later, and in the early dawnings of sense-related life forms, I came to understand how the planets were used to foster the final stages of incarnate forms.

There was something quite unique that was occurring on spiritual levels previous to the birthing of humanity though I was only able to grasp that there was a decision made to have Divinely parented beings appear as individualities here in the material worlds preceding their fully developed appearance upon the highest levels of existence. All that I could understand was that there was a goal little understood by anyone in our worlds throughout the material dimensions, that was yet to occur and in fact would not occur until our material universe had completed its final objectives.

It would be like saying that our parents had decided to wait until our maturity before explaining what we would be doing in the future, and that our future would not be taking place on this planet or place where we had grown up. It would also be like saying that our parents understood we would need a general education on the art of living and using our skills and powers to manifest long before we were allowed to be spontaneous, though the final impression was held by the offspring to be a rare and beautiful gift beyond our wildest imaginings. With that in mind, I proceeded to capture more of the eventual progress intended for us all through the process of incarnation.

I discovered that planets such as our Earth were home to the younger offspring who were present long before time as we know it to be. For example, our solar system is a parenting masculine spirit, and our Earth is the daughter of this same being. In his life expression she lives and moves and has her being here in our dimension as the active personality of the masses. In other words, the feminine life of our planet is a young offspring that is learning to do as her father is doing though her lesson is also experiential as far as she is concerned. She, for example, is experiencing life as we know it with all its strains and limitations of sensibility as well as its loves and compassions. Her overall attributes have manifested through our lives and in this way she has become aware of the use of her will in the ways of practising and attaining to a greater and more powerful expression. In short, she is learning what her potential as a feminine spirit is about and, further, how she will responsibly assume her role as a parenting presence in the late future.

When the Deity of our system first brought about the individualized lives and organisms raised first on our planet, it was intended that such organisms would be a blueprint for all other creatures and beings that would follow. In a very highly miraculous way, the gains of trillions upon trillions of experiential lives could be seen as the working out of this basic blueprint. In the same way, the animal kingdom eventually appeared and demonstrated the gains of a very long gestation period. During this period, the range of sensible contacts possible for all life on our planet began to be expressed in a unified being.

Likewise, the limiting factors of these same creatures, which was responsible for their inability to recognize and establish personal contact with the unseen principalities of the spiritual worlds, had caused a dullness at first in the sense of the world itself. Only later as the time arrived for the expansion of the brain, where it was now possible for the innate laws of retention between individualized lives to function, was it possible to establish the first moments of intentional though instinctive self remembering.

Though the animal kingdom was the first to establish a sense of memory, it was many millennia before it was possible for a creature to establish innate sight and contact with memorable occasions.

At a much later date in the third stage of Earth's development, and only through direct intervention, was it possible for humankind to take their place in the world of appearances and contact. From that time forward which was approximately 300,000 years ago, sight such as is ours today came into being by the then established brain.

Dreams were the height of that period and it was then that our race of humanity began speedily to make progress in the mental worlds as well as the emotional and sentient. It was normal then for humankind to greet and meet the many travellers of time and space while unconsciously working with the Divine hosts who had established their home in our world. It was revealed to the fullest then how we have only been on our own for the last 24,000 years as the last moments of contact were made. Retreating to their cities of lights all around the globe, a smaller number of authorities remained and the many who were once present in the establishing of humanity themselves were returning to other objectives elsewhere in our universe.

By the time I had captured the whole of the records of history I came to understand how the cities of light had been elevated from the surface of our planet to a conscious sphere just slightly above our present cities. The time had come for humanity to be left to make their own free-will decisions and to be subject, as many other worlds are, to the final stages of development. Only when the beginning stages of a collective consciousness were being demonstrated by the majority in incarnation would, or could, renewed contact be established once more.

With that in mind I was astonished to discover that the very day I had observed was about to occur where the definition, experience and eventual responsibility of the individual incarnate soul could establish contact. Following such contact, we will come to be established in the kingdom of souls as it is today.

In other systems I had observed how it was only through the appreciative revelation of sentiency that the need for limiting incarnate shapes and forms would be necessary and where renewed contact was re-established. In other worlds I understood how there was no pain or forgetfulness as was the case on Earth and I found that the time and stage of development was unlike our own. Where there is no sense of pain and mortality, there is likewise a slow and general awakening of the individualities to their residing hosts. In such cases, education and systems such as ours regarding capitalism or incentive lifestyles were largely the choice and responsibility of the masses while the resident spiritual hosts were utilized only as guidance to the ends of mass needs.

In every case, there was an eventual development

of forms whereby contact with others was nurtured to a point where individuality became the primary requisite, and at that time the evolving souls of such worlds and spheres of consciousness were made responsible for themselves. Each scenario showed me that there was the goal of the attainment of personal consciousness and further that upon the recognition of other states and stages, one was able to relate sensibly to the presence within oneself for further guidance.

In other words, it was now possible for everyone in our little world to gain contact through sentient development not only with the ultimate presence within themselves but with the host of other principalities throughout our local universe.

I further discovered that first contact is possible only when the majority in incarnation have sufficiently prepared themselves sentiently, which I will explain further in the later chapters, and to extend themselves upwardly towards space.

In our case, we may find that we are only on the edge of discovery and that within a generation of continued interest in space and space travel the necessary technologies and scientific discoveries will be made, thereby enabling us all to brace our maturing selves sufficiently for such contact.

I was shown how the very first serious attempts ever made to travel in space were done in much the same deductive way as humanity has demonstrated. Smaller probes with artificially induced intelligence were released into the upper atmosphere followed by a manned mission into seeming space itself. Later, when certain difficulties were understood, a space-based experimental laboratory was established upon which multiple replicant platforms followed.

Much later, other worlds within the confines of the solar system led to an experiment in lifestyles in space itself which brought about the first travelling space station of its kind. In its turn, these first independent vessels were used to establish a major base at the edge of the solar system. Through continued exploration and study, these first races had begun to establish their own kingdoms in new worlds. Later, and over a very long period of time, it was possible for these original groups to work with other intelligence and to begin their first organized systems of fraternity and fellowship.

This series of events, however, will make it quite possible today for genuine contact to occur shortly following the collective agreement among humanity at large to live in space itself. This means that by the time a platform is established on the moon itself, we will have advanced to the moment of contact which will ultimately bring us all home to the truly existing universe.

As I was pondering these revelations I became very excited and my curiosity led me next to wonder at the role that the feminine spirit was to have and would continue to have on the then present worlds of advanced consciousness and identification. I was unable to complete the thought as I was informed that the time had come for me to meet with my host in the great hall once more, so I turned my full attention towards the meeting at hand.

This time I found myself meeting solely with my guardian and he explained to me that I would soon be leaving but that I would also return here one more time. I sensed that this decision was being made in lieu of what was happening to my body back at the hospital. From the previous exchange of information I had learned about the potential for viewing not only history but also the future of our little system. The ability to preview the outcome of my own life had not occurred to me then but as I turned to leave the presentation hall I wondered if the choice for me to go forward quickly was due to some inside information.

Before I had completed that thought I was told that, while the possibility of looking into the future was quite possible, certain outcomes can be altered and changed so that the record would show these changes only after their occurrence. In other words, or at least the way I understood it then, nothing in the original text of the past had changed to my knowledge though it appeared that I was able to make a difference in my future. When, or why and how was not known to me though I suspected that my continued experiences would reveal the opportunity. It was then that I began to feel that I was soon to return to my life on Earth.

Studies in Sentiency

There was some time left before I was to take leave so I used that time to discover as much about the workings of this outpost as was possible. In one section of the ship I felt moved to enter into what I thought to be a medical treatment area though my access was denied for reasons unknown to me. A few moments later I found myself discovering an interior storage and stock area. I supposed that this was where necessary goods were stored, although I couldn't imagine what, and as I turned towards an exit area I caught a quick glimpse of a docking area where small podlike vessels were kept.

There were also many smaller vehicles that were locked into position behind transparent door hatches. I discovered the transparency by reaching out in an attempt to board one of these smaller units only to find that it was impenetrable. I understood that from inside or out, the transparency was brought about by something to do with the organic material used. Even on the transport vessel, I had noted there seemed to be no walls or entrances I could see, and likewise when inside the vessel I was able to look directly out into space. The outer frame was made of a light pliable magnetic material though I somehow understood that an organic form of artificial intelligence was at work here and upon the parent vessel. I would eventually come to know and understand the workings of the sciences here, though there seemed to be a lingering sense that I could know and understand everything to come with tremendous clarity if only I had just a few more days.

I was pondering how the average thinking person on Earth might respond to all that I was now perceiving, when I realized just how different it might actually be for anyone else whose curiosity was different than mine and how different I had become, having grown accustomed to such startling revelations. I suspect that I would have been overcome by the revelation of a unified and lawful order throughout the universe, though the truth was that I felt very much at home as if I had never really left here. I was just imagining how there would be a diverse reaction followed by diverse interests for the billions of our incarnate worlds when I felt myself being called.

Within a few minutes I was being escorted through an entrance which led to an open portal where a small vehicle was awaiting my arrival. I was stopped just a few feet away from the entrance and to my surprise I felt I was being flooded within a shower of light. This was the first time I had taken note of colours that I had never known. It was as if I were being cleansed and yet I felt very stilled during these moments.

My guardian stepped into the vehicle right behind me and I found us sitting without restraints within a small room. It took less than what seemed like twenty minutes before I was aware that we were about to enter into the atmosphere of a very bright little planet. I supposed we were on auto pilot though I expected that there would have been some kind of instruments before us. Again it was explained to me that the vehicle was not just a vehicle, but that it was also alive. I was determined thereafter that I would discover what that meant and with that in mind I turned my attention to the place at which we were now docking.

I observed closely as we gradually approached a docking area high in the sky and close to the top of a towering facility. There was a city below us and, as it appeared, all the existing buildings were interconnected and afloat midair. The ground view was one of plush beautiful landscapes where grooming was an obvious activity. It was like entering a perfect picture that was coming alive with sound and excitement everywhere.

I had taken note earlier in the drama that the varied environments seemed to have musical properties and now I began to understand how my own sense of excitement and curiosity was responsible for the sounds I was hearing. Not unlike the huge vessel I had just come from, this entire world had been influenced or designed to pick up on every level of communication going on between beings. In my case, my very state of consciousness was mixed with the elements in the air and the results were that I could now hear and be heard differently.

It was as if everyone was exposed by their particular note to everyone else and this added to the quality of interpretation given and received. It was like hearing another person's name since the sound of each were distinct. Like a fingerprint or a voice print, everyone could be known and contacted simply by addressing them according to their tone.

I felt I had gained a new range or breadth of consciousness that continued to expand with each passing moment. I could hear the cycles and breaths of the planet and within minutes, I found I could hear thoughts and impressions wrapped up in consciousness that were flowing like a stream of bliss through the atmosphere. How I was able to understand so easily was explained to me then as a most natural form of direct communication that has long been the means of communion with those who have long advanced beyond the need for speech as we know it. It was a language itself.

Listening to myself, I observed how each impression was very similar to a soundtrack we might expect to find in movies or entertainment, though in this case, each melody was captured according to the way I felt at any one moment. It became obvious with a little experimentation of my own that the interactive environment was also designed to act on and between the states and conditions of one or more things while maintaining the integrity of the whole environment. In other words, there was no allowance for a disturbing effect upon another. I realized that this was not an imposition or a law as such, but rather that this conscious environment was the way in which the climate, temperature, wind and light refraction were being managed. I was definitely on a living planet and there were some rather large and significant differences to that of Earth, but while I was considering the whole I came to be informed that the planet was capable of travel without the need to maintain an orbit as Earth does. Hence the major differences.

This green blue planet was once an established outpost in its own system and having long parented the races that developed in its system, an initiation to a spiritual level had been accomplished. I was told that the same technology that was invested in both vessels that I had questioned earlier was identical to what I was about to experience on the surface of this planet.

Within the flash of a moment, I had been transported along with a number of others who were now within my company along with my guardian, down to the surface below. The surface seemed to shine and glitter though I had not seen or taken note of a Sun source anywhere. Though the surface was hard, I sensed that I was still somehow standing a few inches above it.

'Here you can do anything!' I heard next. Turning to face my host, I observed as he descended below the surface and then raised himself up about three feet in the air. Following a few other quick movements I came to understand once again that the same organic intelligence I had aspired to become acquainted with was now here before me. I was anxious to experiment further though I was assured there would be plenty of time to get involved following the necessary procedures. We returned to the main entrance to the city above, and simply stepped up to one of the structures entrance points.

I was taken to a reception area that was designed to hold thousands though I was informed that the main body of students and researchers had already come and gone. My guardian indicated that I was to stay in a particular area and then when it was time I would be escorted to dine. I was shown my room and set out to discover more.

There was a chair in one corner of the room where I began my first studies of sentiency. I should state here that I was very anxious to get started on my investigations into the reasons and make-up of the interactive environment. I felt that if I could understand how the organic material was being used, I might very soon find myself capable of returning with a message to my earthbound body. I felt somewhat certain that arrangements had been made in a hurry, and that if I were going to have to take up my body and continue on Earth even for a time, I should do my utter best to learn what I could so that I could at least explain it to someone who could understand on my return.

With that in mind I settled myself. Somehow I felt that by being utterly still and silent I could observe the interaction between my thoughts and the environment itself. Being within a structure also added to the idea I had in mind, since there would be little interference in a capsule of my own.

I was hoping that I could generate some kind of a reaction first, so I took it upon myself to strike out at the chair and then to stop suddenly. After doing so, I took note that the expected bounce or crushing of the material from having struck it with such intent did not occur. I continued to do this though I changed my patterns several times over the ten minutes or so that I persisted.

In each case, there was no reaction so I then allowed myself to sit in the chair. I pressed upon the arm as if to brace myself to stand up but, again, no results. The chair continued to look like a chair and acted like a chair but there was no indentation effect from anything I had done. Even when I pressed and crushed the material in my hands by pinching a small portion, there was no reaction in the materials used.

I then remembered the statement that thought was the responsible agent involved and applied my consciousness to imagining that someone else was sitting in the chair - and then it happened. There was an indentation in the chair that visually indicated someone was either sitting in it or that someone had sat in it and left the chair to look or appear to be well used. When I took away the thought that someone was in the chair, the material seemed to alter to the first condition, although there was no observation made that could answer or suggest what had occurred. It was as if I could change the shape of things which also included the walls in one part of my experiment, though when all was returned to the original condition, I could not explain this either.

I needed more information about this technology so I left the experiment to another time and began to concentrate on the musical aspects of the atmosphere and environment. I focused on some of the earlier processes that I had experienced in the first moments of the afterlife drama and simply listened to the sounds of these moments as they occurred. It struck me that I had not noticed the sounds earlier but now I had a sense of how the activities were managed.

At times, I noted that the varied harmonies and melodies had actually induced a particular impression while at others it was my own reaction to impressions and events that generated these sounds. Still sitting and concentrating while listening to the rhythms of my soul, I detected that the impulses that initiated these sounds were not here in my cubicle, whereas they had existed everywhere else. Now I knew that it was a controlled event that allowed for privacy and only when interaction was desired did it work out to be inductive. I concentrated upon the last image I had of my body as it lay in the hospital and the complete scene was suddenly before me. I was certain that what I was seeing was of the present moment and that, somehow, without having to travel personally to this point, I was able to bring these impressions to life within the cubicle.

This gave me another idea. I tried to touch the bed on which my body was lying and I received a flash impression of the quality of the material. I could even feel the coldness of the sheet that I had touched. I then reached out to touch the lab coat that one of the nurses was wearing and again I could identify the texture and quality of the material. It was then that I saw my relatives enter the room and I suspected from their sentiency that they were not feeling so well about being here.

My father was in deep pain and remorse and I could feel the grief behind his tears. I felt moved to comfort him and as I reached out to him I could feel his thoughts.

He shook inside as he said aloud, 'I think he is going to make it. I feel like he is trying to say something. I don't know how but I think we should just leave him for now and give him some more time.'

He then attempted to talk the nurses into not pulling the plug that afternoon and I could tell that they seemed to feel the same way.

I felt I should call upon my guardian and let him know about the situation I was about to face when he appeared before me. The hologram of the events in the hospital faded and my guardian suggested that I should wait until we were together again shortly before trying more on my own.

In the few minutes remaining before he came to get me, I stood silently within my cubicle and refrained from any new experimentation of my own. It was then that it dawned on me that perhaps there were no communication limitations on anyone who lived here or were a part of these societies and that perhaps it was only in the dense physical body that this was not possible or allowable.

I could easily see why such technologies would be dangerous in the hands of any who are not yet living in the light of one's conscience, and why few could truly be trusted not to misuse the options available to them. I sensed there was no real influence here on the consciousness of anyone, or on the choices being made by anyone, so I assumed by my own condition that negativity was simply a thing to be outgrown.

How we might even arrive at a time on Earth when the masses could be openly trusted without a second thought was not clear to me then though I did understand that through an expansion of consciousness I was able to defeat such impulses altogether. In the end I concluded that only in the material dimensions where the sense of self was being developed would there be a limitation on one's ability to avoid negativity.

It seemed to me that when I had passed through the judgement stages of the afterlife drama, I had been relieved of such limited views and conditions first from the animal tendencies in the human brain, and secondly from the personality errors made over my lifetime. I was certain that when the illusion of mortality had been exposed, only my soul's appetite for expression was left as an option to me.

I further recalled how my consciousness went through another expansion prior to my stay on the space vessel and how just before coming to this awakened planet I had been cleansed by a shower of light. As I searched myself I discovered that I was now free of the historic encumbrances of the incarnate life along with its memories and that I had also recalled all my former lives until that time. When I noticed these transitions through reviewing them, I came to see how the sense of responsibility for being true to my nature had been renewed many times through the life incarnations and likewise from my stay between incarnations. I could not find any reason to believe that there was any negativity to be found in my nature even long ago when I first ventured to our beautiful little planet called Earth.

I found myself adjusting the new lessons and, though there were a few missing impressions in the overall puzzle of the big picture, I concluded that the universe was pure to begin with and that only after the experiment in time and space had been made by the dynastic families of ageless times was there a dual impression of reality. I further concluded that the Fall and humanity's negativity was due primarily to the innate historic influences of our earliest incarnations as creatures.

Somehow, the negativity and suffering of our world were tied to the evolving form in which we incarnated. Somewhere in the memory conditions of the brain, the animal nature was continuing to play a role in the expression of the human form. I was certain to find the answers to this along with a further understanding of light technologies but I was now informed that it was time to dine.

The Mission

I moved to the area suggested and waited for my host to arrive. We entered a large auditorium-style room where at least 700-800 individuals were also waiting to dine. As I looked around, I noted that the majority of souls present had taken on a similar look as to my own. I was assured that this was so because we were all members of the same family. I was almost alarmed to find that I was dining now with descendants of my own family, or race as it is best expressed, and that I had not recognized it earlier.

I had no memory of my first place of origin much less the updated interpretation of their roles or places in these heavenly societies but I was informed that only the former earthbound incarnate lives had been recalled and that, in order to know and remember, I would have to enter into the spiritual worlds by passing through another release or initiation. I sensed that this might not be possible now as time was short in regard to my incarnate condition and that going any further would mean that there would be no return.

I was correct in assuming that there could be no return thereafter and that I would certainly have to make another choice but the true reason for my being prevented from doing so was of deeper significance. I listened, as did the others who were dining with us, as my guide continued.

It was suggested that after coming to Earth I had decided to acquaint with the incarnate conditions in order to understand the general theme and to alleviate certain conditions upon those who were going to incarnate here in the future. I especially wanted to understand the limitations on the psyche and the developing personalities that had taken shape in the world then and so several in a series of incarnations had been planned.

I had immersed myself in the incarnate world on several occasions to help the spiritual authorities in making their decisions. I was further told that after the last series of incarnations, I had come to develop a complete understanding of the make-up and design of the human psyche. As well, I had come to identify the conditions that were hindering the eventual awakening of the masses and had learnt that much more work in the field of sentient development was necessary.

A decision had been made by which I was free to choose whether I would stay longer in this sphere or move on. I had apparently agreed to stay in order to aid the masses in the upcoming transformation of their society following the initiation of the planet and of the masses themselves. By working through thought forms, I would be establishing direct communion with some few who would be most responsible in North America. It was my intention then to remain out of incarnation and to act as an intervening guide and an impressionable instructor. I was also informed that I had chosen to remain until the 24th century when I would take up my last incarnation in form though this time with a full awareness at birth of the processes into which I had earlier been initiated.

It was not intended that my own incarnation was to come to an end at this particular moment, and though the momentum would not be lost, a great deal of skill over the centuries would have generated a host of new liberating conditions which would have to be acted upon.

It seemed that I had achieved such a high degree of understanding for humanity and their conditioned problems that I could not refuse to accept the position. Apparently, I had come to identify the underlying conditions of the mind and brain upon the conscious development of the individual, which meant I was suited for the transition process and would be invaluable to others working on their own particular theme in other groups upon the planet.

While my study had been specialized, and had afforded a more comprehensive association of the direct impediments of any individual, there were others working with economists, industry, government and institutions relative to the growth and continued development of humanity at large. By combining our interpretations it would be possible effectively to educate many people because certain revelations would be unfolding naturally, generated by world conditions.

It was as if my direct impressions of an individual's personal psychology or of a group's ideals and goals could be bridged. In other situations it was possible to affect current events while having a clear interpretation of the long-term effect upon the masses.

Influencing the masses was a normal technique and there had been many who had developed mastership in the process of serving and aiding the mass spiritual need at different times; however the present century had become vitally active on mental levels and the emotional encumbrances of the masses were diminishing in a timely manner.

A major problem at the present time in our world was that the urge to union, and the spiritual interest of the masses had changed most dramatically directly after the two world wars.

It was evident that the masses had come to understand the speeded-up processes of information processing on the individual, but that they had no idea as to the symptoms and transitions in consciousness while under stress, that would take place simultaneously. It was certain to most that unless the masses were to gain control of their own nature, and to begin to understand the processes inferred through psychological studies, an abstraction of one's mind and even the sense of conscience in many would become subjectively dismissed. This would lead to an inability to recognize the dangers posed by a new technology that was about to be revealed nearing the turn of the century. In its turn, the masses would fall subject to preoccupations with lifestyle more than with the imminent appearance of the soul in man.

It was true that the masses had come to make use of television, radio and other forms of information to produce tremendous effects in the world at large, though these vehicles of education were primarily under the control and guise of less selfless groups. The material world's wealth was of more import then and so it was that the medium of television and radio had unintentionally come to condition the brain, mind and conscious development of the masses.

Not enough of an explanation was given to the youth in their day as to the proper use of these media and more fiction than fact was the immediate appetite of the curious and young. Everything that could be taught in regard to the nature of humanity or of an individual was simply overlooked and only the satisfaction of the viewers through entertainment was sought.

The masses had been subject to an expansion of consciousness which led to many discoveries during and directly after the Second World War, but the direct invention of television signalled the fact that an indirect event of consciousness had begun. On one level, the masses were stimulated into a fanciful mindfulness, resulting in an increase in glamour and delusion. The collective psyche became conditioned to seeing the world within the grammar of mental movies and this mental habit eventually reached a static plateau where further development came to a halt. For some this meant greater discovery, greater invention, a clearer view of objectivity, and a widening of the mind. Yet for many more, it became an unwitting trap. Having an objective consciousness, one can remain free of being trapped by mental impressions and a weakening of the objective consciousness may help to explain how it was that many advanced beings were captured by the mass psyche.

Many well-advanced and authoritative beings had come to take their incarnation in form during this period in an attempt to make contact and to instruct in the spiritual sciences, though these same beings became subject to the same impediments of incorrect knowledge as had the general masses. Although they had developed the concentration necessary to follow through on their respective gifts, many of these souls were prevented from so doing by the mass appetite for self-expression and the cult of elevating and worshipping the 'unique personality'. This meant that they were subject to a most difficult path to recover their enlightenment in their later years.

I was being shown in this review by my host that my talents to educate the human race were not to be overlooked. I also sensed that a greater truth was not being mentioned at this same time as the conversation changed. I still had not understood what I might have known if I was to go further and beyond the actual reach of my own soul. Only the sense that I would be giving up my rights to work in the denser spheres had occurred to me during the conversation, and this I suspected because of the fact that the spiritual spheres could not directly be entered without passing through the next initiation.

What would I learn then that would make all of what I was now dealing with change? I couldn't say then but I did have the lingering feeling that I myself may have been the reason. Something about me, about first choices, about my role in the world's present situation, was being graciously kept from me.

I sensed that I would understand the matter better very soon since the decision to stay, as I had earlier suspected, was about to be made. In my mind, the information would come to be revealed since I was having to choose to stay or return to Earth.

The Decision

I was being escorted back to my cubicle following the dining experience with unknown relatives when my guide suggested we speak further. Upon entry into my cubicle the environment opened up and we were both standing at the foot of my hospital bed.

At that particular moment, the doctors had come into the room and advised the nursing staff that they were about to go ahead with the planned procedures. The signature they needed to go ahead with unplugging the life-support systems had been given and the doctors were talking about the decision itself. After some discussion as to the past four days since my arrival, they agreed to observe carefully and had made back-up plans. I sensed as did my guide that they all had an air of uncertainty. It seemed that no one individual wanted to proceed too quickly and that perhaps the decision to wait might be made. It was at that exact moment that my host began to speak.

I entered into full conscious union with him and, as it was occurring, I took note of a principle truth. It was as if I had now entered into a mysterious level of existence unknown to me beforehand. As the images of the hospital room vanished, giving way to the new condition, I observed how there was a prevailing stillness and, within seconds I began to feel the impulses of a word breaking through the veil of silence.

In the next instant I felt as if I were falling and had at one point been lifted up and out of an infinite well. As I gained my focus once more I discovered the word had produced these three general effects upon my consciousness. From the moment I had seemingly fell to the moment I was gaining focus again, I heard three sounds unite into one. There was an elongated A as in awe, which caused me to feel the falling theme, and then a silent O as in ooohhhhuuu, followed up by the M as in mmmhhhmmm. In the end moment of focus, I was overcome by a shaft of living light streaming downwards through my crown and out of my forehead. There appeared a voice saying 'Gracious Peace'.

The light was rising up and out of my head and it felt as if something had been placed on my head while a downward draft of energy had soothed me within this light. It was as if I had opened up in three different areas of my soul's body and was releasing or unleashing a rhythm unknown to me before. I knew what gracious peace was following the event. It was a state of consciousness beyond anything I had known and in fact it had gone beyond consciousness itself as I understood it, and had become an awakened ability that I came to call pure reason. It was as if I need not even use symbolic forms of communication any longer and was enlivened in this light of bliss and rapture.

In this state, I could remain very still and silent forever while acting directly upon whatever I willed. I learned to see this state as an advanced condition of will which was responsible for the genius-like effect upon my own consciousness. I called it 'Identified' then, and was satisfied that I at least could understand what had taken place. I had been initiated into the spiritual realms and for a short time I was able to see and commune with greater beings. Greater yet than those I had come to understand to be the parenting authorities of our local universe. Even this form of divinity which was without shape and form itself was above all others and I expected no less than direct communion with God.

I was advised by my guide that indeed we were now in the company of the elders of the spiritual spheres and that the state experienced by me was to be a permanent opportunity from this point on, or at least until I returned once more to close the doors behind me. This meant that, at some point in the not too distant future, I would complete my objectives and return to my place of being.

In the next moment I heard a voice like a gentle whisper in my consciousness, though I received no visual clue as to the originator. I simply knew that I was listening to the voice of perfection. I was informed that each individuality has within themselves a foundation of truth and that this foundation was the very spark of life that was generated in the first sounding of the word in the material universe. Within the sound of the perfect word there was the guarantee of such a foundation and that upon this word all was built, transformed and then liberated.

I took it that my very life essence was that foundational truth and that by emulating the sound and the word I had earned here I would always have contact with the supreme principalities of all life. I also understood that this was the case for all living beings, and that the structure of thought-generated forms used throughout the universal career of any one individual were the conditioning features of their own uniqueness.

I knew that within a moment of liberation, there was also the moment of limitation, within the moment of expression there was impression and so on. I understood this to be a revelation of the actualized processes of all things and beings alike and that by understanding the sound of any one being, a perfect interpretation of the future progress of that individual could be known.

As an analogy, were we to take our entire language and divide the words into a specific order, certain conditions could be understood. In the case of the alphabet we know that c follows b and that y precedes z. Likewise, if an individual was at the c level of evolution then another who was at the y position could see the experiences needed to complete the task. It was a simple understanding and model to follow because, since our processes are somewhat linear to us, the obvious conclusion was that wisdom was gained through experience and the wiser would be the more experienced.

In this case however, it was intended that I understand how expansions of consciousness were designed in our educational adventure in eternity. Even though this was understood, it did not mean that it was not necessary to complete the experiences themselves. In my case this meant that even though I had already developed to the point where I was free from the need to incarnate as were others in my time, there were still experiences that should be sought after while it was possible, and that these should remain somewhat of a surprise beforehand.

I was not informed as to the correct choice for the future but I did know that there was a greater need for me to attend to the first objectives even though my choice to not return could be made.

Continuing on in the spiritual heights, I had begun to feel that pure inspiration was flooding my consciousness. It was as if a continuous flow of information, along with the ramifications of what was exposed so easily, was quenching my thirst for complete union. I felt I was beginning to understand the nature of those to be found within or upon these heights and then I knew. I belonged here but for the very reason I had decided on Earth as my home long ago, I also knew that much more could be accomplished.

My own needs or desires were unimportant to me, though I must admit that my personal ambitions for my self were more than I would have preferred to have admitted. Even then I had begun to negate my own self-importance with the more I received from the universal fount. I found myself learning more here in ten minutes than I had managed to glean in hundreds of years elsewhere. This was the source I had always utilized in my life in deep meditation, though only now did I understand that inspiration itself was the language of the gods.

The intention to inspire self and others had been my founding ambition and all my goals were based on this, so as the revelations came to a close, I made it a point always to remember this moment of contact and to live on the rhythm of inspiration alone. I knew that from this moment on, all I would ever need would be given when the rhythm of inspiration was captured and

I decided to accept any or all conditions that might determine the choice ahead.

Once more the environment changed within the room and I was back with my host in the hospital. We knew that hesitation was upon the minds of those attending my body and so the procedure began to occur, though very methodically. Without concern for the situation I began to concentrate upon my body and within moments I could feel myself nearer than I had anticipated. Once the breathing unit was slowed down, the room came to a complete silence. It was as if there were a sign or a sense among the staff to stop the procedure though it wasn't until my body began to show signs of a struggle that the pace picked up.

Everyone present began to wonder what they should do when the doctor turned the unit back on to normal respiration. I remember hearing this same doctor say, 'He's not ready yet. He was trying to breathe on his own. That's a good sign. I say let's leave him alone for a few more hours and we will see how he is tomorrow.'

My family was informed that I had struggled to breathe on my own so the procedure was stopped and there was a great sigh of relief on my father's face while others were simply confused. In the next moment my host and I were speaking to one another as we departed from the scene. I recall a part of our conversation that followed and, without asking me if I had decided to return, he simply implied that I had made the right choice. Going further, my host suggested that it might now be possible for me to engage in my earlier experiments on sentiency for a time and that we should later return together to the hospital room to plan out the stages and conditions necessary for my return.

I hadn't voiced my opinion to him but I was still left in the state of illumination and inspiration that was gained earlier. I believe he simply knew without my saying so as it must have been most noticeable to him that I was very different now.

I was feeling very mature and wilful then though the wilful aspect was more of an immovable conviction. I was bound to follow the course prescribed and to ignore all other alternatives without hesitation or second guessing and if I could have returned right then and there I suppose I would have done so. In fact, there was a pleasurable sense of relief that was a response to the impressions of inspiration I was then considering that made me want all the more to make certain that all of my experiences in the afterlife would be easily recalled. I had much more to offer humanity in inspired ways than I had ever expected, and the notion of returning and aiding others in the understanding of their own imperishable journey was electrifying to say the least.

A Moment of Union

Within that same hour following the sensational experience of being renewed in a sea of Divine inspiration, I was off throughout the city to expand my horizons. I entered into the meditative state that was appropriated in my last moments of contact within the spiritual realms so as to enhance the very rhythm I wished to maintain functionally upon my return.

It appeared to me then that I was now seeing with different eyes and hearing with different ears as I sought to experience the living world in which I now existed. I could hear and sense the overall conditions of this world and I further realized that education was of primary importance here above all else. With this theme in mind I sought out the areas where education was taking place and moved there as quickly as I could. I selected one specific group of individuals who had spent a great deal of time here becoming acquainted with the very science I had been so anxious to learn more about and began a conversation with a number of them.

We were outside in a park setting and we sat for about two hours and shared information that I felt would help me understand the sentiency involved. I should say here that sentiency means a sensitive response to impressions. It is that particular ability we all have to feel, to know or to sense the condition of another at various times. It is also what we use with regard to our sense perceptions to interpret the events of life. If you were to be able to identify another's mood, attitude, disposition, countenance or anything about a person that was picked up on by your brain and senses, then that is the sentient attribute.

With this in mind, one might wonder how it is that we can simply tell what state or condition another's mind health was in. By observing strangers in our world, we might sense something to be true about them such as whether or not they were trustworthy or not. In short, it is the ability to sense the registration of impressions themselves. We are all sentient beings when one considers that there would be nothing to take note of were it not for our senses. This law applies throughout the entire field of life in our universe and has been aptly called the affinity principle by physicists. Even an atom can tell what is on the mind of other atoms though their overall consciousness is not like ours in the fact that we know we exist and it becomes meaningful to us. In the case of an atom it is more like being asleep where everything works accordingly but we do not awaken to realize we exist.

In my particular case, I was seeking to understand how one sentient or sense-related being such as is true for man as well as souls, could read the depths of another's heart and soul. If for example I wanted to understand what someone was hiding from others, to what degree could this be revealed? How correct would I be? How could I be sure?

In another example I had been accustomed to understanding how certain misinterpretations of one's own nature and life could cause a limitation sentiently in another. This and much more along these lines was very important to me since I knew we were all constantly registering our state of being at any moment by simply existing. We all have an influence on life wherever we may find ourselves and in turn we are all influenced. The how and what of sentiency was what we spoke about the entire time. A few examples of the technology were used to demonstrate as I watched closely.

One of the students moved his hand lightly into the air and then closed his fist for a moment and then opened it again. In his hand I saw a ball, shaped like a planet. In the next moment he explained how he would use this model to demonstrate the sentiency involved and then he willed the various influences within a planet to take shape. The sphere of energy shaped as a ball then turned into millions of parts though the shapes were more square and rectangular at this time. He then described how millions of lives make up a single part in appearance to our eyes and that each part was reliant on the other parts as they shared a common tone or rhythm. In this, I understood more clearly how an atom would change its behaviour so as to connect with the goal of the thinker. It would be like saying to many atoms of various frequencies that you want them all to act like one you have in mind and then - voilà! - they take shape as you desired. Once the common frequency had been established the shaping processes became easily controlled.

I realized then that it was a matter of information transference and a willingness on the part of another form to take interest in establishing the desired outcome. In this way I saw how a simple thought could be the defining agent and how, upon acceptance, other atoms would assume the same condition as the one brought about in thinking or developing an idea, the result of which would be an image in mind space of the very idea.

I should say here that my own receptivity and interest were the responsive agent that made the merging of our collective consciousness work then and there in the park. Likewise we were all becoming the very thing we had agreed to speak about. In this same way I began to understand how thoughts and ideas over time could develop with or without any accuracy. One could imagine something to be correct when indeed it was not. Going further I found my answers to the neurological conditions of atoms and molecules and how information was a constant receptive ideal. In fact, many of the intelligent lives that make up the system within the body of man have themselves the natural capacity to take shape wherever and whenever the need was intentional.

My interests were well satisfied within the two-hour period and in the end I came to see the subtle workings of an innate intelligence in each and every living thing. I saw how inspiration was the key to all things generated, shaped or demonstrated. And further yet, I saw how the Divine originator of our lives in the material worlds was most central in each unit of life.

There was no limit to what we might think or acquire from inspirational sources, but I believed fully that inspiration was more than a form of communion and that it was a life-giving truth that embodied the nature of the great and perfect ones. There were so many conclusions that I could now make with regard to the universe but the most inspired impressions to me then were the fact that there was something beyond energy and it was that quality of life that was central to every given experience and individuality.

Certainly we are one being with many faces, though the individuality that was developed historically was the greatest event of all. To have been established as one in the universe of many where no two are identical except in rhythmic life expression was sufficient for me. It was simply miraculous to know that what we think does take shape and manifest as experience or sometimes as objects and other times as events involving the whole of the human race.

We are impressionable beings, capable of communicating our knowledge in exacting impressions that can uplift others wherever there is a receptive ear. This law of receptivity became my next interest as I had well understood how possible it was to prevent ourselves from being inspired as well. To me, this was one of the biggest and most crucial problems with humanity today apart from the need for a greater education. It was their overall disinterestedness! Where there is no interest in being inspired or learning, the sentient attributes would remain in check, waiting for the day of liberation when the powers of the soul and of the spirit within could be safely utilized.

The objective of every spiritual individuality or principality in our human world of limited expression and manifestation was to inspire the uninspired! I recalled how vitally important it was to wait for certain agreement before any attempt to inspire or communicate openly and freely could begin, though now I knew how fragile the undeveloped minds and personalities of our world truly are.

I could see how impressions led to hindrances and eventual arguments, and how frustration through disagreement could lead to acts of violence among different races; however, I also saw how these same conditions could be reversed, allowing the soul to manifest and escape the spheres of material development.

I recalled how at one point I had been speaking to one of the students when he said, 'Imagine what you will and be prepared to pay for that imagined manifestation.' Certainly - and ironically - were it not for the limitations of our sentient powers through ignorance and because of the body in which we incarnate, the universe would have destroyed itself. Imagine having a child that is born with these same well-developed powers associated with sentiency and then imagine that whatever the child imagines coming true instantly. What would happen to anyone whom the child decided should change? The implications warrant a deeper look than we would normally consider as it is true that our shortcomings are mostly due to neglect and ignorance of our true nature, which was and remains a requisite for control of our sentient attributes. Hence the single law of non-imposition in the diverse universe.

Education, inspiration and experience, combined with the dulled but informing sentient attributes of a being in incarnation, were the perfect means by which a Divine offspring could mature without harm and under a watchful protective eye.

Our maturity and likewise our independence were of great import to the responsible hosts of humanity and it was with this understanding that I chose to return to Earth and take up the form I had left behind on the tarred pavement days earlier.

It was much later when I was digesting the ramifications of the sentient attributes of the universe and the unique signature tone to the triple word I had heard aloud in the heavens, that my host returned to me. We were speaking of my new insights and how the pieces of the puzzle were coming together so quickly, when my host commented on the comparable rhythms between myself and the truly Divine source from whom the inspiration was received. I understood him completely then and I was astonished likewise by his comment.

What he was implying, as it was pleasantly recognized between us both in that instant, was that we now shared a common Divine insight; an undeniable truth; a one-minded awareness of life as it is; that we did know something now about the nature of the great ones, having been receptive to them. I also understood and took the gesture and inference to be a welcome to the fraternity of those who knew the correctness of truth thereafter as I sensed a personal acquaintance with him consciously.

It was the first memory I had of ever sharing a moment with a knower and lover of the truth and it was even more miraculous to find that our hearts could feel the shape of impressions and qualify the condition of their appearances. If we chose, it was possible for us to feel and to see as does Deity, as our final attainment knowable was to be as close in personal expression and beingness to the nature of the One Life that we could. Certainly the sweet truth of one-mindedness was just as profound.

There was a momentary pause, as I felt him look deeply into me and I likewise adjusted myself. Then a great moment occurred for me. It was a moment of union with another being in progress and this was unlike any other sense of being known. This was a part of that very special pleasure in reality of knowing eternal truths in synchronicity. It was a feeling of being known and knowing! I can only explain it to in terms of our both agreeing without saying, so that we both knew and had experienced a greater truth regarding the nature of Divinity that many will eventually come to know, but until then we had the sense of union between ourselves. Along with our agreement in certain truth, we understood the way it was.

The touch of illumination that had occurred when I had earlier felt the downflow of a seeming sea of inspiration had continued to be alight in my central nature and heart. The after-effect was that I had gained a sense of self that was responsible for my now keen sense of correctness. On inspection I discovered I had made a copy or a memory print at the root of my heart in those moments and I was still able to make use of this rhythm. Every moment afterwards, I had seen things in a continuing light of inspiration and when my host suggested the effect I knew he understood that we both had gained the touch of truth within us.

In normal conditions during incarnation there are times when we know how to feel the truth of some people. Even then, and during my limited sensory capability it was undeniable that we could feel the processes in others and understand how they ended up looking and feeling the way they do. It is a fundamental truth regarding our ability to communicate as incarnate and as liberated souls.

I found that my ability to interpret the nature and progress of other individuals in the human kingdom and in the kingdom of souls had been enhanced to the point where my conclusions were very much like those that the Deity would make. To perceive life in the human kingdom as would our attending guides was certainly a greater asset than I had imagined possible. Now I had the ability to feel my way into and through the conditions and limiting factors of a soul in progress and identify the means by which liberation could come about properly. This was to me a very special ability that I felt was given to me rather than having been earned since it was only through contact with the Divine that I had managed to assimilate the actual focus and conscious condition of a more advanced being. I knew that this same ability could be awakened in anyone who so aspired to communicate with the Divine within themselves and that a methodology of approach could easily be understood by the average thinker on Earth.

I sensed that the means by which we grow wiser in our human incarnation was through contact and then comparison of ourselves to others, which is the common experience and methodology everywhere in the living universe. Having said as much, I discovered a working model to aid in the next steps ahead.

I was beginning to prepare myself for the eventual reinstatement of myself into the human world and I sensed the need to review my diagnosis again and again. In this way I felt I would find the most inspired approach to relate to another thinker on my return.

I concluded that consciously to attain to the heights of our potential of Divine expression was the outcome and near final condition that all aspirants to the truth would have come to personally experience and know in order for direct contact to begin on conscious levels. In saying as much, I further knew that assimilation and emulation of the Divine expression of our truly innate attributes were to be the basic approach to attainment of Divine consciousness and countenance.

To be Godlike was the goal. To act as would a Divine one, or to see and understand as do the Divine hosts, is a workable model. One would only need to understand that they had the ability presently to adjust themselves to a particular state where direct inspiration would begin to unfold the basic truths of life itself. It was concluded that everything that one seemed to understand had earlier come to be known through this same method of intentional assimilation and emulation and the more one was driven to goodness or betterment, the more one could see and understand beyond the average thinker. In this way, I chose to remember the methodology in terms that would best suit the thinkers of our incarnate Earth. With that in mind, I began to prepare again for my return.

I was considering how each offspring of the original Divine couple was given a unique sound, and yet how they all were so similar to the originating word itself when my host decided we should now return to the scene at the hospital.

With a simple gesture my host and I were now within a living hologram of the exacting situation in the hospital where certain tensions had been noted among the staff. I had begun to have problems breathing on my own and it seemed some other sort of experiments along these lines had been tried out earlier that same day but with no satisfaction. I was beginning to enter into a worsening condition and I could feel the pressure on my heart and chest as it was certain that I was having a heart attack. The doctors were working at high speed and I focused on one doctor as he attempted to restart my heart.

I looked directly into the eyes of my host and wondered if I might now return when he assured me that it would not be necessary. I could feel the doctor's fist pounding on my chest and I had a sense of interfering with his activities. I could feel myself tempted to return and to plead with him to stop when my host drew upon my attention and prevented me from directly interfering. It was then that I noticed several entities approaching and beginning to influence the team while two others attended to my body. Within half an hour, I was stable again and everyone was relieved including myself.

My host informed me that my body was being

guarded naturally and that it was the choice to return that I had already made that gave way to the rights and law of my protective hosts to attend to me. In aiding in the continuity of my body, I was also to understand that they would remain for a time on my return to adjust to the given situations of health and conscious continuity. I understood that I would be able to expect further assistance in recovering much of what I was now experiencing in brain consciousness as this was to be a rather difficult task ahead for me.

It dawned on me then that my consciousness, free of human form, was to remain intact though it would be very difficult effectively to create and manage the conditioning factors of the brain on my return. I contemplated the matter and wondered if I could recall everything I had experienced. For a time, I was intent on dealing with the potential struggle to bridging the conditions of the brain and my own consciousness.

I was certainly not as conscious before the drama in the afterlife began while still in form, and so the expected effect of the expansions of consciousness on the brain were not yet knowable. Only on my return to body would these things be possible. I recall then how it was that I had sensed some urgency in my attempt to make certain that all would remain in memory, and now I could see why. I believe my host sensed my next thought with regard to the condition of the brain following the impacts and trauma as well as my own distance, because he then began to suggest what was awaiting me in the future, well into the recovering years ahead.

The Way Ahead

I was given twelve years of information about my immediate future as I remained quiet and responsive to what followed. I was shown a moment in the immediate future where certain physical disabilities would continue to make my progress on return very difficult. Certain long periods of recovery and rehabilitation along with further surgical interventions were to be expected, and I recalled then how I almost changed my mind. Certainly from where I was in the inner spheres of existence, there was no limitation, pain or stress whatsoever, and naturally it would be acceptable to return to my body under such conditions; however, I was not so enthusiastic after learning that I would have a very long period of continued pain to deal with.

I was shown how these limitations would interfere somewhat in my overall zeal as my devitalized body required much more time before repairs were made and a sufficient lifestyle could be founded. A further investigation revealed that I would also find myself without assistance in the future and the period of financial poverty to follow was not yet determined. It was explained that I would have to find a way and means to support myself but that the greater picture and outcome was only based on my having met certain criteria on my return.

This meant that unless I could identify and make the correct choices as conditions occurred, opportunities could be lost. Now I was beginning to see how very difficult it would be to meet the demand for what I desired to do on my return. It was also quite possible that failure could occur and, given such a condition, there would be opportunities for me to change my direction and actually release myself from form. Failure on my own part to live the necessary lifestyle, as well as to understand the necessary timing while living in a spontaneous world of uncertain events, made the objective all the more difficult than I would have expected.

From what I had learned thus far, I could see that certain outcomes in world affairs were definite, yet I also understood that certain changes or events could interfere with such outcomes and from that point on an abstraction in potential outcomes thereafter would be all the more difficult to achieve.

From this information I imagined a model which I had hoped to recall in the distant future. In my model of the future, I created a series of impressions that were already known to me with regard to the future. For instance, I knew that by the year 2048, the consciousness of the masses would be then equal to the requisite stages of enlightenment, and that a further greater cycle of 2150 years later, the condition for humanity would be illumination. Further, I noted that within 6000 years, the whole of humanity would have been raised out of the material worlds and that our present populace of souls would be complete with regard to the final objective.

By imagining these outcome impressions like a picture screen at a drive-in theatre, and spacing them in specific time sequences, I could identify the guaranteed outcomes of the future. Doing so with my own life, I could see what would have to be attained every seven years and knew that at certain points certain requirements would need to be fulfilled so that I myself was involved in the future picture guaranteed by the law of evolution in the material worlds.

In order for me to sustain myself and to achieve my goals, I would have an initial 31/2 years to overcome the physical difficulties and begin the process of integrating my soul with my body consciousness and personality. After the 7th year, I would have to meet the conditions necessary to pass through a spiritual initiation where an expansion of consciousness would allow for the furtherance of my goal and objective. If I could make this certain then it would be possible by the 12th year of extended opportunity in form to transcend those conditions in form which would prevent the greater initiation in the 14th year. By making the initiation occur before the 14th year and no later, the goal would be guaranteed from that point on.

I should say here that I was fully aware of the fact that I would continue to have contact at least with my host, and that certain questions regarding choices would be left to me alone. There could be no interference or tampering as was the law for all others in incarnation, and although I had the advantage of contact, the unknown would have to be discovered along the way through natural progress. I was grateful for the advantage of continued contact though I sensed then that somehow I was going to repeat my own afterlife process and initiations once more, though in and through the limitations of a physical body.

Inspiration was the key, I thought. To remember the moment of inspiration meant everything to me. All I would have to do to regain contact or to recall the data and experiences that I had now undergone was to assimilate the rhythm of gracious peace and then the flow of inspiration would follow. This was all I could depend on and, with that in mind, I sought to recall certain revelations about my future when the time would come to make a change in direction, or to choose accordingly.

I remember being shown my father's death and it was important to recall certain events such as this one because a decision to target certain goals would have to have been made previously if all was to work as desired. Another instance was a vision of myself living in an apartment with a friend unknown to me then named Michael. Still more visions with an accompanying warning were shown to me up to the 12th year. If I had not attained the goal by then, I was shown how an accident on a major highway would occur and I would be leaving my body.

The outcome either way was worthy of consideration. Even if I failed in my lifetime to complete my goals, it would not be truly seen as a failure. The attempt was worth it all and I could make a small difference; however, it was inevitable either way that humanity would meet the intended goal regardless of anything else that would occur in the world. Certain outcomes were inevitable, though for certain periods one's free-will choices could make their lifestyle more difficult than need be.

In all that I was shown, there was an air of urgency and a slight warning remained in my memory. How effectively I would be able to recall these moments was unknown to me and there was to be no further revelations apart from those regarding the progress of the masses in the attempts to meet the stage required at the turn of the century where consciousness would be

expanded for the majority, and a new era of enlightenment would ensue.

In these revelations I was shown how a crisis of
conscience on a worldwide level would begin to take
effect and with certain conditions being met or not, the
lifestyle of the masses would change for the better or
for the worst. If the masses were not able to identify or
relate to the current events of these times then a short-
er period of despair and futility would come about
where the crisis of conscience would be known thereafter as the event of the century. The end of ignorance
in our world and eventual contact in the first half of the
next century would still occur, though until that time,
life could be quite difficult for many.

The key element of this transition and global initiation would depend solely on a change in the mass
consciousness with regard to the word 'accusation'.

I learned then that accusation, and to be an accuser by habit, had always led to destruction and sorrow
worldwide; that the grave and cruel tendencies of
human nature had always led to punishment of the
individual and of the masses; that from accusing,
charging, humiliating and then punishing an individual we had continued to breach our potential for contact with the Divinity rooted at the very core of the
individual's heart; that wars were started, due to a lack
of conscience, by simple accusation and the implied
threat of punishment; and that humanity had learned
to punish each other in both subtle and obvious ways
daily, all of which was preventing a spirit of understanding from emerging.

We had always been too quick to judge, criticize
and punish the unenlightened, and this condition was

now at its heights of intolerance and control in the world, even though the lessons of war had been hard learned by many. A period of time was now upon humanity and by automatically desiring to punish instead of understanding in our daily lives and in our justice systems, the unrecognized souls in process were being prevented from the very opportunity that was Divinely decreed long ago.

Humanity was, on a personal level, to make decisions regarding certain current events of these days where the outcome was to be of greater understanding for our natural processes of mental and emotional development at the least, instead of the conditioned habit of punishment. Separative notions of a global community could not begin to manifest a cooperative global society unless the basic premise of tolerance and understanding for others' shortcomings was implemented.

To kill, maim, imprison and seek vengeance on our neighbour constituted a regressive, stifling condition of the mind of the many. In order for the population to prepare for an expansion of consciousness, a certain clear understanding of our criticisms and accusations followed by the urge to punish would have to be exposed as a dark tendency responsible for much of the horror of our past.

I likewise understood that this period of great sorrow and plight could be avoided and many of the working authorities in our system were fully concentrated upon the awakening of the soul within mankind in order that a greater sense of interpretation and understanding could be ushered in.

Could humanity at large make a personal decision

to oppose a retaliatory response towards their supposed enemies? Could the leaders of our world come together in a united manner to refrain from the continued aspiration to punish and accuse wrongly? Could we in the free world make a decision to avoid punishing those who would like to suppress our lives or could we avoid an outcome yet to occur by gaining certain insights beforehand?

The effort to raise the consciousness of the majority throughout the free world wherever receptivity was to be found was the immediate goal for those whose ability to impress and inspire the masses was possible. In particular, the United States, whose constitution best resembled the correct understanding of the rights of the many, was to be given special attention as in the end this same country and its leaders were the targets of the accuser!

The final conflict between the ignorant and fanatical populations of our world against the free world ideals and its populations was to be where the crisis could be found at its height in the coming years. With this in mind, I realized how I might proceed on my return and was further moved to discover how these negative human tendencies could be overcome in time.

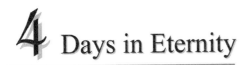

Part III
A Grail Mystery

The Afterlife Drama: Conclusions
on Stages I and II

The second phase of the afterlife experience was quite different from the first for many reasons. In the first stages the main emphasis was the on the resolution of the personality and dealt mainly with the restoration of my conscience, and a return to peace of mind that is a common theme for everyone entering into the conscious spheres of the afterlife realm. Although there were many transitions and events that I had relived for eventual peace of mind to return, I had not yet understood with any clarity what lay behind everything that was being demonstrated.

The unexpected greeting and naturalness experienced with certain entities, guides and hosts demonstrated the fact that we are, at least on Earth, a more recent system and heirs to a vastly intelligent organization of highly advanced ancestral beings.

It was also understood in the first stages that we are indeed imperishable as there was a definite order and protective aspect to the entire arrangement preceding birth in our world, followed by further development of our innate potential thereafter. This simple fact proved to be the most moving of all for me, though I needed more knowledge to understand how this had come into being and it was only in the second stage of the overall drama that this was made apparent.

In the first stages again, I blissfully accepted all that transpired and had little control other than through my own innate curiosity of the actual processes or events. In these experiences I had simply allowed everything to take place, while in the second stage I was able to conduct myself accordingly.

To some degree I was able to follow through on my own self-generated experiences. This verified for me that certain persuasive elements were initiated in the first stage in order to prepare me for the continuance of my innate interests. This, I found, was very revealing since I came to understand the subtleties of a justice system involved, which in the second stage was beginning to show itself. In the second stages, there was no tampering or interference with my own interests and much of what followed was directly in line with my own curiosity. In short, I discovered the limitations upon certain higher authorities to interfere with my own free will regarding my interest in self-development.

Throughout the second stages, the theme was one of remembering and reacquainting with situations and experiences I had come to know at other times in my earthly career. This was new information to me and, much like finding out that we are imperishable beings, I likewise appreciated and was completely moved by the fact that our overall progress was not as binding as I had once thought it to be. It was the sense that we could condition ourselves and our personalities to such a degree that, without the aid of restoring ourselves anew through a series of lives, we might not find our way out. This had been an unconscious fear of my own that had come into being from attempting to digest the possibility of reincarnation while living unaware of certain aspects of human existence. I had once thought that all could be lost regarding our memory but such was not so. Indeed all that is true remains within our scope and ultimately affects the development of our redeveloped personality in the new life.

Only the truth was carried forward into the next life. In this way we gather our experiences in each life as treasures held in our unconsciousness, and until the day occurs where the personality has begun to make contact with the soul itself, all that has been earned and learned comes forward in one grand integration.

There was one point that I captured much later, but I feel is worth mentioning here so as to make certain points clear as the book unfolds. It was the fact that the evolution of consciousness, partnered by our personality tendencies in any one period or life, inferred that the first task for the soul that is outward bound is to salvage the personality itself. I found this very interesting as the ramifications were such that failure to succeed in the afterlife process meant certain return to the incarnate worlds. From one angle it might mean to some that the afterlife processes could be targeted intentionally so as to ensure that the need to develop another personality would not be necessary.

I pondered this at great length until I understood the perfection of such a system. When I realized that so many personalities are absorbed into the final one I understood a familiar concept. The first personality to be salvaged was also the first moment of direct conscious awareness in eternity. Likewise this meant that the last personality life would be the first one in which we succeeded. However we look at it, the main thrust or understanding of our lot as humans was that we were to develop certain qualities within our personality identity that were initiated by the soul in order to remember ourselves once and for all. On the day that we truly awaken to eternity we then have the first notion of a fact suggesting that it will be our last life if we so choose.

Knowing that this was to be my last life and knowing that I would now and forever remember my first awakened moments here in our little system, I began to feel somewhat sentimental about Earth herself.

It was knowing that the moment of triumph had already occurred for me and that even greater triumphs would follow gave me an incredible sense of conviction and compassion overall for those who had not yet awakened to their true inheritance. In these moments I was moved to celebrate the majesty, perfection and potential glory of all the unsuspecting personalities of our world and I longed thereafter to return. Whether or not those I had come to know and love in the material world would choose to make this their last life seemed to be a paramount issue.

As I have suggested earlier, the second stage differed

greatly from the first and, nearing the end of the second stage of the afterlife drama, I began to see how I had now come to a more responsible position than I could have ever suspected. I saw that there was much to do and suspected that returning to my body was not going to be the all-embracing, wonderful exercise I would have expected. My sense of responsibility was growing as I learned in the second stage just how responsible each of my contacts were as individualities. Could I attain to the necessary selflessness to accomplish my own objectives along with aiding in the overall plan of many of the authorities already at work in our world?

Could I succeed in my efforts following my return and negate my own interests at all times during the impending period ahead? Only future circumstances as they unfolded spontaneously would reveal the answer.

The Afterlife Drama: Stage III

The third stage of my afterlife drama was one of education and preparation along the lines of justice and originality. The art of living was the setting lesson for the next stage preceding my return.

I was preparing to return to the city in the sky as I had come to call it then, and was meditating upon the voice and the inspiration that came to me so freely when once more I found my way back to the greatest moment of contact thus far.

Practising silent meditation: I   The steeple

I recalled how at the age of ten I used to sit in the steeple of a church one block away from my home. It was a cold, snowy night and my reason for climbing up to the steeple was a direct result of an unrecognized appetite for silence that had occurred may times throughout my mortal life. My father had asked me to run to the store a few blocks from home, and on the way back I had gone up to the steeple as I had often done. I was familiar with the then darkened stairwell as on many earlier occasions during masses, I had set out to discover the secrets within the church.

I had come to believe by this young age that there were secret icons and perhaps secret passages in the church that were only known to certain priests or authorities of the church and I was determined to discover them for myself.

On a previous occasion while doing my job as an altar boy, I had listened with amazement as one priest spoke of the cross that Jesus supposedly had been hung upon and how the church had dug it up some time ago and sent pieces out to all the other churches for sake of performing miracles. When I had enquired as to the whereabouts of this church's piece of the cross he demanded that I curtail my curiosity and not tell anyone what had been suggested or I would suffer accordingly for breaking God's will. I was frightened to think of what punishment I would receive but even then I thought that it would do no harm for me to see this piece of the cross as my intent was only to feel closer to the truth itself. Claiming reverence for God and certainly for his messengers, I felt that I could assume the privilege without defiling anyone in the process, and so I set out to discover the secretive icons.

In the church steeple that night, I thought I had found a means by which I could become inspired by God. As I looked out over the neighbourhood I became utterly silent. In fact, I had made it a goal to silence myself to the point that I could not even hear myself breathing. In these moments I refrained completely from any tendency towards self-talk and simply opened my eyes and stood still.

After some minutes I began to see something I had not noticed earlier. It appeared to me that I could understand what was happening in every house I was able to see from my lofty position. I felt as if I had an eye for discovery regarding people and their lifestyles and felt inspired as I began to see that similar situations were occurring in each and every home.

Although I had not travelled beyond a few blocks from home during my first ten years of life, and without the aid of television, I seemed to recognize a system, a process, and a general theme that I supposed was worldwide. Everyone has a home, a family, a job. Everyone goes home and eats, speaks and then sleeps, only to repeat the same events day after day, I thought. I came to look upon them as if they were ants who lived in colonies and repeated the same processes every day to no apparent end other than basic survival.

There must be more to life than going and coming, I thought. There has to be. With that in mind I would return to silence and build on my first conclusions though I sensed that certain conclusions could and should be tested if I was to have definitely spoken or made contact with God. When I felt that I had gained insight I then returned home quickly so as to continue the process in the privacy of my room.

In the continuing meditation back in my cubicle, I had once more unearthed the first impressions of inspiration in my life and the method of silencing myself

totally and avoiding any unnecessary imaginative formats proved as exacting a methodology even now as it
had all those years ago. In order to regain the sensibility I had known when being identified with my celestial
Divine host, I used the same method I had taught myself
back then. It seemed to me that the most natural part of
the whole process had been so easily uncovered in my
youth and many similar accounts throughout my mortal
life came to mind as I continued.

Practising silent meditation: II Detroit

I was eleven years old and was playing with my young
cousin from Detroit when my uncle had asked if he
could take me home with him as a companion for his
daughter for a couple of weeks.

My mother instantly replied nastily, 'No! No way!'

I should say here that my mother had always antago-
nized us as siblings throughout our life at home and the
mere suggestion that I could be free from her wicked
appetite for punishment for two weeks was too much for
her to bear. Hearing her response I was saddened and
went to my room where I cried for a time and found
myself asking God to intervene.

In doing so, I remembered that answers could only be
gained when a certain silence had been attained first.
Quickly I found my silence and began to seek inspiration. Within a few moments I felt I had my answer and
having asked for intervention I approached my father
directly.

'Dad,' I said, 'Mom would be happier if I went
because she always complains when I am around, and
the summer is just starting. Besides, Cindy and I are

good friends and I promise not to do anything bad. Just one week please?'

My father looked at my mother and for the first time in our families history he intervened and said, 'Hurry up and get your clothes before I change my mind.'

My mother was quick to argue with my father and a slight fight broke out then as I hurried to gather anything I felt I could wear on my vacation in Detroit. As it turned out, I met my oldest living aunt who was in her last days and ended up spending most of my time with her during the day while my uncle went to work. Apart from a one-day trip to the millionaire's house where my uncle worked as a bodyguard, I had spent little time with my cousin.

It was on this short vacation that I discovered how others were more objective and had a greater measure of happiness in their lives than what I had come to learn from my mother. On many occasions my aunt would correct me and tell me how I could think more objectively without worrying all the time if I would be punished.

Though the conversations were simple they meant so much to me. I told her of my story about how I tried to talk to God all the time and was showing her how I did it by being silent one day and when she tried the same suggested method, I was rewarded with a statement that took hold of me and gave me a greater ambition to continue.

'Wayne,' she said, 'you are going to be someone very special one day. I can see that. I am a very old lady but you are the first boy I have ever met who knows so much about love and kindness and manners, and I have learned a lot in my old age so you have to believe me. Your life is special. Now when I die I want you to smile and know that I will talk to God about your life and, believe me, I know about your mother and I will make sure she doesn't harm you or your sister any more.'

I was ablaze with astonishment and cried aloud as I thanked her. My aunt truly was a sweetheart and a giving soul who had endured much in her long life, though she knew about my mother and that made all the difference in the world. She was the first living being to help me understand that I was sane. That I was more than was suggested by the names that my mother would call us every day. This was also the first time I was not embarrassed, humiliated or left to feel unintelligent.

When the vacation was over I returned home and thereafter I was stronger and had more of a sense of conviction than ever before. Though new arguments began between my mother and myself, I had learned to forget myself and pursue her when she began to strike out at us, especially my sister who was blind and disabled. It was also the first time that I felt my method of silence and stillness when attempting to contact the presence within was indeed realistic. Because of her impressions and advice, I had begun to claim my independence silently and harmlessly.

Practising silent meditation: III Arizona and other events

Another time was in Arizona at the age of 15. On several occasions I would sit outside and far away from any population where I would open my mouth and just let it stay open though relaxed as I entered into deep silence.

I would observe the stars and I always felt as if I were being given an education in the art of living. Though I never thought of this moment of inspiration in religious ways, I felt that I was simply accepting and reverent. How it worked I never knew until the afterlife experiences made it possible to see clearly.

One day I crossed a bridge above some rapids. It was only wide enough for one vehicle so I was walking along one edge while a car waited. Before I was halfway across, a couple of younger men started to yell at me to hurry and then it happened. The car came rushing on to the bridge and the driver intentionally moved his vehicle right up to the very edge of the roadway, making it impossible for me to continue. The four young men inside began to reach out the windows and were leaning quite a ways outside the car in an attempt to push me over the edge. As the car came close enough to hit my legs I closed my eyes in deepest silence and asked for assistance.

Then and there the car went over the edge of the bridge, plunging five feet into the rapids. Everyone was safe afterwards and no harm had come to them, though the car washed away for a bit and then stood on end in the middle of the stream.

At another more dangerous time, while sightseeing in the States, I had found myself trapped in the back of a transport truck. The driver decided he was going to teach me a lesson for not getting involved with him sexually and he locked me into the back of his emptied truck. Once again I asked for intervention through silence and when the next morning I heard him unlock the truck doors I lay still upon the blankets used for protecting his cargo. I was sweating profusely with nerves but he interpreted it as my being ill. As he ran back to the centre where he was picking up his log for the next day, I ran out and into the cab where I found a gun and some loose change. I ran into the offices where he was and threw down his gun in the direction of the dispatcher while yelling aloud that he had tried to kidnap and sexually assault me. With that, I ran for the highway where I was immediately given a ride.

On another occasion I had been discovered at a neighbourhood party by a group of bikers who decided they were going to demonstrate some of their strength and skills on me. I was on the ground and was being struck in the face persistently when I decided to go silent. In the next instant I felt as if an angel had reached out and pulled me to my feet as they began to run. When I looked about there was not a soul to be found.

I can't say for sure that such intervention has been due to my own invitation, but I can say that these interventions were commonplace for many years and the silence I had come to depend on so much had likewise become an effective method of learning all that I had come to understand.

It was through the silencing of my own voice and receptively awaiting a moment of inspiration that I had unconsciously come to learn the art of living, and now in the presence of a truly Divine appearance I was reminded of the many times that objective silence had encouraged connection.

The Empress

As I continued to meditate in my cubicle, I was rewarded by the appearance of an unfathomable feminine personage. It was as if she stepped right out of my silence and into my consciousness. I was somewhat alarmed at her appearance as I had never felt so exposed and unprepared.

Because of the influential expression of her own nature and her unfathomable beauty I felt somewhat incomplete and distanced from myself in comparison to her maturity. It was as if I had looked straight into her eyes and was able to see through to her true nature in those moments and all that I could do was adore her. I have never felt so compelled to reach out and, if I had, I was sure that I would have surrendered something of myself. I felt as if she were responsible for my present situation and as I continued to observe her, I seemed to recognize her rhythm. I had known this same rhythm so many times before without suspecting it was a feminine quality. Within moments I realized that she was and had always been very instrumental in my own little life.

Without saying a word, I sensed that my continuing survival had much to do with her though I could not say to what degree or for what reason. As I continued to feel drawn to her I couldn't help but note how divinely perfect she was. She did not have a tangible body, nor could I reach out and touch her, but she was very much living and glowing in appearance.

It was her magnetism that captured my need to share something with her, and the feeling of wanting to give her something was having a deepening effect on me sentiently. I could not and did not want to end this purest of moments in eternity with her, and only when I gave in to the yearning to surrender did I discover just what it was that I wanted. I wanted to die. I simply wanted to give her whatever I had that would be best utilized by her for whatever her objectives might be.

But in allowing this feeling to overcome me, I felt as

if I were coming to life instead of dying. With every moment that passed, I felt as if I were uncovering some one great truth that was itself a mystery of mysteries. Again, with still no form of communication taking place other than sentient contact, I began to feel that I was emerging from behind some unrecognized impenetrable wall. I began to fill up and expand beyond my own borders of self with a peace and grace that I did not want to end.

A few moments passed by very slowly until I came to a point of stability and as I looked upon her one more time, I felt that I understood something of a passion that I had never known beforehand. I felt sacrificial. It was not that I wanted to be so, nor that I should be so, but simply that I did. I understood then that at the very root of myself, there was an underlying motive ultimately to forget myself and to give all that I had to her.

I was in love with her at once certainly, though it was a love that did not raise the impulse to hold or possess or even give in to her. Instead, I felt a Divine sense of love for the first time. The presence of this love had become like a flame in my heart and in my head. I felt as if I had found that which I had come into being to discover and that no more need be done. It was a love in which I was able to rest and relish. There was a sense of jubilance, deep compassion, selflessness and, above all, sanctity. It was of a purity and a stillness from which all things seemed to come. In such a moment I recognized something further about her very nature and could understand the how and why of our existence itself.

In short, I had come to learn something about a greater love that was unlike anything previously imaginable or touchable, but that was life-giving. It was as if I had been showered and cleansed to a point of utter revitalization and zeal. I thought I could smell the presence of flowers all about me and it was as if the scents of the environment had been established to emulate her very enlightenment as well as to establish a Divine rapport between us.

When she extended her hand to me, I thought that I would enter into the highest of the highest realms of existence. Still no words were spoken even though I was certain that we shared the same moment consciously, and as I reached out to touch her hand I began to see in my mind's eye how the universe had come into being. A stream of life-giving water came flowing out of her palm, as did an array of flowers that came to rest all about her. To her right there appeared a waterfall that seemed three levels high and I felt I should walk into the waterfall - so I did.

In the next minutes I was given a vision of the flowers flowing from out of her palm again and I observed how it was a symbol of her Divine motive and love for her consort that had given way to the material dimensions of time and space. We were the children of her children. She was the mother of our material universe. As I remained in awe, I saw how the flowers came to represent the showering of her attributes of imperishability and benevolence along with a feminine quality which I could not name. I could only sense an inclusiveness about her that meant everything to me and served to give me a total picture of a perfect love beyond comparison that was effectively manifest by her alone.

I continued to remain quietly enthralled as she revealed the ambitions and motives of her manifestation of our universe. I saw how a microscopic world of intense activity had caused a field of appearance built of the substance of consciousness and light, that was impelled by the originating word and voice of her consort as they were enveloped in an endless embrace. I saw how the quality of her nature had nurtured the first semblances of individualized life within her universal womb. Further yet, I saw how it was mostly her innate nature that was being demonstrated in each and every new life that found its way to the surface of our material dimension. It was her mystery, her embrace and her nature that were being passed on to her children. It was her expressed wish that was manifesting as an appearance while the male or masculine aspects and attributes of her consort were mostly responsible for the more invisible qualities and properties of consciousness itself.

I also came to see how the intended outcome, following the long gestation period of our manifest universe, was to have brought forward a completed body of manifestation upon spiritual and Divine levels for the originating couple. As I observed the intended manifestation of her Dynastic family of families, I saw how it was to be that through the illumination and perfection of these offspring, and through the establishment of their kingdom in the material universe, a Divinely decreed existence would come into fruition.

I also understood that beyond this point no further revelation was possible. It was only to the point of having birthed and completed the task of perfecting the dynamic skills of their offspring that an innumerable race of Divine offspring will have come into their own that was to be known. Beyond this point, when the material universe has come to its ends, there will be another revelation of their will for the continued eternities to come and only then may the will of the great ones and of the greatest one be known. Until then, I understood that a family was at the root of the originating motive. Through a highly unfathomable motive of purest intent, we have all come into being and our quest in the universe for now was to aid in the furtherance of this perfected purpose, plan and will.

I was continuing to uphold myself in her light as I came to identify, at least to my own capacity then, that each of us in the present world of activity and manifestation has a very important place in the overall scheme and motives of the Divine.

Regardless of how we might change, shape, rearrange, or adjust ourselves throughout our maturing cycles, we will all establish the illuminative outcome predetermined on and for our behalf. With this in mind, I came to see all of the souls of the universe as eventual masters of our Divinity.

I was given the sense that my own life had more importance to it than I had come to know as a solitary individual, and it was the greater sense of inclusiveness I had first taken note of within her expression that I came to acquaint with a collective consciousness hitherto unrecognized.

As swiftly as she had first appeared she ended the session by giving me a smile to remember forever. Before it was over though, I had come to understand how entry into the highest levels of consciousness and existence was only possible by passing through another seeming death of the soul itself.

I had come to understand how the human body was a vehicle for the spirit that was born out of the great embrace between herself and her consort, and that the soul was simply the manifest spiritual vehicle of our individuality and experience. With this in mind, our objectives were first to attain as a human in incarnation and then attain union with the soul itself. The next stage of development towards our Divine expression and identity comes when the lessons and lifestyle of the soul have been known and sufficiently experienced so that union with the originating spirit is possible.

At this point we will experience the loss of our precious sentient soul in much the same way that we are relieved of our bodies through death, though the fear and uncertainty usually experienced with regards our first death will not be as such when the time comes to enter into our final inheritances and further advancement within the family of Divine beings.

I was feeling as if I were beginning to reorganize my whole being as the view of the universe from this experiential height was so clear and obvious to me. For many months that followed I continued to resort to this particular event and those revelations as a source of inspiration and further enquiry as there were so many objective results that I was unable to gather the whole in just those few moments.

Long after my return to my body, I came to understand the greater truths and mysteries of the ageless wisdom that had survived in text in our world and I was never again left to feel alone.

Returning to the event itself, I had come to feel ultimately privileged to have shared in this great revelation and visitation, though I also felt that this would not be the last opportunity for contact with her again. Somehow, I had sensed that she was going to mean much more to me, and would have much to do with the outcome of my return to human life than was inferred at the time.

I was meditating upon her image and vital rhythm

following the visitation when it dawned on me that there was more than one Dynastic feminine presence in our universe and that these others likewise were responsible for the diversity within all corners of our extended worlds. Even the feminine presence in our world was now beginning to take shape in my mind as the direct offspring of a Divine family that had existed and were well about their business long before the appearances of the universe as we know it.

I was gleaning much more of the exacting situation when I received one more impression of the feminine presence I took to be the Mother of all life, and in that moment I saw how her first born were the heads of the families. In this I began to understand the mystery of the Grail.

The Divine Bloodline

I was already aware that there was a disagreement in the early manifestation of our universe between certain individualities of our similar world lifestyles, when a fall or a decision to refrain from the first task of existence was undertaken. I was likewise certain that intervention had occurred from the spiritual heights, but I was surprised to see that certain of those who had no reason to incarnate in the developing spheres had done so. I chose to give much more time and consideration to these instances upon my return to the vessel-like city in space afterwards as I felt that I had the answers but was not able to integrate them without further knowledge.

I was leaving for the vessel within the passage of about an hour following a series of conversations about the Empress, as I came to call her, with the younger individuals I had come to know here on the living planet.

I remember making an assumption about the apparent frailty of the innumerable lives of the universe and how perhaps just one simple gesture out of time could change the whole of eternity for great long periods when I experienced a dawning. I supposed that it was possible for someone to enter into our worlds from a greater height within the spiritual realms if only to adjust or inform our world of the truth regarding our origins when I remembered how I was taught as a child of so many Divinely inspired prophets and seers as well as the anticipated return of a messiah. These memories began to organize and in a few moments I felt I was gathering another inspired opinion of my own. Could it be that just such a thing had already occurred in our history?

Certainly, and according to the Divine law as I had now come to understand it, someone could have made the sacrifice to come to our very small and seemingly less important world which would make perfect sense, though I knew that just such a group of individuals would have to give up the rights to their own influential powers on such high levels and would have to live as we all do. They would be expected to be born into a forgetfulness as we all are, and would have no special privileges such as guaranteed health and opportunity by which they would be recognized or known to anyone at all.

I realized that much of what I had learned to be the heaven like worlds of purgatory, hell and paradise were merely assumptions and not to be taken as true fact. Finally, because of my own experience with the aforementioned facts, I was awakened to the fact that it had been so. Certainly, the sacrifice had occurred many times over though the religious corruption and misuse of power over the centuries were largely responsible for the errors in interpretation.

A Divine messenger, according to law, would not have suggested such ignorant and misunderstood Divine values and also would not have promoted themselves to any degree by which a church or institution would be created anew. Religion is not the means by which the truth was contacted - I had come to know this to be true in the larger picture - but a methodology of contact could be taught by which an individual could come to know and identify the fact of the Divine within themselves and in others.

In such a case where one had achieved such contact, there would be no discriminating of one group or race from another. There would be no accusation of any incarnate soul that was bound to the unenlightenment and forgetfulness of their true spiritual identity and of their inevitable inheritances. Further, there would be no punishment or need for a crusade in which millions had been actually murdered and tortured for their beliefs. The burning of Alexandria would not have been a Divinely decreed event. The forsaking of violence would have been most natural except for self-defence, as was the case in the great wars of our century. Love, respect, decency and understanding of others' shortcomings would have been an affordable opinion, and the effort to become aware of our morality and responsibility to the family of humanity at large would have been the key ingredient of the main message.

If in fact we had been advised by a truly Divine messenger, and if the advice had been taken to be a methodology of approach to the Divine in us all, there would most certainly be the key impression that we are all indeed Divine in origin. The notion that some are an offence to God, or that some are disposable in God's eyes, is absolutely irresponsible.

With these examples and many more I had in mind at the time, I realized that something was missing of great importance. Even if the message had been misunderstood and taken advantage of politically or religiously in order to enhance the control of certain individual kings and leaders of the day, something would have continued to demonstrate the objective truth that indeed we are living within a universe of perfect justice and law. Further, a simple assumption that a Divine messenger would naturally be only one of a greater number beyond our present knowledge, and that given the fact that any of these being married or having had children during their lives, would be of great moment.

It was then, according to all that I had known and experienced, that I understood how it was that a Divine bloodline and heritage would and should exist among humanity. In time, this family of direct decedents should have grown in number and would be most obvious to many of a scholastic intellect. I remembered further that there was talk in my own incarnate life about a secretive group known as Masons and Templars who claimed lineage and bloodline to the actual family of Jesus and James, his brother.

On closer inspection, I found that the intent for intervention and the eventuation of a bloodline was indeed a fact, though the bloodline began long before the actual appearance of even David and Solomon. Long ago in Egypt, where pharaohs were depicted and honoured as priest kings, a bloodline had been established right up to the present generation of reigning monarchs. Could this originating bloodline of Divine/human intervention be the actual grail mystery and what of the secret that was so great and that had been lost?

When I enquired of my host, I discovered that such was very true and it was expected that within time, every living soul in the incarnate world on Earth would have been eventually introduced to this same family at birth. I was told that the separative accounts of racial and religious division had begun along such lines and themes, and that the originating seed of the most Divine, even though it was already a part of us all, was of great moment in the original wisdom and teachings long ago.

These great secrets, I was told, were about how the lineage was passed down through initiation to those who were preferred for long periods of history, and it was a great secret within the societies of these specific religious groups, but that after the appearance of Jesus and James, certain families had been integrated into all of the nations of the world. The continued secrecy was due to the fact that the safeguarding of our very societies was of great import for the last two millennia. This information in no way could change the fact that we were all Divine though there certainly was some advantages to having been born of the intervening spiritual host that was first established among our races on Earth.

I came to understand that shortly after the turn of this century, these facts would be made public and that such a revelation would mean much to the world and further still that these truths would be responsible for putting our history into true perspective for the first time.

I realized then how the truth had been suppressed in order to suit the agenda of the corrupt few who had their own ideas for modern Christianity. The fact that the mass population was of less import to the Divine than were others was a ridiculous and unjustified lie by which much suffering and ignorance had occurred. Finally I had come to understand that in the far distant past of our unrecorded racial history, there had been an attempt to undermine the natural spiritual processes of humanity, and that intervention through the bestowal of certain spiritual authorities had been directed by the greater authorities of our local universe. In this same act, a family of direct descendants of a certain Dynastic family had been co-generated, thereby allowing for contact once again with the spiritual hosts of our world.

It seemed that humanity, and life on our planet as we know it today, was in jeopardy, and that by these specific interventions we were once again liberated and it was now possible for us to ascend to our heritage and inheritance. A further lesson had been gleaned as I listened to my host, and it was the simple fact that death on our planet was the direct result of the earliest negative interference, and that in the very near future we would enjoy the restoration of an immortal race once more.

In the end, I understood how humanity was now under the direct protective interests of the Divine, and that the mysteries of the Grail were the actual secrets of our true spiritual identity, immortality and, most of all, about a great love and embrace between a Divine couple most responsible for our development.

I was relieved to see that the plan for humanity was of tremendous import to the Divine themselves, and that the end of evil, ignorance and death was the great agenda for the immediate period of time that we all now share.

With this in mind I decided to invest in a period of solitude in the moments ahead, in order to digest what I had come to learn overall. It was then that we arrived on the city in the sky for the last time before I returned.

The Dream of Gold

As expected, I was told that we were to dine in a room that could be found on the upper levels of the city. I found time to respond and adjust to the newest information and was quite excited to be attending dinner.

Once more I was treated to a definitely Divine meal that seemed to rejuvenate my sentient form. The discussion during this period was mostly about originality and the art of spontaneity which had a tremendous influence on me. On my return to my designated room I chose to go for a short walk outside on the deck which looked over the expanding levels below.

As I strolled along the outer perimeter of the deck, I noticed how the remaining few levels on top of the vessel were emitting specific rays of pure light in enriched colours with which I was not familiar. I made a note to myself to return here the next day if it was possible and with that in mind I returned to my room to sleep the wonderful sleep of the soul. I should say here that the sleep was deep and pure, and that though I had not lost consciousness at all, I could see a pulsing effect radiating off my form that reminded me then of the same lights I had seen issuing from the uppermost area of the city. I contemplated what they might be from and then fell even deeper into a totally refreshing and enriching sleep of bliss.

As I awoke just a few hours later, I found that I had been dreaming. Although the dream was much more conscious than the usual type of glamour and illusiveness that one would expect in the incarnate world, I still sensed that I was involved in a dreamlike experience!

This particular dream had something to do with the lights I had noticed not only upon the upper decks after dining earlier, but also from the radiating lights coming from my own less dense form. Somehow the connection was made and the dream to the best of my recollection was about desire itself. I found myself walking through what appeared to be a supersensible shopping area. In the first groups of quasi stores, I was instructed to choose whatever I desired according to my liking or interest.

Even during the dream there was a lingering sense of detachment from the objects I observed which made me feel as if I was passing through some sort of test. The first store that I walked into was radiating a greenish blue hue and everything in the store was the identical colour. I leaned over to look into the glass-covered display counters and observed rings, bracelets, and jewellery which were of spectacular design. Each piece had or seemed to have an appealing aspect of its own and I was tempted to investigate further by asking to touch some of the few pieces I found highly artistic and unusual.

In the next quasi store-front, the colour was orange and everything in the store was coloured accordingly. Here I found wallets, purses, luggage, and apparel that one would expect to find in a store for travellers in an airport. I had the overwhelming feeling that again I was to pick or choose according to my desire and when I asked how I would pay for anything I had liked I received an unusual response. This is what made me feel that I was indeed within a dream and was not as conscious as I would normally have been. The response was that everything was free. Although I had not chosen anything by this time, I noticed that there were others in my dream and that they were involved in the same process as myself. The only difference was that they seemed to linger and upon realizing that there was no price to pay, they were collecting several items.

In the third store which was of the colour yellow, there were gift items of rare quality. Each item seemed to be alive or in some way it appeared that they were pieces of living art. One could somehow collect these as special pieces for a collection. It was then that I began to see that although I had found the items very alluring and interesting, I simply was not interested.

I hesitated at one point when I thought I was looking into a mirror that was producing a yellowish light from the polished glass. Apparently, as I was told by the attendant in this store, the mirror was highly prized as one could use it to see into others and find anything they wanted to know about anyone they chose to consider. I felt confused then and as I walked out of this one store, I came to understand that I must be in a dream as I know of no reason why I would want a mirror by which I could spy on others with.

I was beginning to feel a little perplexed and as I continued, I sensed further that there was something influencing me to feel drawn to these items in each store. I also felt that I must be making some kind of mistake as I was overlooking the items in which all the other shoppers were interested. I noticed how I was now being watched very carefully by a large number of other shoppers at the entrance to the mall, and I remember thinking aloud to them all, 'Where would I put it all? What home do I have to make use of such things?' I recall how puzzled they all seemed as they continued to stare at me with an overall look of suspicion.   Is it that I'm acting differently from the others? I thought quickly. Or could it be that I'm not catching on to what's going on? Or perhaps I'm failing a test. The sense of a test continued though I did not feel I was at all interested. When I walked into the next store which was of a deep indigo colour, the attendant spoke to me and suggested that I was to pick out whatever I liked and that I deserved to collect all that I wanted as it was some kind of reward for having done so well. She continued to encourage me, trying to convince me of my worth, and I began to feel I was being misled. I responded by suggesting that aside from not finding anything I really wanted, I could not fathom what I had done to be rewarded.

Her response was, 'You will find out when you finally pick something. After that, you will understand, so go ahead. You have to pick something. Everyone does!'

I was feeling a bit confused and wanted desperately to believe her, though I couldn't find anything suitable even in this colour which I found very tempting. I remember feeling very thirsty and asked where I might get a drink and then the attendant returned with a beautiful glass that sparkled in the indigo colour. The fluid seemed so tempting that I immediately drank until the entire glass was empty. I was amazed at how quenching the drink was and when I asked what it was the attendant said, 'Eternity.'

The taste remained with me for the entire dream and I couldn't seem to get it out of my mind as it was so very good and the taste was unlike any other. I remember wondering if I had taken a drink of something that was restoring my sense of youth then and there as I moved on to the next store. Here I noticed the colour gold and was awed at its brilliance. When I went to touch a small piece of gold it seemed to roll in my fingers and then return to its original shape.

Once more I touched another larger piece and felt my

fingers slip effortlessly into the gold bar. Again, on removing my hand, the brick returned to its original shape. I asked the attendant why the gold seemed so real yet so soft.

'Oh, I see, yes,' he replied. 'The gold is very unusual and it has special properties as well.'

I looked at him for a moment and sensed that he was very interested in giving away his gold to me.

In fact, as I hesitated he asked quickly, 'Would you like to take all that you see here? You can if you like. There is more than we need here and few ever come to this store.'

When I asked him why few would come here he implied that others found it less appealing for some reason. Then and there I felt that I must be the only one here who was so unusual and perhaps I had chosen the colour gold simply because I was greedy for everything else. My attention was captured when he asked me to step into the store a little more where I at once noticed an open door that seemed to be the exit at the back of the store itself. As I did so, the attendant smiled and asked me to step behind the counter. I was wondering why I should but it seemed that he was asking a favour of me so I agreed.

I stood behind the counter and reached in to pick up a piece of gold that he pointed out to me. When I went to pass it to him he suggested I look more closely at the piece. I saw that the gold had begun to resonate with a humming sound and it began to feel very warm yet as soft as butter. The attendant asked if I might like to cover for him for a while as he needed to go out. He also told me that all the gold was meant for me and he had only been waiting for my appearance that day.

I watched intently as he walked away, but after what seemed like hours I began to feel I had been left on my own and that I had somehow been deserted. As I looked at the exit in the back of the store I noticed that the door-frame had some kind of statement etched into it though I could not make it out. I was attempting to leave the store when I was confronted by a very tall, beautiful male spiritual entity. Though he didn't speak, I sensed that he was advising me to stay here for a time and that when the gold was gone he would return to greet me. In the next instant he was gone.

This was when the dream ended and I was curious as to what it might have meant though I tried to let it go from my mind and prepared for the morning greeting from my host.

The Test

I was thinking about my return to my body and all of the ramifications that would require my full attention very soon when I was notified that I was to attend a short get together in a private section of the vessel.

My host greeted me with a smile as I entered the room and asked how I was feeling; I sensed we were about to speak about my leaving for home soon. I was then introduced to five other individuals who were going to aid me in the following hours to prepare for my journey. It was decided that it would be in my best interest to go with these same individuals so that my own consciousness could be prepared for the events ahead.

Apparently, I was going to a briefing where I would be given a set of procedures which would assist me on my return. The ultimate goal was to make certain that I could retain the full import of what had occurred throughout my experience in the afterlife worlds.

I had no idea then that I was about to receive an education in the dynamics of those specific transitional processes which were commonly used to restore an advancing soul in a newer form. It was suggested before the commencement of these activities that everyone who participated in incarnation on conscious levels was to understand and then take sole responsibility to guide themselves from one state to another after the initial procedures had begun. After hearing this I envisioned a process that most resembled the learning and training stages that astronaut's might be subject to preceding a launch.

I learned much later that the process was solely related to the condition of one's consciousness during transition and had nothing to do with the actual procedures themselves. Until then I was to pay attention to the dynamics for other reasons that were about to be revealed.

I left the room with all four individuals. We moved towards an elevator to enter the upper decks of the vessel which thrilled me. I was asked to enter and remain in a room until their return. When I was finally greeted by one of the four instructors, I automatically followed.

As we entered the area where the briefing was to take place I noticed a hallway within the main area that led to where the lights seen earlier were pulsating. Before I could enquire about them I was instructed simply to enter this same corridor and maintain a rhythm of ease about myself the whole time. My guide inferred that I would be subject to certain impressions which were to be considered as responses to my own active consciousness and that following these first impressions a series of events would follow from which certain information regarding my own apparent condition could be understood better.

I was further told that the area I was to enter had been designed to illustrate the uniqueness of any one individual and from those results, a series of further investigations would establish what need be done to aid me upon my return. Expecting nothing, and understanding very little of what was about to occur, I began to make my way into the corridor ahead.

My first observation was the design of the ceiling and interior walls that were narrow and tall in the beginning and quickly changed to wide and short, followed by angles and unusual designs protruding from the ceiling. I suspected that the overall design was as purposeful as was the lighting throughout the entire area, and I soon discovered that I was beginning to feel different with each approaching step I made.

For some reason unknown to me, I was feeling a kind of pressure upon my consciousness and my senses themselves. I slowed down so that I was barely moving as I wanted to see if the changes that were occurring within me could be identified, and I discovered that certain mood states became most prominent regardless of my desire to change or alter my own disposition, attitude or mood.

It became obvious that the intention was to bring about certain effective states to produce a connection and that a story was being told by walking through the area without resistance of any kind on my part. Soon, I came to another area that made me feel as if I were travelling downwards even though the floor was obviously not altered and remained unchanged. Here the sound of my own nature began to have an impact on me as did the walls and ceiling heights.

I continued on in this way for quite some time before I finally realized that my consciousness was being tested in some way. For all I knew at the time, I was being influenced to recall certain mood states which ultimately changed my thinking, and yet I was unable to determine how these varied states were so effective. Regardless of my will to stay calm and open-minded, I was subject most to the patterns within this now obvious maze. I wondered if I was moving through a labyrinth as it was the only image I could muster up at the time and then as I turned with the walkway to the extreme right I found myself climbing upwards towards a very small doorway ahead. Beyond the doorway I stepped into a circular room and moved to the centre of the room where a single chair had been placed.

When I sat down I was then subject to images and impressions that ran through my mind that appeared to be connected to the movement of certain lights within the room. As one colour of light would appear and then another, without any specific pattern that I could make out, I began to realize that my own perceptions were being exposed to me.

At one point I decided to concentrate upon history, having chosen to consider the subject of war and peace as the basis of my interest. In the following moment, I watched as my mind projected a series of events running through linear time. It reminded me of much of what I had experienced in the first (stage I) revelations of the afterlife experiences. The big difference then was that I was now able to identify the changes in light that matched my feeling responses to the images.

It was as if every feeling I had about the subject at

hand would introduce a certain colour of light and as the impressions continued, so too would the lights change and alter accordingly. It was then that I realized how the lights were merely the projection of feelings and states while the sounds were more akin to the impact on my consciousness of the events themselves. In short, I came to see the workings of my own innate life being exposed through the rendering of light and sound.

Once I became accustomed to this I felt I was free to think and observe anything I desired, and with that in mind I kept my eyes concentrated upon the interaction of several colours that always seemed to be dancing around a single colour of indigo or electric blue, regardless of my individual thoughts. Here I came to understand that we all have a host rhythm that varies very little over time and I took it to be my host signature. It was as if I now knew myself by the expression of colour alone.

I was very excited then to see how every word, thought, idea, concept or perception was influenced overall by my host rhythm and colour of electric blue. I could also see that each change of feeling produced a new colour or set of colours and that each attempt to hold myself in one state ultimately changed the colours themselves. In other words, I could imagine an event that had actually taken place in my life and then I could see how I had internally responded to it at the time, while being able to change the original conclusion I had made to a more sensible one. It was an amazing tool for change, I thought, but even more than that, I marvelled at the thought of having exact awareness of every inner reaction and response to every minute experience in consciousness.

I continued in this way and eventually learned to still

my conscious activity so that I could see the precise measurement made in any given situation. With that in mind I would speed up the action, then slow it down for the sake of clarification. From these experiences, I was beginning to assemble a working model by which I could continue to utilize this process without having to resort to the aid of the equipment being used.

By the time I had finished these sessions I had come to understand how a perfect form of justice had been appropriated by all living beings within the makeup of their own bodies. Arising out of the ability to stop and hold an impression at length, I could identify how incorrect assumptions could and had in fact generated a condition of unease and discomfort consciously for myself and all other thinkers.

In this way I also saw how former misinterpretations of people in general, or of their personal behaviour, had a direct connection to the biochemical production of states that were devitalizing and less rewarding. Likewise I could now see how it was possible to deal with an unresolved past issue and upon identifying the incorrect conclusion made in haste or through early childhood conditioning, it was possible to release oneself.

I remembered then how the feeling of being imprisoned by my own conclusions had such a definite effect on my mood or state of mind in the past, and because of the test and opportunity at hand then, I was now able to clarify just how much everything was truly a matter of conscience.

I was pondering the reality that I suspected earlier in the afterlife experiences regarding my conscience and my relationship to it, when I noted that my host rhythm and colour would change when an unresolved issue was at hand. In other words, if I was at peace with my conscience, my overall rhythm and love for life remained intact; if not, the discoloration of my host rhythm was evident and, likewise, my general sense of satisfaction with life overall diminished.

Even though I had not realized it beforehand, the innate sense of conscience within humankind was a predetermined aspect of our divinity that acted like a compass within the human brain and body to allow for a more instinctive connection between the basic law of the universe and our own chosen appetites. One's conscience was thus a medium of contact and rapport between the personality and the soul where the difference between right and wrong could be identified on mental and emotional levels as a means of intervention on behalf of the evolving soul itself. The colour of conscience I now understood to be one's own host rhythm while the colour of the Divine spark of Deity within us all is gold.

It was in the later part of the test that I discovered an unqualified and unchanging rhythm within the lights and behind my own host rhythm. It was the truly spiritual me. This was represented by the colour gold and at the exact moment I noticed this I recalled the previous night's dream. I purposefully re-enacted this dream as I had remembered it, and I noticed that there did not seem to be any error on my part in remembering the dream. In fact, it appeared then to have not been a dream at all but rather a factual impression arising out of my own innate nature. On further investigation it became apparent to me that having chosen certain colours over others, I was now being subject to the same sort of situation. I then sought out the colour gold on its own and when I did, I had brought the memory of the Empress to conscious view at the same moment.

I had not expected anything but when this memory was tapped or triggered as it were, I realized that it was the rhythm of inspiration! Now I began to put words to the colours and suddenly everything became transparently obvious.

In the end, I translated the dream to mean that when I had attained the quality of inspiration necessary to complete my objective, I would then be able to understand what was written upon the threshold of the afterlife beyond the realm of the soul. Certainly it was a Divine impression of the future I recalled. This meant that somehow I would be acquiring wisdom more than the general appetites of the body or mind when back in my world as a human, and that at a certain point of attainment, nothing else need be done and I would be able to enter into the kingdom of the spirit itself.

I understood the interpretation to be something akin to the following: 'Naught but the truth prevails!'
I pondered these words for a time while holding on to the colour gold and attempting to discard all other colours that appeared. In the following moments I remember seeing a vision of someone taking a small piece of gold from me and then placing it in their right palm, at which point the individual went through a transformation in appearance and quality not unlike the Empress herself. I was amazed as the vision continued. Another individual came to me and, upon receiving an even smaller piece of this fine gold and following their transformation, they stepped out of the exit doorway and into invisibility. One after another came and to each a portion of their own was given until the very last one came and then

when there was nothing left to give I saw myself pass through that same doorway into eternity.

Once again I was overcome as the meaning behind the dream became more specific. My interpretation was that through the attainment of a certain quality and measure of wisdom, and only then after sharing this wisdom or giving to each their own, would I be leaving the worlds of the soul. I further came to realize after this vision was completed that I was likewise to remain until a certain time, when it would be very possible for others to make that leap from the soul to the spiritual kingdoms. For me, it was as if I now understood the larger portion of the work ahead and I was satisfied to know in advance that through hard work and true conviction I was to play a small part in the overall purposes, plans and will of the Divine Feminine spirit I had come to know personally.

The tests were over for a time and my host entered into the circular room where I had remained seated. We spoke for a time about my own discoveries and it was apparent to me that he was pleased with the response to the tests and it was then that he suggested it was possible for me to enquire as to the results and findings that were being analysed.

Without hesitation I agreed and then followed my host out of the room. We entered what seemed to be a working laboratory where the four individuals that I had been greeted by earlier that morning were preparing to reveal the findings.

I remained quiet for the time that passed and listened intensely as I came to understand the diagnosis.

As I had suspected, the corridor was designed to produce a response from me to the impressions that were forcibly introduced. I was then shown a scale of reaction and responses to the initiated impressions which were numbered in the hundreds. It was a graph like model of expected results and my own responses were indicated throughout the scale accordingly. In this way, I understood the explanations to mean that I was advancing sufficiently though on an instinctive level. In a few cases I was somewhat limited.

In the end I understood that certain expressions and responses had yet to be developed sufficiently for me to be able to retain the full measure of the afterlife experience in brain consciousness on my return. Due to these few shortcomings which were perceived as blocks in my memory body, a certain education along the lines that I had invented for myself during the actual event could be initiated to alleviate some of the hindrances to full recall.

In the case of other more ancient instincts which were not of my own making but rather of the brain, and of the emotional body for the most part, there was little I could do with the remaining time except to impress such memories upon my consciousness which in effect would come to mind for me in the future. There was also another choice which was made thereafter though in this particular case I would not be able to act upon the condition knowingly and would have to rely on my accompanying guide.

It was made known to me that I would be able to maintain contact with my original guide on my return but that I would have to invoke him accordingly when it came time for me to recall other events. To do this and to be certain of the outcome, I would have to be sure to remember a single statement beforehand. I remember returning to my room that afternoon saying to myself over and over again: 'The truth is imperishable.'

Could I remember this statement at just the right moment? Would I remember the words correctly? Could I say these words in the same state intended for the outcome to be a full recall of the events themselves? What if I were to say these words at the correct moment but in the incorrect state?

I spent a great deal of time attempting to burn the thought into my memory and even though I trusted the process and those who were directing it, I couldn't help but to repeat them over and over again. Well, as it actually turned out, I did remember but my timing was a bit off and so was the state, though it did not matter because when the time came for me to initiate the stages that followed, I had already attained the necessary conditions. It was well into the second year of recovery after my return that I had remembered and there was only a small sense of a nagging or incompleteness that I felt about myself then, so all was well.

Returning now to the diagnostic review and planning that had occurred that afternoon on the vessel, I was in a real hurry to get back to that room where I could play a little more with the light technology and to learn as much as I could, as I sensed that my return was now imminent. My hosts affirmed my aspiration and even stayed on to help me with certain insights that were gained along the way and so it was that I remained in the circular room for most of the rest of that day.

I was told that there was to be a major meeting the next morning having to do with my final preparation and to apply the finishing touches, though I was assured that I was using the remaining time effectively as I ventured back to the circular room.

After sitting down, I asked my host if it were possible

to experience other states of consciousness by having them introduced to me, or if it were possible to experience the actual states of consciousness if only for a time of my own choosing. The reply was affirmative and with that in mind I asked to be shown the difference between my own state and condition of consciousness and that of some of the Masters that I had observed. In the end, my host suggested that I try the experience he thought best first, and then once that was understood it might be better to graduate from one level to another in a series.

In full agreement I quieted myself with the intention of being impressed and, to some degree, compelled to respond in kind. As expected, the lights began to respond to my given condition when I started and, for a time, I just allowed myself to enter into various moods in order to reacquaint myself with the colours that indicated such conditions. In this way, I sought to prepare myself to understand my own nature and the make-up of the experiences I had gained in order to attain my own state of consciousness beginning with my youth.

Stages of Consciousness

The first stage of my chosen experience proved worthy as I came to understand how I had awakened in time and through natural experience from a sleepy consciousness towards a focus in consciousness as a young adult. It was obvious that I had come through a very dreamy stage of awareness from five to twelve years of age and that there were many impressions of a traumatic period while attempting to deal with an aggressive and dark influence. Even though this period was violent and unnecessary, a certain conditioning and enticement to focus on the overall situation did add to my ability to free myself eventually from certain idiosyncracies.

It seemed that having to deal with such trauma at a young age had actually worked to my personal benefit as a young adult. Through the interpretive quality of the lights and colours of this period, I was able to see a growing sense of conviction that was established emotionally first and later on the mental levels. I was unafraid and had begun to perceive the abuse in my youth as less of a threat and more of a personal mental problem on the part of the adults in my environment.

By the time I was 21, I had a very favourable emotional stability, and a growing sentient control of my own aspirations. My overall changes came more from the 23rd to the 27th year of adult life. This was when definite measures had begun on my part to manage the impressions that were a part of the makeup and character of my own mind use. At 27 years of age I had already established an integrative personality and my mind use was manageable, due mainly to my interests then in self-accountability.

It seemed that I was not just keeping tabs on myself throughout the years but that I had also unconsciously determined to defeat certain aspects of my own expression which were deemed unfavourable. A high moral standard of accountability was most responsible for the eventual steadying of my own mind which in turn produced the effect necessary for the brain to meet requisites of an advancing conscious condition.

I was delighted to see that all of my former pain and agony, anxiety and duress had been sufficient information on which to establish a foundation of self-accountability and what surprised me most then was the fact that, through mere thinking over time, I was able to gain a consciousness unlike my own peers. In short, I was amazed to discover that it was intended for us all to meet the demands of our experiences in life by presenting ourselves with options on our given responses and behaviour.

I had already known to some degree that we have the power to choose to affect our behaviour and perceptions through self-accountability though I had not known that there was a reciprocal condition that likewise established the neurological conditions which were themselves the key to integrating our consciousness above and beyond our own mind use. This meant that through the use of mind, and through self-talk over a period of years, we had either talked ourselves into or out of our own behavioural situations. Into or out of our own beliefs. And into or out of our own balanced perspectives.

Overall, I came to see how our chosen conclusions were responsible for our overall health and peace of mind throughout our lives. If I had been more negative or less objective, then the gains of the brain, neuronetwork and our physiological realities would be less receptive to an expansion of consciousness even though the requisite experiences had sufficiently occurred. In such a case, one would have been hindered from the natural unfolding of their own consciousness by these shortcomings. Only by the gains of a more objective perspective of life, human behaviour and of ourselves, was it possible for an incarnate soul to attain to the awakening stages of and through the expansions of consciousness designed to have been brought to the fore on our behalf.

It was quite clear to me that through our ignorance of

our own nature and the nature of those whom we chose to know, we would most certainly be subject to less objective experiences designed to suit our advancement. The more pain the more gain? I found that pain was not the intended outcome though often one's resistance to change was very capable of producing the illusion of self-affliction.

The next stages of consciousness were expansions which were identical to those I had experienced in the afterlife.

In order to explain the overall revelations that I was able to capture that day, I should like to suggest the general stages of an expanding consciousness at this point. I should suggest first, however, that the explanation to follow should be taken as typical or regular in its design, though there are a number of variances depending on any individual at any time in their incarnation. Hence, this is a general outline of the expected results of an evolving consciousness that is nearest the final stages of development in the material worlds of conscious evolution.

It was clear to me that our human cycle of evolution regarding consciousness itself could be determined by establishing seven complete cycles of seven years each for the sake of clarity alone. Of course there are greater sub-cycles of 31/2 years, and still more cyclic patterns all the way down to the passage of a single day or hour in which a cyclic influence was present and accounted for.

With this in mind I will spend a little time explaining what one might expect to observe in each cycle, beginning with the first.

First cycle: 0-7 years

In the first seven years of growth and development, the general theme is the development of the brain, its mechanisms and, most of all, the relationship of sense perceptions and instincts. The most obvious to the average reader may well be that of the body instinct development. While less attention to the developing psyche or personality is apparent in the aforementioned statement, the most important aspect to the soul is the work upon physical levels dealing with responses, reactions and interpretations of events and experiences that primarily suffice to explain instincts as they relate to conscious development.

As I came to understand these cycles, the most interesting surface fact was that of the ability of the brain to be a fault-finder. I have chosen this term intentionally since it expresses the idea behind the operative and objective development of the brain and likewise the advancing personality tendencies. It seemed that the brain was the basic provider through its mechanisms of the first glimpse of learned psychological tendencies and, as such, the child should be seen to be preoccupied with finding solutions or simply making associations of likes and dislikes.

The ability of the brain to register the impression of threat or danger stands to be the foremost instinctive response where a child would begin to interpret the outer world of appearances with respect towards safety and continuity. The brain has the overall responsibility to assure the continuity of the young life and to make certain that specific impressions of threat to the whole life in particular is identified and acted upon. Hence the obvious and apparent response of crying, running away or hesitation on the part of the child, whenever the sense of a threat becomes apparent.

We can also find this to be a feature in the adult who has not yet overcome the brain consciousness and is most noticeable when we hear or feel that we want to just run away, escape, disappear or seek the safety of a trusted friend or adult. Our fears of aloneness, of those who lack conscience, of the unknown, of personal harm and terror, of death and punishment, are some of the basic outcomes of these initial fault-finding qualities of the brain mixed with our innate animal instincts.

Our responses that develop in these years are more apt to be to follow the line of least resistance and to run, hide, lie, pretend or become angry when threatened. In this way, the child grows to become conditioned according to the instinctive animalistic qualities of humankind, and this likewise begins to shape their personal expression along these lines. The less shy individual will respond somewhat differently and may even approach confrontation directly if taught to do so as a response, or the shy child may tend to be quiet and fearful under threat and likewise develop their expression according to the taught responses of the parents.

In each case, whether shy or assertive, learned responses are often unlike the impressions that the brain would have us follow, as the parent attempts to teach response for other than developmental reasons, and has little insight into the tempered styles of response education that we might find in learned or scholastic circles of education. In short, the child learns to manage their responses to threats in the environment and this shapes the first expressions of the working personality involved.

The development of the body and its mechanisms of course are also subject to a large degree to the trained or instinctive responses of threat to the individual child.

In short, the first seven years of life for the child, aside from most of what we already know to be true, is sense-related development and includes the instinctive tendencies that will follow accordingly.

From the perspective of the soul, however, the beginning of the fault-finding tendencies in the child are of great importance. There is a tremendous need for the child to maintain emotional and mental balance while being subject to threats themselves. If there is a leaning towards a less objective fault-finding aptitude, then this suggests a developing limitation in the future for the child to maintain objectivity itself. In such cases, the fault-finding qualities of invention and creativity are frequently adjusted and sometimes lost to promote the repulsion of others in general. In other words, those who are subjective fault-finders tend to develop a pattern of complaint, criticism and of punishment, in place of understanding.

This first development of subjective or objective impressionism is of most import for the entire period. It is also during the first cycle, and often at about the fifth year of development, that the soul finds its way into the mechanism of the brain and begins to work with the instincts and emotions until the fourteenth year. The hope then is to impress upon the mind of the young child the creative aspects of an objective imagination.

Working with the idea that the soul tends to desire a purely objective consciousness in the final outcome, one may begin to see the opposition and challenge to this spiritually stated objective as it works out in the first seven years of our youth. The obvious challenge to the development of a purely objective consciousness may also be recognized by considering our own past while asking ourselves these questions:

* Was it ever your intent in youth to look for the worst in people from the start?
* Was it your nature in youth to strike out and to punish others?
* Even though you were taught to disapprove of others for various reasons, did you tend to adjust to these directions or did you find it easier to accept another being's shortcomings?

The obvious dual character of the questions selected are just a few of the situation experiences where a child comes to know that something is right or wrong regardless of what is being taught. More often than not, we end up being much like our teachers in our youth though there are few who would deny the fact that there was an internal battle for objectivity at play in most of their memories.

The very sense of the soul occurs first in the sensibility developed for interpreting one's own true nature. With that in mind, one might find that years of keeping tabs on themselves happens to be due to the recognition of one's true nature as it relates to the expression of a growing personality. It has been my experience to find that most thinkers of today claim a quality of harmlessness with regard to their true nature, even though they may suffer the expression of a less objective lifestyle in adulthood.

Second cycle: 7-14 years
From 7 to 14, the main emphasis of the soul with regard to its overall objective is to bring about a balance between the developing personality and the emotional body. This is the first stage of initiation and development of an integrative personality. In this stage, the emotional body is of greatest import as the meaning of life and the fears of the instinctive body tend to battle for the high ground.

This is when the condition of 'being true to one's own nature' is challenged by the desire nature of the thinker. Doing what is innately correct or following one's conscience as a guide is often discarded for the opportunity to possess, control and dominate; while the fears developed in the first cycle have to some degree caused a hesitation of choice in the thinker, desire becomes stronger than fear itself for a time. This is a most active phase of the soul and the creative aspects of the awakened personality are now coming to fruition, even though the emotional body rules.

What older children feel during this cycle is often of great moment while everything else does not matter, and a selfish aspect of the developing identity begins to squander experiences and objects that are useful to attract and to appease. It is a young version of the instinctive impulse towards relationship and often plays itself out on the instinctive emotional level alone.

The soul's main interest is to assist in the building of a greater sense of identity and sexuality in a balanced and objective way rather than an intrusive, demeaning and humiliating character stage of development.
This is often when the punishing aspects of a fault-finding personality comes into being and can be quite dan-

gerous or alarming to those who are most responsible for the development of the child.

Third cycle: 14-21 years

Overall, the 14th year signals the beginning of the identity stage of consciousness. A self-consciousness now takes over during these years and finishes its development in the next stage between the age of 14 and 21. If a spiritual sensibility for creativity or inventiveness is brought to the fore of the emotional body, then the eventuating attributes of the soul can likewise begin to appear in the expression of the developing personality at this time.

Self-consciousness, or a sense of self that is separate from all others, begins to dominate the mental aspects of the personality, and certainly takes over the emotional body from this point onwards. At 14 the child thinks of themselves as being independent and begins to approach a more realistic mode of self-accountability regardless of the conditioning that has taken place earlier.

In short, the soul is now prepared to aid the growing sense of self-consciousness towards becoming a personality level of consciousness and so it seeks to impress fundamentals of the spirit upon the mind of the thinker. In this way, the still small voice of conscience can begin to be understood by the thinker in times of emotional importance. If there is a longing for spiritual values, and I do not mean institutional religions, then the soul has the great opportunity of working more closely on mental and emotional levels at this time. In the case where the habit of subjective impressionism is still dominating, there is little the soul can do except wait for the day of opportunity.

From the age of 14 to 21, the whole emphasis is the balancing of the emotional body, and the full development of the personality overall. For those who are aspiring towards objective reasoning, another important feature of the mind also comes into being at this stage as the personality is now prepared for a greater initiation of the personality and the soul itself. This is often not completed before the 28th year though in many cases, particularly our generation of information processing, the personality is ready for the first stages of spiritual consciousness. This later statement does not mean that the young adult of 21 is soul conscious but that a spiritual consciousness akin to the soul is beginning to intervene in the use of mind, and inspiration begins to uplift the advancing thinker. So, for these seven years the aspiration to inspire the personality begins and, at the least, the emergence of a developed personality begins to express its nature in the outer world of appearances.

Fourth cycle: 21-28 years

Between the ages of 21 and 28, the soul seeks to end the process of development along personality lines and begins to work on spiritual orientation on the mental levels. This means that a balanced and well-managed use of mind must come into play along with the prior harnessing of the desire nature and emotional body. When the emotional body is at rest, and the intuition is working to some degree as the mind becomes functionally manageable, it is then possible for the innate mystery of one's own nature to be discovered.

A direct interest in the mind or of the nature of man, and often of the spiritual aspects and attribute qualities of notably great artists and thinkers, becomes of interest. A study of self begins midway at the age of 25 and may continue, though the first impressions and accountability of the self is of most importance to the soul.

Fifth cycle: 28-35 years

A crisis stage is reached at the age of 28: it is make it or break it time. In most cases, the personality has not yet been completed by this stage and priority is given to this development during the next seven years. The actual experiences of the individual tend to surround the unaccomplished aspirations of the soul, and all efforts are thrown upon the personality that must accomplish the goal. In such cases the soul returns to the work of instinctive development regarding the unresolved lessons of the past.

This suggests that what was taught to the thinker in the first seven years must now be brought to light over the next seven years so as to correct the impediments accrued. If this is not affordable, or in the case of certain conditioning that has taken place formerly, the soul may remain quiet and wait until the next incarnation to begin the next stages again. In most cases, a re-evaluation or reassessment of the past must come to fruition before the individual is 49 in order to maintain the personality gains of the life.

The age of 28, however, is the turning point in development for the soul as the personality should have sufficient experience by this time to attain to the enlightenment designed to bring about the highest form of consciousness attainable in form. Planetary consciousness entails the understanding of the nature of the evolution of humanity, the triune aspects of the Divine nature, and to some degree it requires one's expressed ability to communicate with deity by the age of 35.

Sixth cycle: 35-42 years

From 35 to 42 the aspiration of the soul is to manifest its powers of thought-form building and manifestation through service to humanity, or to at least be of service through attribute expression while understanding the devoted aspirations of the soul itself. This is often called soul consciousness or awakened spiritual consciousness and is not regarded as simply being an awareness as is often the big mistake of many.

Instead, the consciousness of the individual has become expansive enough to provide evidence of imperishability and verification as to the identity of the masses as being Divine. It is more of a soul consciousness with verification of the further facts but does not suggest that the individual understands the workings of the universe to any degree at all. Unless processes themselves are being studied and the nature of the mind and consciousness itself are also studied, there can be no attainment in form of the final initiation. This is as far as one need proceed to depart successfully from our world and be free of the need for incarnation so long as soul consciousness is attained.

Seventh cycle: 42-49 years

Between the ages of 42 and 49, and only if all has proceeded correctly, and only if the individual has begun to understand the receptive responsive modes of meditation through service to humanity, can union with the soul and Deity take place in form. This is a rather difficult stage of development and there are still four more initiations possible for man beyond this in form, though it is not in our generation that other than a few would be able to attain such an initiation as God consciousness.

For sake of clarity I should suggest here that we grow through a sense/instinct quality of consciousness to an emotional/desire nature consciousness, and then on to a more emotional/mental identity stage, followed by self-consciousness and eventually planetary, cosmic and then God consciousness.

Each expansive quality requires the registration of certain experiences that qualify the diverse interpretive skills of our sense perceptions until the time when we enter into the mental worlds where the definition of self and consciousness itself is sensed and understood through maturity of response. In some small way we could see ourselves as masters in the making as it becomes obvious that our ability to master our interpretation of self and the world is the requisite outcome.

As for myself, I perceived the advancing soul to be a student in the foundational schools of conscious development, where the major task of the soul was to become wise. With this in mind I began to see how difficult the task was of attaining to an all-inclusive sense of collective consciousness while living unaware in the world of suffering and uncertainty.

It was quite understandable to me then that the average individual, subject to an already conditioned world, would have great difficulty establishing themselves as a spiritual entity.

The School of Earth

I

By the time I had finished my adventure and exercise with the various states of consciousness possible for us all, I was feeling quite overwhelmed and a definite compassion and affliction arose from within me. There seemed to be so much that the average thinker would have to learn in order to attain soul consciousness other than to remain devoted to the path, and I felt perplexed when it came to children as I came to understand how the majority were being conditioned so early in life by unwitting parents.

Suffer the little children? If only we had known I thought. With a sense of deep compassion for the children of our world, I began to contemplate how it would be possible that an educational programme for children could begin. After a time I came to realize that only after the adult population was able to capture the essential truths of their own nature could the lesson of sentiency be taught to their offspring.

It was when I was able to define sentiency itself in the following hours of my initial experiences that I came to identify a possible approach to aiding the children of our world. In seeing sentiency as the sensitive response to impressions themselves, I was able to formulate a plan which could eventually come to the attention of the parent. I should also say that in having had these experiences previously, I was more apt to predict the future of humanity as each generation represented a transition in consciousness itself; the next global expansion for humanity, as I had learned, was now on the visible horizon.

I found that there were a series of words that, when

focused on one at a time, would allow the requisite experience in interpretation and eventual perceptual transitions to aid in the actual expansion of consciousness to follow. I found 72 words that best represented the graded stages of development and the understanding as well as experience necessary for a complete understanding of the methodology. By focusing on one word each year, it would be possible for someone to attain to the enlightened consciousness of the soul by the age of 49. By continuing along in this same theoretical process of word states, the individual could complete the requisite progress of the soul.

Going further, I recognized that having the opinion that we are all masters in the making, and that we are in a school where it was deemed we become wise to our own nature, one could understand that certain tests of character were the main emphasis of every experience. When it came to dreams, even then the tests of character were most obvious as most dreams are related to how one deals with circumstances related to their conscience. Premeditation was also, and could be seen as, a test of one's character and conscience, and it was upon this theme that I was allowed to understand that a series of thought forms were beginning to form in my consciousness. These thoughts I hoped would survive the return to brain consciousness upon my return where it would then be possible to investigate further.

It was knowing that every experience would have something to do with a character test of one's conscience that I perceived to be worthy of my efforts towards bringing about the cessation of certain ignorances in the world that were directly linked to children. If the children of the world could be taught to seek wise council from within themselves at a certain date, and if the parents were more familiar with impressionism, then there was good reason to study this theory further.

II

On my return to the centre where the former analysis had taken place, I discussed my findings with two of the four individuals present and was given the impression that I was indeed on the right track and with that in mind I asked the next questions regarding my own progress.

I was told that everything possible was being done to aid me in transferring the gains of my conscious experiences here and then into brain consciousness on my return.

I remember continuing my thoughts while seeking further inspiration as I returned to my private room late that afternoon when, once again, my host called upon me.

He came to take me to the main centre of the vessel where a larger population was to be found. Here, he thought, we or I could come to understand the everyday activities of those who resided upon this vessel and from these experiences I might then discover more of my own interests and curiosities which were already being actualized.

There is really no way that I can explain how satisfied and thrilled I was that afternoon as I soon found out that my presence on the vessel was known widely. It was as if I were greeted by the main population in a way that one might expect when visiting heads of state were greeted with a fanfare on Earth. It was not as if my presence was significant or special in any way whatsoever, though I was made to feel as if I was being welcomed home.

I was specifically greeted and then attended to by several individuals who immediately whisked me away in a small vehicle. It was an open-seated vehicle that moved along a seeming magnetic track and it was as if we were floating everywhere we went. I was stunned to discover the immensity and size of the vessel at this point and came to understand that more than 70 million people were living here and raising families at the same time.

I came to converse most closely with a couple who had been living upon the vessel for more then fifty years of our time, and in particular their two children who appeared to be in their teens. It was through this couple that I came to understand the educational processes and lifestyles of the many upon the vessel which enhanced my perception of those living in forms less dense than our own and without the fear of death. Apparently, it was possible for these individuals to maintain their bodies as long as they chose and, likewise, the children matured very quickly though they maintained their youthful appearances for longer periods than I had suspected. It was also evident that no second thought was given to their bodies or appearances as lifestyle was the governing motive of life for them all.

I was shown to their residences and found that there was very little that anyone needed to attend to and that the main thrust of their lifestyle was education alone. The children were expected to discover their given potential nature, as was the same for children on Earth, though it certainly was a utopia of their own. Here, I understood, a fully awakened awareness and consciousness of eternity was being lived out which foretold the future of humanity in one overall glimpse.

What I was now seeing and experiencing was exactly

what the Earth's population would come to within the next 1500 years. Though few of the residents had ever ventured towards living an incarnate life as was my choice, they were completely aware of the choice and differences and the main topic of discussion was more about Earth life. How it was to be subject to mortality, uncertainty, pain and suffering, yet now that I was free from all this, they wanted to know what the difference was for me.

I did notice one slight difference between these individuals and myself and it was my particular ability to appreciate the liberating condition of life without the mortal form. It seemed that they were in no special hurry to learn more or to accomplish more as they perceived events in larger terms and as an eventuating process, while I was definitely vitally interested in learning their lessons with the intention of going beyond where they had already advanced. I learned here how it was that through the specific incarnation of life in our world, we come to feel more vitally active and impelled to proceed beyond the basic proposition of the semblance of paradise.

I was informed by my host at one high point when I sought to understand the questions I felt they should have already transcended that I too had once questioned the differences and the values gained by entering into the limited worlds of sentient expression. I was a little stunned to recall that indeed I had once lived just like these groups of individuals and had sought to further myself by coming to our little system in the far distant past.

There was good reason certainly for coming here though on a personal basis alone, the fact remained that I had chosen to experience a lifestyle that is not generally found throughout our universe. Very few systems have ever passed through the evolutionary cycle where it was necessary to continue in a form such as ours, and it was through futility, pain and suffering that the gains were becoming most obvious.

Those who chose to maintain the lifestyle of the soul, as was revealed on the vessel and on certain spheres, were less inclined to proceed through evolution at the pace and expected quality of expression that we do once we have taken the plunge into the illusion of mortality. It was now possible for those who had taken the plunge to proceed directly to the next levels of acquaintance with the higher spheres of diverse beings and entities all the way to the formless worlds of Divinity. As for those who were born on the souls level, they rarely chose to descend and their progress was generally longer.

Once again, there was some evidence to suggest that through separation from our own Divine consciousness for several lives in the incarnate worlds, we would be enabled to begin our journey to the ends of our universe and beyond, having the advantage of knowing all the levels of material experience and communication. In this way, we had the fruitful ability to identify the exacting position and stage of consciousness that all others were capable of at any time if we so chose.

In other words, by living on Earth for a sufficient period of our evolutionary time, we would excel in our capacity to earn the rights to pass through many a world without having to partake of the lifestyle there. We were saving time in our progress and gaining much with regards to the basic motive and understanding of the outcome of the universe itself. All of our education on Earth would one day prove to be specifically valuable when it comes to intentional action and service to the

Divine will of the Great Ones overall. In my own small way, I felt I had gained the requisites for direct communion with the Divine worlds and the hosts therein, as well as having gained the opportunity to be of service beyond my own self-interests. As far as I was concerned, I was just happy to forget myself and to find a greater sense of purpose by being of some value to those less advantaged.

I learned later that day that many souls from our world would often opt to remain here or on one of the other systems where the lifestyle in the kingdom of souls was closely similar to these. I could easily understand why as I too continued to have a longing for love and for relationship as did the many on these vessels and spheres. Life in the kingdom of the souls proved to be very tempting indeed.

In another set of conclusions that day I learned that there were many other levels I had not yet experienced where those who were completing their goal on Earth would eventually come to stay for long periods before taking up the interest in advancing beyond the kingdom of the souls altogether.

The Dream of Life: II

I was saying my goodbyes later that evening to a large group who had attended a dinner together in one area of the vessel that greatly resembled a restaurant when my host surprised me by saying that we were now leaving for Earth!

I remember being taken by surprise but not letting it affect me as I kept my sight upon those whom I had come to know. In the next few moments, I was surrounded by three distinctly memorable guides. They were the same guides who brought me here and as I turned with a question in my mind that was directed towards my host on the vessel, I began to feel that we were moving swiftly away from the city-like vessel in the sky.

'Am I to be given other information or should I trust that my return is prepared?' I shouted aloud, and the reply came in a form of inspiration as I felt myself moving backwards and outwards into the open space of the universe.

I was recalling an impression about time itself as something had been mentioned hours earlier about the past and I distinctly remember feeling somehow that I was returning to the past and not the present.

My assumptions were validated on my return as I enquired along these lines immediately preceding our entrance into the city of lights within our Earth's atmosphere. To my surprise, my guide began to advise me on the situation in the hospital and was very anxious to tell me that everything was prepared and that we would have more time together immediately following the impending events.

Having suggested that I felt it had been more than a week or so since my leave, my guide responded by inferring consciously that far more time was spent where I had been, though only four days had passed in real time for my body. He explained further how it was that there was no time as I had understood it where I had been, and in fact, he was surprised that I had not discovered this on my own.

It was inferred that time itself was evaluated in various ways and for various reasons beyond those associations relative to earthly incarnation. I was somewhat overwhelmed to discover that the true facts of time as I had understood it was equivalent to 52 years of study. I couldn't imagine how that was possible at first, though after listening to my guide and checking myself thoroughly I found that it was true. It was stated that if I were to have studied along these lines of sentient and conscious development in a relative educational institute, and if I had likewise gained the experience that would naturally necessitate a complete understanding as was now mine, that 52 years of human life would have been necessary.

I was further startled to discover that the actual time spent in the presence of the Feminine Principality, and the direct inspiration of a quality resembling pure reason, could be reckoned to be about 14 years.

Could I have spent as much time as that? I wondered, while continuing to listen.

It was then that I understood how time was an evaluation of progress on conscious levels. The differences in comprehension, aptitude and the overall ability to express all that I had learned could not have happened most certainly in just five days of Earth-time experience. It was definitely true and evidentiary. As I attended to what my guide was telling me, I realized that even my ability to listen had changed dramatically. I was also careful to observe the type of visual impressions which corresponded to each statement made by my guide, and thus I noticed even more how much had changed.

Now I was able to understand the sense of urgency depicted by my hosts and guides throughout the final moment preceding my direct return to body. It was much more than a few days of experience in the afterlife that my companions were intent on preserving most carefully for and on my behalf. It was also the transitions and initiations which seemed to have occurred so naturally within such a short amount of apparent time, and the unification of my former life memories historically which were so very important.

For a few minutes longer I pondered and qualified measurements within myself which seemed so automatic to me now, and realized that I had simply taken it all for granted and that it was the most natural aspect of our continuity when free of the limiting senses of the body. We simply and automatically adjust without question while accepting the gains of attributes and qualities that would otherwise be perceived as miraculous if such things were to occur in the material worlds.

Another truth that I found utterly valuable and inspirational was that time, in the material worlds as we know it most naturally today, does not exist! Rather, we are timeless entities that have in effect returned to the material worlds for our experience and education on our nature and the nature of the universe itself. Before we come to this world we are alive in the present! The present exists as the spiritual formless realms. It is there that we are first eventuated and eventually, when the time is right, we enter into the dream worlds of the material dimensions.

To illustrate this, imagine that you are a child that has come into being in the most advanced society within the universe. In your world you would be learning the 'how to' of your potential while being nurtured and raised within a highly technical world where light can be tamed, bent, shaped and altered to suit any type of experiment or model preferred.

Now imagine that your parents one fine day decide that it is right for you to begin to see the history of existence in the overall universe of universes. Having said so, your parents introduce you to a holographic screen that appears in your room which is going to be used for your curiosity. They tell you that you can imagine whatever you will and the answer appears on the screen with full explanations and all you need is a few starting exercises and examples.

The first example then might be that a time is chosen when the universe was just beginning to be discovered by intelligent beings who used to live on planets. So now your parents command the screen to show you a time and a place where the first spiritual beings might have come to learn most of what they know today.

Suddenly, the screen projects the image of a planet called Earth. The year is 2000. An explanation is then given by the supercomputer that suggests that Earth in that year was just beginning to notice that there were other beings in the universe and that for hundreds of thousands of years earlier, these people thought that they were the only ones alive in the whole universe.

Imagine next why you might be smiling since you are that child and the idea seems so unlikely. Next, imagine that your parents tell you the best time to use the time screen is when you sleep because in your sleep you can engage in the past and walk upon the planet you have just seen and see the events as they truly were. Now imagine that after one hour of Divine sleep, you awaken to tell your parents about the evening's dream work. Now imagine why your parents might appear to be so happy that you have discovered how to live in the past when you tell them that you actually were born and lived a life of 87 years before you died of kidney failure.

If we could understand that the entire history of the

material universe is what you see when you look up at the sky tonight, it might also be possible to see that you are truly in the present and have projected yourself here for educational reasons, until the sufficient educational aspirations are met. The body of the child in the story would represent your true Divine self which in fact, is presently concentrated upon the greater picture than your personality and brain consciousness has yet to comprehend.

Time, would be the equivalent of sentient experience and consciousness. Your parents would be the Grail couple, and the past itself would be the memory of the One Great Architect of Life.

Through this story, I hope to show that in as much as we awaken in the morning from a seemingly real-ife dream experience to discover that we have actually only been seeking answers to our general curiosity and interests through dreaming, such is also true when the dream of the incarnate experience is over for the soul. Further still, when the soul awakens to the spiritual worlds, then too will the other worlds be merely a formerly shared memory and dream of the One Great Dreamer!

Though each experience and each moment is truly original, and is in fact a true-life experience, so too are all the moments of experience in all other dream worlds. In this way I came to understand how we are all in more than one place and time in the same instant, and that it is our true destiny to awaken fully to the ever-present worlds of the Divine while living in the dream of life itself!

Going further, my guide suggested that within the next week or so, I would come to understand this most vividly as I would have a greater sensibility of my body at that time.

It seemed that I was now going to return to my body time though I was somehow going to be able to maintain my consciousness on the present mental plane regardless of what might happen thereafter to my physical condition. My guide continued to say that within the hour I would be experiencing the limitations of my body once more and he then suggested that I would be sleeping for a time before I came to realize that it was all over.

I would have preferred to return fully conscious but, as was suggested then, this would not be in my best interest. When all was said and done, I expected that I might feel groggy but that full consciousness would not be lost in the transition so long as I was able to maintain a balanced and receptive rhythm at the exacting moments of transference.

What I expected next was to experience time in three specific ways upon my return. I first expected to identify some differences in brain consciousness at first which might make me feel that my experiences were either slowing down or speeding up. I then expected that regardless of the conditions, I would eventually or shortly thereafter, begin to feel time consciously as being different than the time in the body. As for the clock, movement and sentiency, I imagined only that I would be able to sense myself on three specific levels. How different would I be now regards feelings, emotions, moods, attitudes and even in thinking as I was now accustomed to, not having to imagine and think in the old ways?

The Wasteland Will Be Restored

I The 22 Cities of Light

Before I had finished tabulating the conditions expected, I found that we had already entered the city and I discovered that the lights below us that night were from London, England. As I concentrated my focus towards the surface I saw planes circling the city below and with a more intense aspiration I found that I could see people up close as if I were standing right beside them.

We were heading for a specific location to dine that evening so I gave up my focus and decided to return to this when the opportunity became available later that night.

The three guides who had brought me back to the city in the sky that evening had parted ways and I was left with my own guide who had been with me from the first moment of the afterlife experience. I remember speaking to him on a much more private level that evening as we entered the central area of this particular city. It was not the first city of lights that I had encountered a few days earlier but rather a smaller one that was very similar in appearance.

I remember speaking about the number of cities that were like palaces when viewed from above, and how they were intentionally dispersed throughout the world in order to suit the varied differences in objectives overall. Then and there it seemed, I began to see a direct correspondence between the levels on the vessel and the objective placement of these cities.

There were 22 cities in all, though aside from being a founding residence for souls in between lives, or between worlds in transition, the most outstanding differences were to be found in the preoccupation of the resident authorities working on behalf of humanity overall.

II The Seven Words of Power

As much as there were seven levels of consciousness to attain preceding the kingdom of the soul and spirit levels, there were seven words of power that best described the quality and expression of the 49 differing expressions and influences of these authorities.

The best way for me to describe these power words is to suggest that there are seven qualities that can be identified among many within mankind:

1. Will
2. Love/Wisdom
3. Intelligence
4. Harmony/Friction
5. Concrete Knowledge
6. Devotion
7. Ceremony

Imagine for a moment that there are three major qualities that can be easily noted such as Will, Love and Intelligence. Due to these three qualities in any given moment one might appear to be wilfully, lovingly intelligent, or in another order we might observe one to be predominantly intelligently wilful and sometimes loving.

When one thinks of these three primary attributes as personality qualities found in a given expression, it might then be possible to see how one may be polarized expressly in any specific one of the three, which would cause a slight change in the personality disposition and expression. Now, observing these slight changes in an individual's quality of expression, we can begin to add the remaining four so that as an example we may find one personality to be as such, 'a loving and intelligent harmonious personality who is devoted wilfully to the aspirations of learning and teaching within the arts of drama and theatre'. Another proposition might suggest an individual who is less loving and more troubled who creates friction everywhere they go because their will is not intelligently controlled through gains of education, though they do love ritual and are often devoted to their desire nature and self-pleasure.

Perhaps in these two varied personality situations one can see how all seven words are at work and have an effect upon each other as well as the overall expression in time of the individual. In the case where an individual is found to be soul conscious, we could expect to find a wide variety of intelligent, selfless lovers of humanity who wilfully devote themselves to education and the objective progress of a harmonious world through creativity, art, literature and ceremony.

These seven qualities, found within every man, woman and child, can be seen as eventuating powers on high spiritual levels. As the soul approaches the overall objective of Divine expression in our world, each word begins to take shape as an attribute and then a power, and when the full manifestation of the soul is complete we then see the power words I have attempted to ascribe to the resident authorities on Earth.

It is the task of these authorities first to express their attributes accordingly, as it relates to the overall purpose, plan and will of Deity, and then to influence or intervene on behalf of society in inspirational ways. In the case of the word Love for example, we would find that the main objective of certain authorities would be to influence social, ideological, institutional and even economic institutions in such an inspirational way as to have the very attribute of love and wisdom come to full manifestation through each and every other soul who tends to listen to the inner council of self through that specific attribute.

Certainly there is much more that these types do with regards service to humanity, though the main point I have chosen to express here is that the focus is upon the attributes of the soul, and the mirrored institutions which are helpful or useful in the main thrust of the overall plan of Divinity to reach out and to aid all souls in the primary objective of enlightenment.

Unknowingly, whenever an individual tends to specialize in any one particular interest in life, they have in their own way identified, at least to those who are trained observers, the particular group that they are most closely related to in nature. In these ways, the unconscious masses are able to discover their innate calling as well as the specific skills expressly acquired through their eventuation and manifestation in our world. Likewise, in the city of lights, certain qualified authorities of varying attributes maintain their focus upon that specific number of the population which are akin to themselves.

III   The Spirit of America

In the end, I understood that within each city, all the varied qualities were present though their strength in numbers varied from one to the other. In certain populations such as the United States, concrete knowledge, devotion, intelligence, ceremony and love are the strongest tendencies. In this way, I came to see how the US was spiritually eventuated to provide the best environment for incarnating souls along the lines of least resistance over the past few centuries.

In fact, it was when I was beginning to feel a more personal relationship occurring between myself and my guide, as we entered the very core of the city, that I recognized a familiar rhythm. It was as if I could see the face of the Feminine Principality again though in consciousness. The air about us seemed to whisper the very mood of the inner city. It was as if the core area was the consciousness of the city. I saw then how America came into being spiritually.

From having been in her presence much earlier, I was immediately struck to have noticed that the same feeling or constitution of the city was similar to her presence. There was so much of a reminder of her presence there. When I began to focus on her face in those moments, I was given a series of visions. A revelation of her presence in our world came into focus then as I watched and listened.

The words 'The wasteland will be restored' were all I heard as I was then given to see a period of time, nearing the end of the first millennium around AD 1000. A small number of men and women gathered together in a meeting hall and planned with all their given wealth to set out and purposefully discover La Merica. It was a place they expected to find the kingdom and cities of light, where Divinity in the person could be met, touched and known; a place where they could begin the plan to restore the wasteland. It was to be land west of the known world that had been known to them for several generations.

In the following impressions, a fleet of ships set out in numbers of three and five. Their arrival in the land called America occurred at this same time and was kept a secret for as long as possible.

Wealth and wisdom were the foundations of this society for the next several centuries and they likewise enjoyed contact with the peoples of the Americas. With this wealth and foreknowledge, plans to establish the United States of America were made. As the centuries continued, each family had kept the secrets of the birthing of a Divine feminine spirit alive in their records and written histories to this day.

I was then shown how the very families involved in the beginning were the actual descendants of others going back well into the past and that their records were already being kept a secret. These records were valid impressions of the true history of humanity as written and accounted for by the earliest members of the Grail sects.

The expected prophetic revelations of this particular group were about the reunion in the heavens of the Bride and the Bridegroom. Their expected revelation was that of a Divine couple that would have a child, and that this male child would marry the daughter of a Feminine Principality likewise. In the material worlds, this meant that a man and a woman would meet and give birth to a Feminine Principality by which the seed of truth and the bloodline of truth could eventually generate a humanity of Divinity. Through their presence in this world and through their eventual recognition, a similar condition in the spiritual worlds would likewise be occurring. In the spiritual realms, the true bridegroom would be released from his duties to humanity and would thereafter partake of his marriage in the cosmos and return to the Dynastic threshold of his own inheritance.

I was also shown how this was similar to another

occurrence taking place simultaneously in the highest levels of the heavens as well.

The entire universe would be experiencing a great single moment that would bring about the cessation of evil in the material worlds and that through the restoration of conscience, our consciousness would be awakened to the universe throughout. On this given day, the whole of life would be lifted up to a closer plane of existence where the greater nature of The One could be known ever more intimately.

A moment later I saw the actual history of the United States come into being, and as the decades passed I began to see the eventuated moment when the birth of a Feminine Principality came into being with the signing of the Declaration of Independence. The attribute of Love/Wisdom was the spirit of the agreement, and this spirit began to gather from out of the hearts and souls of the many over centuries of effort and sacrifice.

She immersed herself deeply within the embodied constitution. She then spread her youth upon the growing masses as they came to the call of freedom from abroad. She was truly heaven on Earth to those who revered her, though in a short time she became subject likewise to her nation's invention. With every slight of injustice and every hand of ignorance that rose up within her, she came to experience our lives and sojourned in her plight towards her and our spiritual guests.

It was the masses within her form with whom she shared her wisdom and her love, and in her growing spiritual maturity she nurtured a nation of souls through grief and triumph. It was her attributes that shaped our collective aspiration which built the spirit within us all, and in times of violence and war, it was she who shared her conscientiousness with the world at large. She lifted up those who fell in her name, though she was not known, and gave them a place in her Divinity. These are called her attendants, her knights, and her Judges. Others are embraced in her countenance, as they so choose, to aid her in her own plans.

I saw next how the feminine spirit of America became initiated into the spiritual realms and, with her Divine love, how they share the moment of her continued objective. I saw how the nation was consciously influenced through her selfless intent to become more objective with every generation and how in this last generation, she has come to her moment of triumph as the world's keeper. Through America, her attributes and qualities will continue to manifest the next generation of enlightened souls, and in the time of restoration, she will come to be known finally for her presence and her influences. On that day I was shown how humanity will eventually come to ascend to her home and be sustained in her Dynasty.

I was deeply overcome then and though I was likewise awed and amazed once more, I had begun to feel ever more freedom than I had known possible.

The Light of the World

I was about to return to my body though now I had a vision to keep and I knew then that I would not forget. As I digested the revelation gained at the city's core, I sought to maintain the vision of the Empress, in order to keep all that I had gained from her initial contact so that upon my return to the body I would be able to appreciate these impressions again.

It was as if I were now gaining a more inclusive impression of all that I had come to realize and experience in the afterlife, more so than I had expected to upon my return. It seemed that the closer I came to my body, the more I was gleaning of reality. I suspected then that I would also appreciate certain of my gains much more after my return because I would have the immediate opportunity to advance my perspective among the uncertain masses.

With that in mind, I had become all the more convinced that it truly was in my best interests now to actually return so as to put everything into final perspective and to begin on that foundation to move towards a greater goal and quest. Deep within me, I had also begun to feel that I wanted to know and participate more in the unfolding story of the Grail history and I was somewhat anxious to establish contact with certain known members of that society.

So much information and so much more the greater inclusiveness had continued to attract me back towards my final return, though I was yet to see why my guide had brought me to the city's core other than to demonstrate the living quality of a spiritual being that could be discovered sentiently at the root of every nation and within every heart and soul upon the Earth. Everywhere that one finds themselves could now be seen and expected to reveal the given nature of some one spiritual being that represents the overall consciousness of the many within its given boundary. As it was here in the core area of the city, so too were there spiritual beings within and without our universe. Whether they were representatives of a national consciousness or of the overall consciousness of humanity at large, even up to the Great Architect of The Universe, all of these beings were representatives of our collective consciousness.

I imagined how it was that we lived and moved and had our being within the spiritual manifestation of One great life, and how all spiritual beings themselves were likewise living, moving and being within the great One life as well. In short, I felt a common ground for every individual and an importance for each individual likewise. I knew that if the truth were known that death was an illusion, how every individual who passed out of incarnation would come to be overwhelmed by the events and lifestyles of the Divine. I suppose I had a wish list long before I decided to return and this became more obvious as I began to consider those I had left behind on Earth.

My guide suggested that we be seated for a time and shortly thereafter, we were visited by two very beautiful and highly influential entities. They had the look of men on Earth, though they were brilliant and youthful, wise and still. Their countenance was such that I was given to assimilate their condition as they approached and seated themselves. I looked into the eyes of one of these men and noticed a capacity for great power as his eyes relaxed into mine. There was no sense of threat but more of a protectorate. I felt I had met one who was from the greater realm of spirit.

To my surprise, it was explained that such was true and that the main preoccupation of the one male was to maintain the inner council of masters here within our world. It was his objective to guarantee the continuity of the greater powers upon Earth and to intervene when necessary on behalf not only of humanity but of the resident society of masters alike.

I felt as if I were in the presence of a Divine life that should be known or at least recognized, and I sought by listening and maintaining silence to discover his familiar yet unrecognized rhythm.

I was unable to say what it was, or to put my finger upon the impression I sought to reveal about this mysterious and beautiful entity, though I did gather his rhythm into my own soul.

I remember a brief conversation and after raising my glass to participate in an invocative blessing of sorts, I began to feel I was rising into the air above our table. In this same moment, I found that we were all rising together above the city and within the flash of a single moment, we were above the city of London, Ontario.

I felt that I was to recall the words and images I had practised into my consciousness when the male spirit reached out to me and touched me upon my shoulder. My consciousness opened in that moment and I saw myself standing to the right of this entity from a high position in space overlooking the brilliant Earth, and while feeling the rejuvenating rays of the Sun from behind, I heard the final words. 'I am the light of the world!'

I was overcome by his blissful and gentle touch that seemed so fatherly, and trusted that I could let go as I found myself moving across the sky and down into the hospital where my body lay in silence. Within a single moment, I was back in my body and was then overcome by the smells, scents and tastes of mortality once again. It was a distasteful process from that moment on and as I tried to maintain my vision. I found that I could not remain conscious enough to capture the interest of the attending nurses and doctor in my room.

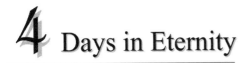

Part IV
Return To Form

Awakening

More than a full day had passed by without my recognition since the first moments of returning to my body, though it was unclear as to how much time was spent unconscious then, as even the first glimpses of the room I was in were fleeting at best. I remember the first awakened conversation I had which were about the second week in my stay at the hospital, and it was then that a certain measure of confusion had begun. An attending nurse noticed my awakening on her rounds and called the doctors quickly to my room. I recall attempting to ask her what day it was and what hour of the day it might be when I noticed the devitalization of my body.

With each word, I found myself struggling with my breath to generate a sound. I was unable to voice even a single word. The responding pain in my throat became most obvious to me and I was unable to sit up as I had presumed to. In fact, every attempted movement on my part was met with a resulting crisis of consciousness. I was unable to move or speak without feeling as if I were about to lose consciousness totally, and so it took me about twenty minutes or so to adjust to what was now so obvious.

As I continued to struggle to maintain a calmness about me, I realized that my body was very frail and that my weakness was such that I was unable to participate in the conversations that followed as the doctors entered into my room.

The first doctor to speak to me asked me if I remembered my name and for a brief moment I couldn't remember it. As I attempted to answer him, he took on a puzzling look which caused me to take greater note of his overall countenance and I began to see many things at once that created a crisis of consciousness for me that I had no way of expecting. As I looked into his eyes he asked me what day it was and if I could tell him how old I was, only to note that I was unable to identify these answers for him aloud.

Every time I tried to speak aloud I would begin to slip into unconsciousness again, and I became more interested in what I was seeing in him than in anything else that was taking place at the time.

It was as if I was seeing into his life. His private life. His home life. His career as a doctor, and his sense of personal resolve with himself were clearly evident to me! I also noted his compassion and surprise for me that I had indeed awakened at all. In fact, it was more of what he did not say aloud that helped me to realize what was happening to me more than anything he said aloud!

As I looked out at the others that stood about and listened, I noted that likewise, I was communicating with them all though not verbally and somehow to my great surprise, I was able to understand the less visible yet meaningful conditions of my very caretakers.

I was so insightfully excited that I began to tell them about my experiences in the afterlife and how important it was to me to know how long I had been unconscious when one of the doctors leaned over to me and suggested that they understood and that I should try to not speak at the time.

I then picked up on a conversation that was occurring among them as a few departed from my bedside. A series of investigative tests were being ordered immediately and there was some talk about the possibility that I had lost my ability to speak. Certain procedures began just as quickly as blood tests were taken, and monitors were brought into my room and adjusted to accommodate something that was about to begin. I felt as if I could expect some procedure to commence as this same doctor returned to me and told me about my present condition.

leaned over into my sight and said, 'You have been with us for a while now and you have overcome a great ordeal so far. When you first came to us in the emergency ward, we thought you were dead, though you proved us wrong and after a long night of surgery you once again proved your will to live by recovering beyond our expectations. We all think of you as our miracle patient right now and it is a wonder at all that you are with us now. Do you understand me so far?'

I motioned to affirm that I did and he proceeded.

'In the beginning, we just thought of you as the victim of an accident where you had been run over by a car, but we now feel as if we know you as we have come to know your family and each of us has taken a special interest in seeing you through these hard times.

'It will continue to take your will to live to help us in the weeks ahead and to be honest with you now, I must tell you that your chances of survival are still fifty-fifty. We are going to do some tests very soon so that we can understand what you might now be going through since we were unable to tell without your being conscious before. I need to ask you now if you understand the nature of your health and if you are in any pain?'

I nodded yes and moved my hand about, attempting to point out the source of the pain but could not control my arm or hand once in the air. The doctor reached out and suggested it was alright and that he would soon be giving me something for my pain but that he wanted me to stay awake for as long as possible or at least until certain tests were done which I also agreed to with a nod.

He then went on to explain in greater detail by saying, 'We've been monitoring your lungs closely and it seems that when the car hit you the first time, certain ribs were broken and a few of these broken ribs pierced the wall of your lungs and then the blood flowed freely into your lungs which caused the first dangerous situation. In such cases, many drown in the blood because they're unable to breathe any longer, but in your case we managed to drain your lungs and get you started up again.

'You had a couple of heart attacks under the immediate stress which is quite normal though there is an apparent abscess in your lungs now that we fear may bring about a new problem for us. We know you are not very strong yet, but even so, we may have to operate on your lungs to clear up this abscess.

'What I am proposing is that we wait a few days and see first before we decide to head to the operating room, OK? You also had some damage done in the abdomen and we had to do some work on your pancreas, spleen, kidney, liver, and pretty much all of your internal organs were affected. In such cases of trauma, we were surprised with how well you held up even though you had a major coronary contusion, and though we had to give your heart a chance to recover first hand, we were able to wash out your abdomen, so you may find some sensitive areas of your body and some scarring from the surgery as well.

'We also have to keep you on insulin until your pancreas recovers and we have you on other drugs to help out the lungs as well as your adrenal glands. Unfortunately we could not save one of them as it was crushed up against your kidney, so we're giving you cortisone for that. You may be experiencing a bit of a fever as well now since we're still draining the fluids from the abdomen as a bacterial problem has come about there, but we feel you're doing well enough to get past that right now.

'The important part is your lungs. The people will soon come from X-ray and we'll be able to tell you more afterwards.'

After a few reassuring smiles and glances, the doctor left me to the nurses who were preparing to change the dressings on my body. A few moments later, I felt the nurses struggling to remove dressings from my hip, stomach, arm and then the right side of my face and fore-head. As I observed, I noticed the gashes and scars that were forming on my stomach and hip underneath the dressings and wondered how my face might now look.

It became more obvious with each passing moment that I was really not in any condition yet to begin to relate to anyone about my afterlife experiences and then I turned my attention upon my body which now appeared so skeletal to me. I had apparently lost over 90 pounds and my musculature was being used by my body to supplement the energy requirements of survival.

I looked at my hands and saw long fingers, bones, and knuckles without the usual flesh, and I attempted to ask for a mirror. My plea was not understood and I could not muster the energy to write. Even my hands were apparently traumatized and blood loss had caused a great pain in the intended use of my hand overall. I sensed that my nose was frozen as the oxygen mask remained upon my face but when the dressings on my face were attended to, another doctor came to aid the nurses.

This doctor was a dermatologist and was overseeing the recovery of my wounds and lacerations upon my face and hip. He explained that he was attempting to prevent as much scarring as possible by debriding the skin every other day. This too was a very painful process and I began to sense that I just wanted them all to leave me alone for a time so that I could gather my thoughts together.

Immersion in Experience

So much was happening and so fast, though unlike the

afterlife experiences, I was now subject to pain and anxiety once more which made dealing with the rush of information much more difficult. It was in this conceptual interpretation that I began to take personal notes on the differences that existed before the accident, during the afterlife experiences, and now having to deal with my mortal form once more.

I remember quietly repeating a statement to myself as the dressings were completed for the time being. I had expected there was going to be pain again, but even though I knew this in the afterlife, without the actual return to form, I was not able to appreciate the fullness of experience itself. It was as if I were continuing the afterlife experiences even now back in my mortal body, as what I had learned and taken for granted consciously was not experiential and made so much more sense of itself.

I had concluded that even though there was a continuity to life, wisdom was not of value without the exacting moment of true experience to back it up. 'First we experience understanding and then later, we understand experience!' For me, this was a reconnecting moment. A great conceptual breakthrough that was now affecting my very brain and body, for which I had understood the need in incarnate terms, but now in true conscious terms, Wisdom brought about an awakening within the brain as well. Now I was beginning to truly understand much more than I thought possible even in the greatest moments of Divine potential and reality. Now, Divinity, imperishability, incarnation, and the confusion of knowledge without experience had verified how wisdom was actually gained as a Divine experience through manifestation into the world of pain and seeming futility.

As I pondered the premise that understanding can come about preceding the understanding gained through the factual immersion in experience itself, I became mindfully aware of the differences in the vast scheme of experiential existences and the causes for the misinterpretations of a lifetime. Likewise, I now knew that I truly was continuing on in the afterlife experiences even though I was using a familiar body.

With that in mind I began to concentrate away from my pain and into the remembering of the afterlife experiences as if to recover more of what I had missed earlier. And I began to prepare myself for even more confusion as I sensed that my conscious memory was different from my brain-conscious memory. It seemed that my human memories left in the brain and body were now interacting and as the expansion in consciousness could now be felt and identified, I was unaware of what would now occur for me as I was now also subject to the past.

Though I was resolved in the death to my life, I was still subject to the unresolved memories that remained in form and that were only now beginning to meld together. It was some time during that first evening of consciousness in the critical care unit that I began to take notes on certain seeming mysterious occurrences that would eventually lead to another set of conclusions that would effectively change my life forever more.

Seeing the Human and Divine

I

A middle-aged man came into the room around 2 a.m. and I overheard the nurses saying that he had been run over by a car, was a diabetic, and that his blood pressure was giving him trouble. I tried desperately to look over at him as he lay only a few feet away from me and noticed him changing colour. He was deeply purple as he first arrived and as I looked again later in the evening, he had turned a yellowish colour.

I heard his breathing becoming distressed and tried to reach my buzzer to call the nurses then but was unable to due to general weakness. I began to concentrate on him and was feeling deeply compassionate for him when I was reminded of the events that would follow for him in the afterlife. It was then that I noted that I was able to identify with his soul as I had done with many in the afterlife and, upon doing so, I was informed that the decision for him to leave had already been made.

I waited patiently to see if he would look over at me through the night but he did not and it was just after dawn that I saw him attempt to get up from his bed and noticed that he was caught up in a dream at that moment and was attempting to leave his body by simply physically walking out. I was amazed to see this as my own death had been sudden and somewhat shocking, while his was gradual and contact had already been appropriated.

Within the first moments of his attempted walk, he collapsed into the side of my bed and I felt so badly for him wishing I could reach out to him and let him know, but then he let go, fell to the floor, rolled over and with one single breath, he leaped forward and out of his body. I watched as his light moved about the room and then after a group of brighter lights appeared, he and they formed a circle and withdrew from the dimension. I noticed how little time had passed and that his guide had taken him in a dream state into the light that was no longer visible to me. Another moment passed and I wondered how much contact I could still have and I realized I had not made another attempt since my return to communicate with my guides until then.

Within a few minutes I had quieted my mind sufficiently, and recalling the rhythm I had felt in the afterlife, I attempted to commune with my guide. To my surprise, I began to feel free from my body with each passing meditative moment. I continued this until I felt I was beginning to endanger my own life as I sensed a familiar clamminess and distaste in my throat and mouth. I rested in that mode and attempted to envision my guide. In doing so, I felt the stirring in my head of energy that was akin to the nature of the originating sound I had once heard on the pavement. Within seconds, I was speaking again to my guide about those who were dying in the hospital and the gentleman I had felt so close to who had just died beside me earlier.

II

Once into the deeper portion of my meditation upon my guide, I had envisioned the city of lights above the Earth's surface and found myself in the core of the city again, though I knew that the setting did not require as much from me to actually begin to communicate. As we sat together, the background scenes disappeared and we were alone together and in deep conversation about the unique processes others undergo in their individualized and unique formats at the time of departure from the form.

My guide aided me by sharing what I would call inspirational visions, which shed more of a revelatory light on former happenings. In the case of this middle-aged man, for example, my guide identified the feeling of his rhythm that I had qualified within myself and showed me exactly what the individual went through on conscious levels during that time. I noted how this man felt he was typically at home and had felt he had over-slept and to his surprise, he felt very heavy and weighted down upon his usual morning awakening.

Though he did not have a direct awareness that he was actually dying, he was attempting to do as he normally would in his routine day while his soul managed the entire process for him. At one point, he had concluded to himself that his body was still asleep and thought perhaps he had risen from bed too quickly which then triggered an impression in his mind that he should sit back and gather himself then and there, expecting only to awaken more sufficiently.

To his surprise, he couldn't understand why he continued to feel so heavy and, although he was in no pain, he felt he was carrying himself and began to feel dizzy. Once he had settled, and this is when he fell, he thought to laugh at himself for losing his balance. He then tried to speak aloud as if calling upon his wife, and he had actually seen her before him in his kitchen as the environment of his own suggestion continued to have a dreamy effect upon him.

There was no immediate sense or sound for him, similar to what I had experienced in the first moments of my own death, though he did begin to feel vital and healthy in the final moments and was simply overcome by a feeling of awe and beauty. Without a question, he simply moved towards the spiritual host that appeared to him then as if an old friend had come to visit him. He was elated and wondrous mentally then and within the few moments it took for him to leave his body, he was within a new environment and having what seemed to him to be a long conversation about the younger periods of his life.

My guide went further as my curiosity had come to the fore and he began to shed light on certain aspects that I wished clarity on. My guide then showed me how the rhythm of this soul in particular was beginning to progress and with each change in the rhythm, a greater revelation would come into being. Eventually, I was left to understand how we pass through a graded series of feelings that actually acquaint the individual soul with the greater truths.

In much the same way that we can observe someone who is saddened for a time and then within minutes their mood and disposition has changed, I was able to see the variations of every passing moment and the outcome for the soul in the afterlife. Having observed this again and again in the case of others, and then comparing these to my own previous experiences, from which I was able to capture the predictable aspect of the passage of a soul from one moment in human life to an awakening to the fact of eternity as the soul itself graduates the rhythm on behalf of the individual to this point, I was able to predict the next conscious moments ahead in another soul's life by maintaining their rhythm.

This made so much more sense to me as I was curious as to how I was able to see two things at once now that I had returned to form. It was when I first came to communicate with the attending staff and doctor in the critical care unit that I had noticed the Divine and the human interacting together, though unknown to the individual at hand.

I was shown how my brain consciousness was used to the habit of evaluation and conduct with another thinker, yet now I was also able to see the soul within the individual as well. It was like looking at a glorified impression of the same individual who, in human terms, looked very grey and diminished in comparison.

This ability to see the two together and to identify the variations between these two enabled me further to see just how close to the point of conscious attainment we are. I could literally see what one need do and understand to make the personality self appear more like the Divine self overall. It was this new attribute that followed me back into the form which allowed me to see the whole world in a light unlike any other I had experienced beforehand.

Not even in the afterlife did such a revelation occur to me, and how this ability had came into being took up most of the remaining conversation between myself and my guide. By the end of the conversation I was able to identify the means by which an individual's rhythm could be envisioned and held so as to capture the eventuating conditions of their future. Much later this turned out to be the greatest skill I would eventually come to use in all that I did thereafter. It was as if now that I knew the feeling of the soul within, I could identify the characteristics that were hindering or preventing the individual from attaining an integrative association. Having the ability to identify this in exacting facts would be of great use in the future as I planned to make use of this gain in specific ways that I will mention later in this chapter.

III

I did go further that night to enquire as to why I was beginning to feel the normal anxiety of being around others in the world again and found out that I had been able to maintain my own peace of mind and rhythm in spite of the unsuspecting noise of the unenlightened in my environment. On my return, and with a full and complete sense of resolve, I had innately chosen to keep this rhythm with each passing moment.

However, I had not noted earlier that this anxiety arose from my being disturbed by the mixed messages and sounds of others voices that were less objective. When I was left to myself, I was able to return to the same mind set and consciousness I had gained in the afterlife experience, though now, in the presence of many others, I was struggling to get used to less objective forms of communication which were acting upon my overall health and well-being.

I had taken note of the general stress, tiredness, nervousness and anxiety that were being displayed by the staff around me which was having a direct effect upon my own chemistry as a result. Learning to deal with those who were not resolved became a new experience to me altogether. In fact, it was several months later that I had finally come to master the actual influence and effect that others had upon me sentiently, though in the meantime the need to understand impressionism as a science had now come to be a major project during this same period.

I had come to understand much more clearly, and actually quite differently now, that the world was filled with the noise of the confused and uncertain masses, and that the peace I had come to cherish and respect so much was difficult to detect in others to a degree which I found surprising. My view of the world was rapidly changing now as I came to immerse myself deeper into the lifestyle of an incarnate soul. I pledged myself that evening to maintain contact with my guide on a regular basis daily and, with that in mind, I fell to sleep with the assurance I had only moments before my return to form.

Ignoring the pain and chemical challenges that my body passed through so frequently now, I was able to bring about the rhythm gained in the afterlife and it was this habit that I cultivated daily until the need for remembering it was no longer necessary.

Attempting Communication

It was very early in the morning of the second day of full consciousness for me now when the nursing staff entered my room and began to go about the general business of changing dressings and tending to the natural processes of the day. One of the nurses looked at me and made a comment on my appearance and stated that it was a new event for her to see me actually awake as she had come to know me in my sleep only.

She was very pleasant and genuinely good-natured which caused me to smile in response and so I chose to attempt to communicate with her more directly. After flagging my hands about in an attempt to request that she bring me a pen and paper, she agreed and calmly aided me in my attempt to write for the first time.

I wrote as I had when I was in grade 2, I thought. It was very difficult and quite painful to write even a single letter that was readable, but I persisted and succeeded eventually to write the words:

Man died. I saw. Was good.

She looked questioningly at me until it struck me that she would not have understood what I meant and so I quickly reached for the pen again and wrote:

Saw man die. No pain in death. This is good. Was happy.

'Oh,' she sighed quaintly and with a generous smile. 'Yes! I understand. Yes, it is good when they don't suffer so much.'

After she left the room, I knew I would have to keep much of what I knew and saw to myself which led me to ponder the ramifications of my intended communication for the remainder of the day. I chose then to keep my conclusions to myself until I was in a better position to explain further. This turned out to be a very wise choice as the days passed and I came to realize the more. I had just been too anxious and enthusiastic for my own good then, and when I received the news later in the same day that some permanent damage to my voice was irreparable, I began to feel disconsolate.

Apparently, when on the first evening that I arrived at the hospital, A decision to intubate was made, which really turned out to be a life-saving procedure. Unknown to the doctors then, I had suffered a fractured larynx and some nerve damage to the vocal chords which went unnoticed until this time. The doctor who told me this suggested that these things sometimes turn out to be temporary, and in most cases it was possible for a person to speak though after a longer recovery period.

He promised to send in a specialist that afternoon to see me but I sensed from him then that he was just trying to keep up my will to live, and that it was his feeling that I might take the news badly which would not be in my best interests to have to grapple with. I also noted that his countenance had changed from a bluish to a yellowy brown and almost shadowy colour as he attempted to cover up. I understood what that meant and appreciated his interpretation, though I was now faced with a grave situation. How was I ever to communicate all that I had now come to know if I were to be mute for the remainder of my time?

I spent several hours lingering in deep meditation before I called upon my guide to assist me in the situation and it was well into the next day before I attempted to communicate with anyone again.

I found out that much more was being kept from me at the time and that there might be a change of plans over the next few days for which I began to prepare myself. If I was to leave now, I was going to finish my life properly this time, and that is all that crossed my mind as I prepared to die again.

The news had reached other staff members before long and the way I was approached during those times when my dressings were changed or when being washed and cared for was different. I noticed a quiet despondency in some, and a conspiracy to hide the facts from me in others as the hours passed, and then I chose to write out a statement to let them all know that I had already come to grips with the news and was happy to have been given the privilege to have time left.

It was my opinion then that having time to deal with the fact that one was to die was much better than to be subject to an unprepared, striking or quick death. In my case, the more time left to prepare the better! I still had the chance to see my daughter and family once more before I died, and this gave me the idea to write out my thoughts to them at least if only to let them know that I had indeed come to discover the truth and that I now saw death as a great release from a temporal burden.

The news spread quickly that I had most likely lost my voice for good and that I might now also lose a lung. With this news also came the concern that I was too weak to survive surgery and that the abdominal infection was getting worse. My doctor told me that it was a matter of hours and that I should prepare just in case. I was satisfied that I had finally been told the whole story and knew what I might be facing but I was also very saddened that I might not ever be able to tell them what was ahead for us all in the unending future.

Around the fourth week the doctors decided there was no more time left and that surgery was imminent. I had been told that the very next morning, around 6 a.m, I would be taken to surgery and with that in mind, I decided to make an appeal to my guide to aid me in leaving my body before the morning had arrived. I knew this was possible and had decided that this was the right thing to do, at least until I met a very charming and beautiful soul that very night.

She was a nun who had happened by my room and coincidentally had heard about my situation. She understood I was unable to speak aloud and we tried to communicate through what little writing I could produce as we went along. By this time I had been given a special writing pad that allowed me to erase the entire page when desired as I used up more space.

My writing had improved though there was still the missing element of character in my words that made it difficult for many to understand the meaning behind them. This nun, however, had no difficulty in understanding and as she spoke to me I found she was covering much of what I would have suggested aloud. She was very natural and something about her pure innocence reminded me of the Feminine Principality I had come to discover in the afterlife. I chose to trust her with my private thoughts and began to tell her the story of the Empress.

She was filled with delight as I suspected she might be and as I looked to see that she was understanding my story to be out of the realm of religious preoccupation, she looked into my eyes and said, 'Please, go on. It doesn't matter what religion I am. I sense you have a new view of these things, and I am really interested to hear more.'

The conversation was delightful and I felt grateful for her presence that evening. Just before she left, she reached into the large pockets of her gown and pulled out a plastic bottle that appeared to be filled with water. She surprised me then as she looked over her shoulder suspiciously so as not to be seen and then I felt the splash and coolness of the water upon my chest.

She quickly asked me to keep the moment between us for a time while explaining she had obtained the water from a friend of hers who had sent it from Lourdes in France. She smiled when she asked me if I believed in miracles while suggesting further that I should think of myself as a miracle itself and as I nodded yes to her, she seemed overjoyed.

'Perhaps tomorrow,' she said, 'I will see that you need not risk the surgery. Tonight, think upon the Lady you spoke to me of and invoke her to aid you in your work ahead. I know you have much to do and there is justice in my using the whole bottle this time so I will come back to see you tomorrow and we shall both see, alright?'

She left the room as quickly and as quietly as she had entered and I noted that two hours had passed by. As she had suggested, I had already intended to enter into meditation, though for different reasons that evening and with a new question in mind I prepared myself for the contact I was now most ready for.

Intervention

As I began to meditate, I contemplated the innumerable revelations that had taken place in just four weeks and mostly in the last two weeks of my return when it dawned on me just how much I had come to learn. Within two weeks, I was able to identify the exacting condition of the patients, their visitors, my own family and everyone that came into my range of sight and feeling. I was able to see the world they had built for themselves out of the mental substance that dreams are made of. I was also able to identify what conditions would come to be experiences in short time for all the ones I chose to study at length and the sense of Divinity in others was now gaining stability in my sight and focus. I was on the verge of integrating all of these attributes and newer skills into conscious applications even though I was unable to speak and might never speak again.

As I pondered the extremely gratifying privileges of having lived beyond the afterlife, only to return and to find the world for the first time, I began to cry from deep within myself. I had come to discover a great truth about existence that was beyond anything I had ever heard of in any other individual's life, historically or otherwise. I was now beginning to feel great sorrow for humanity and I knew how afraid that everyone really was under the surface of their appearances of strength and conviction.

The illusion of mortality and the limited perspectives of life in spite of the world's greatest scientific discoveries - and yes, the children, I thought.

The children! How awful it is to see them being gradually immersed into the illusion of the world at large and how much unnecessary pain must they continue to endure!

My thoughts kept on as I saw the world unfold before me once again and I was within the presence of my host guide by the time I had finished weeping.
A silence came upon us both for a time before I was able to communicate, and I felt healed as I relaxed and listened to what he implied next.

The affliction and loss I was feeling for the children of the world were not uncommon as I discovered and understood fully for the first time what the suffering of the soul was about. Though I had come to meet and identify with the many souls who tend to the affairs of humanity on a moment-to-moment basis, I was now able to share in the common affliction that was theirs as they sought to intervene under the limitations of the law.

I was given the opportunity to enter deeper into the meditation where I then joined consciously with the many who were working along the same lines as my host was, and in the cumulative vision I came to see how my former experience was personalized and now had become a power of its own on this level of consciousness. I could intervene even now as I lay in the hospital. My life need not be negated due to the disabling effects of the body. There was much to do and though I was continuing to learn more on a daily basis, as if I were continuing in the afterlife itself, there was still time to do what could be done.

When the session was over, I was not aware of what tomorrow would bring and I was moved to turn on the television right then and there. As I did, a story was unfolding about a group of people who had escaped Vietnam and were on their way in an overloaded boat to Hong Kong. As the story played out, it focused on a particular family and I realized I could reach out and do more. I recall then how I began to relax into my pain throughout my body so that I was now able to feel the full brunt of the pain and, as I continued, I began to focus on the child I had seen in the documentary and began to invoke the aid of my host and the souls I had shared group consciousness with. I reached out to this child and began to alter his rhythm.

The evening's events had come to an end and I prepared myself silently for the call to the operating room. I checked the time at one point and realized it was past 7 a.m. I began to wonder what was happening and, as I did so, I heard a voice ask where I could be found. A staff member from X-ray turned the corner into my room and shortly thereafter a group of five individuals entered the room.

My doctor stepped forward and advised me that he had chosen to take an X-ray of my lungs while I remained in bed as he was hoping that something might have changed, which I found profoundly unusual. It took several minutes to raise my body into the air as I had many life-support systems hooked up to my body including the pumps which were keeping my lungs inflated at the time.

After experiencing a great deal of pain, though I suppressed my anxiety as much as possible, I was once again lifted into the air following the X-ray examination. I felt overcome then and began to lose consciousness as my blood pressure altered drastically. My doctor's urgency increased: he had to make a decision, though I wasn't sure what had happened.

'I think we should operate here in this room right now!' he said. 'I don't think you will be strong enough to make it to the OR right now and something has to be done.' He asked for my permission and suddenly the room began to transform itself as I watched the monitors being replaced and equipment being rushed in. The staff put on their robes and focused on my left arm where they intended to take a clean blood sample in preparation. The attendant from X-ray arrived, along with another set of doctors. It was explained that I required a special anaesthetist since my adrenals were insufficient but that the X-ray suggested some healing had taken place overnight.

I thought of the nun and then the Empress.

There was a quiet cheer and many smiles behind the masks facing me and I found myself crying aloud with joy. I am sure the doctors did not understand why I was crying but they had no way of knowing how much the news meant to me. From that moment on I sensed intervention in my own life: a choice had been made in my favour.

The doctor proceeded to open the chest wall with a small incision. As he pushed a tube forward into the lung itself, I could hear air being released and my lung collapse. The stench was awful as it appeared that gas was escaping from my lung area and the pump was giving the surgeons difficulty as they tried to inflate the lung again. Suddenly I felt as if I had been blown up from behind as I arched into the air instinctively with excruciating pain. A few moments later, I was given morphine: the pain subsided and I continued to watch the operation.

In the end, a great pressure was released from the abscessed lung and the pumps were working like a clock. A new chance for my lung began as the healing was swift thereafter.

The Healing Process

I Visits from my family

Over the next three weeks I watched and felt the chemical moments of my life and the effects upon my own consciousness of these processes daily. As I studied the healing process I was undergoing, I could see the micro words at work throughout my system and had begun to understand the order and workings of the human form.

I found that I was gaining new insights almost every minute that passed about those subjects that I had never studied earlier in my life. Due mostly to the quality of vision acquired in the afterlife experiences overall I was able to see the activity of an underlying science at work. Something new about my body, and about consciousness itself was continuing to unfold every day. The more I watched and listened to the activities related to my body functions the more I knew, and it was in these first three weeks after the bedside surgery that I came to engage in a specific study outlined by my host, and intended to aid me in the future.

I felt that it didn't matter any more that I might still

die. It was the blending of three worlds into one that was of greatest import for the longest time thereafter. Being able to see the causes behind people's behaviour unbeknown to themselves; the interaction of their personality and desire nature; and the overall process and plan of their conscious evolution was for me the main thrust of my focus and attention.

My family had come to visit over the first month and much had passed in communication though I remembered a vision in the afterlife concerning my father and I was somewhat afraid to let him see what I had written about this on one of his visits.

My relationship with my family prior to the accident was always somewhat tenuous as much remained unresolved regarding my mother and how we had been treated as individuals in the earlier years. My mother's unloving behaviour had continued to remain a large part of the problem as there seemed to be little give in her opinions and, as such, little contact over the years.

My father in particular had always tried to stay out of the situation and offered a semblance of balance behind the scenes when my mother was not around to interfere with his views, though there was very little interaction or bonding before this time. Finding myself in this rather difficult situation, I was eager to see my father and to establish a working relationship with him more than ever, though until now I had no idea just how much he had been keeping to himself.

I was particularly stunned and shocked when my father leaned over on one of his first visits and said quite graciously, 'I've never told you this before, but I always liked you best even though I tried to never favour anyone more than another. Looking at you now, I wish with all my heart, honestly, that I could somehow give you the remaining years that I might have of my life.

'I'm getting older but I am not happy just sitting around listening to your mother all day and if there was anything I could do to give you more life than you seem to have left, I would. I wish you could believe me when I say I love you even though I have never said so before, and I always liked you because you were more certain and independent than the others and I know that if you'd had more time your life would have been great.

'You always had that extra something special even as a kid that no one could explain but it suggested there were greater things ahead of you. I know your mother always made it difficult for you to get ahead but If I could, I would ask God to give you my years.'

He began to cry at the last part of his statement and I was stunned at his sincerity and selflessness at the most important time of my life.

My parents came to see me frequently even though it was a day's drive each time, and it was the beginning of a resolve and a healing between myself and my father that I looked forward to each time I saw him. I had come to express the notion that I had experienced something unusual in my afterlife experiences to him on a few occasions and once he even picked up the book of notes I had managed to write regarding these experiences. Though he never gave me his overall view, I realized he was not certain that this was so but he did humour me and tended to make me think he was right there with me.

I was struggling with myself regarding my father for another reason as I had foreseen his death in the months ahead but was still fearful of telling him, thinking he might not understand.

My mother came with him and at one point she offered her sympathy for my condition though I felt she was weighed down by denial as her conscience remained unresolved. It was hard for her to say she cared as she had preferred not to have to deal with me, especially now in this way. It was hard for her to take back what she had repeated so many times before. I understood her very clearly and sympathized for her as I knew she was limiting her ability to restore her own happiness and to make a change for the better in her life.

Even so, I also knew that she had no way of understanding where to begin or how to approach change after such a long and hard cycle of conditioned misery and unhappiness backed by self-pity. She was so critical, complaining and punishing that she had little room to demonstrate any genuine concern as she was so wrapped up in this condition, but I knew beneath the surface that she was truly suffering her own losses. She too was heartbroken and her soul was clearly afflicted so I took the opportunity to communicate with her soul.

My mother did seem to come around after this time as she sensed there was no regret or judgement on my part, and I made certain that I mentioned nothing in writing that would expose the past or that might embarrass her then.

II The death of my father

It was only five months later, in late November - in fact it was my parents' 32nd anniversary -when my father chose to leave our world. I had sensed it coming long before as I had seen it in the afterlife and was certain that he had made his resolve much earlier, though I still couldn't get over how much he was willing to sacrifice his time so that I might live. I was still stunned by this at the time of his death though it was a very special moment for me when he died.

We were in the same hospital and I had managed to make my way down to his room, though I was still very weak and could not walk more than a few feet without passing out. Once in the room, my father began to tell me about his ordeal with having his first two heart attacks and I realized that he was not being attended to by a specialist but was being cared for by our old family doctor.

He told me that he now understood how I might be feeling since he was now aware of the fact that he might be dying and I smiled in agreement, knowing full well that the matter is less wrenching after one is made aware of death as an imminent factor. He smiled back knowing that we now shared a common insight into people who had no way of knowing what or why we were so happy during such a crisis.

He made fun of himself and his situation as he suggested that he did not know how to resolve those who came to see him with grief and tears, and he continued to make fun of the relatives as he had always done. We were both laughing to the point of tears when my mother arrived in the room.

I left my parents to themselves and tried to communicate with my sister and brothers who had come to see my father then though it was futile to suggest that our father was indeed going to die but that he was very happy to have come to his moment awake, ready and even excited to see if what I had said would turn out to be true. My sister was too grieved to understand and my brothers had no way to understand what I was saying and had in fact wondered if I had lost it all together.

A few moments later, to my surprise, I felt my father calling me and I headed for his room. I passed my mother in the hallway along the way, and I attempted to speak to her but she was unable to make out my whispery sounds.

As I entered the room I felt forced to look at my father directly in the eye as he was stressed as if to tell me something. I felt he was struggling inside to fight off the familiar feeling of death's approach and as I looked into his eyes I began to experience the loss for a time of my newly discovered father.

I held his hand and we touched at each other's hearts completely then and in the same moment I sensed his fear but turned my eye into his sight and passed an impression of the light to him which brought a direct change to his face overall. In the next moment he struggled to continue to hold my hand and began to let go.

As I released his hand and observed the passing moments, I knew he was still awake and I tried to tell him to meet me at the family home. With that in mind, I headed out of the hospital into a waiting taxi and went directly to my mother's home. The family had not yet heard about my father and the nurses were just arriving as I was leaving his room so they had no way of knowing where I was or what I had gone to do.

Within twenty minutes I was at their home and sitting in my father's chair and went into a deep meditation while calling upon my trusted host guide. My father remained awake as I had in my afterlife drama, and was free to proceed within an hour or so after leaving his body. I was concentrating upon his departure and had noticed that I was staring at a picture on the wall of a church interior that he had always cherished for some reason.

It was then that I got the story about the church: it

was where his parents had been married and his mother had been buried there at a young age during the Great Depression; he and others in his family had taken their marriage vows as well. Yet even more than this, it was in this church that he had his first moment of contact and communion with Deity that had begun his search for the truth some fifty years earlier.

Thus I found out that my father had much deeper thoughts about life and death than he had ever suggested aloud. In fact, my father had lived a very concentrated life of focus regarding these truths and had never mentioned this to anyone as he saw such things as improbable conversations with those he had been surrounded by in his later years.

I was given the privilege of discovering how much he had longed for the priesthood in his youth and had remained unmarried until the age of 36 mostly due to his private thinking. I found that there was not a single soul in his life who had any indication that my father had been living a very private life of renunciation and contrition.

He wanted me to have this picture of the church as he had so many memories of a solitary nature locked up in it, and these were his final words at that time to me:

'The picture has to be yours now since you and I are on the same path. I love you more than I could say and I trust we will be together again now that we both know.'

With that, I remained in a quiet silence until the family arrived.

Aid for the Dying

I Sign language

In the five months before my father's death, much had come to pass at the hospital and many new decisions on my remaining time had been made. My daughter had come to visit me though she was too young to remember these moments and I had chosen to remain alone if there was to be any chance of my leaving the hospital at all.

I had also chosen to leave all of my friends behind as they belonged to my previous life and in any case they had not come to visit me. If I was ever to get out of the hospital I would choose to go immediately to British Columbia to see and be with my son for a time.

I had already begun to write out all of the experiences I had gone through in the first four days into the afterlife drama. Though I was still unable to talk, I had received a book from a friend who chose to visit and it was on sign language so that at least I could communicate with someone directly other than through rapid response writing.

I had done very well in studying this book on signing to the point where the nurses who had known me for so long now had begun to act as if I were deaf. It seemed that because I could not talk, without thinking it out for themselves they automatically assumed that I could not hear. They would shape their mouths and speak loudly to me at most times even though each time that they did this I would turn and sign that I was not deaf. They always smiled thereafter but few caught on at all.

I had continued in my meditations and study with all the free time to do so and likewise, by the third month, I had learned to control my blood pressure and most of my body chemistry so that I was able to manage my heath through active meditation. This was very surprising to most of the staff as they were aware of my intent to manage my health in this way and it seemed I was able to do just that which left them curious at best.

There was one particular incident in the third month when I was still in critical condition as my pancreas was still not working well - it appeared I would have to go back to surgery for this and to remove my gall bladder at the same time. A kind of a bacterial slush had taken over inside the abdomen and was now working against my health on the remaining organs and a high temperature kept my health at bay most times.

The situation had begun to change rapidly in this fourth month to the point where I contracted pneumonia. I remember shaking with cold relentlessly while lying under three or four blankets in the height of summer.

My doctor came to visit but did not enter the room and instead leaned into the doorway.

'You going to meditate on this too now?' he asked, with a serious look.

I nodded and smiled back almost defiantly yet humorously as if to say you know I will. He said good luck as he turned away.

I knew from having heard him speaking in the hallway to the staff that he thought this might be it for me and I noticed the entire afternoon as they walked by that no-one came into my room and I was left alone to deal with the inevitable. Two days later I did manage to bring an end to the dangerous period I had entered into and to their surprise again my meditation had paid off. From this point onwards, I was informed by a watchful nurse who seemed to have adopted me by then that the doctors knew it was all up to me, and they had learned to trust me.

After that, whatever I asked for I got.

II Living with the dying

I had begun to make more independent choices and when I asked to be taken outside in a wheelchair for fresh air, they always agreed to it. In certain cases regarding surgery, the staff waited until I felt it was absolutely necessary before they chose to go ahead. Overall, the process and progress of my health and life choices were now mine and it was only a matter of time before I was able to feel I had a home away from home here at the hospital.

I had come to meet so many others who had come and gone during my stay and because my condition was still undefined and somewhat critical, I had the privilege of observing many who had come here to die. In fact, I had come to be so close to the nursing staff on all shifts that I was able to do my own dressings and drainage during the day and was also able to administer my own insulin and manage my cortisone intake.

It was a rather dangerous situation to try to wean myself off the cortisone as my pancreas was not healing well but I sensed that the cortisone itself was mostly responsible for keeping me alive and also for the general weakness of my liver and pancreas. This was confirmed by my doctors and so I had begun a programme of gradual dosage reduction. While this was occurring I prepared myself for other surgeries but in the fifth and sixth month I had asked to be moved to another area within the hospital.

I was in the general ward now though the patients in my room were often more critical cases than usual, and during this time I came to observe and study many who had learned they were dying.

It was at this time, between the second and third months in the hospital, that I had begun to relate to a number of individuals whose lot was very similar to my own. It was not unusual to find that someone in my own room would die - there were at least two to three deaths every week. In many of these cases I had the opportunity to participate with these individuals, their families, friends and care- givers, and also to hear the personal life story of each.

Though there were some few individuals who sought to work directly with the patients who were attempting to come to terms with the inevitable, I also had first-hand exposure to the varied therapeutic process involved in such cases. Overall, I came to see that there was very little real aid or assistance given to anyone who had found that they were not likely to survive. This was mostly due to the fact that there are few who are ever trained to deal with such situations psychologically or otherwise.

While noting that there was a great need for and on behalf of many of these individuals to be able to speak openly about their concerns, fears and emotional griefs, I also understood that it was not likely that many specialists could be found locally, let alone nationally, to deal with such events.

I was privileged to identify certain facts that were common for each and every one of us at this time, and to have been accepted into private affairs and conversations after the families of the patients had left for the day. I found that many of the patients came under stress every day as visiting hours came to pass, and that after the relatives had gone, a great relief and many a sigh of relief could be heard followed by smiles and a certain humour.

It seemed that those who communicated with others who were in the same situation had begun to have a very special and unusual relationship with each other. It was more to the point that we all understood something that we knew, by speaking privately to each other, that those who did not share our situation could never guess about, much less understand or be able to participate in directly.

In one situation, an elderly man had been brought into my room and over a period of about a week, after discovering he was dying of cancer, he began to open up to me and the others as if we were a sort of brotherhood. He spoke and referred to us many times as comrades, much like the very good friends he had fought with in the Great War. It was obvious to us all that he was trying to tell us that he was glad to know that we were seeing and experiencing the same situation together for he understood that through it we had all come to establish a very special relationship.

Not unlike others who came and went, it seemed that the remaining patients like myself were a growing fraternity of supporters who had much information to offer. Many a night we would continue to communicate into the early morning hours.

Our conversations would always start with a review of each others' situation, such as what we were suffering, when we expected to die, how long it might be, how we were dealing with it and how we saw our family and loved ones who came to visit. On many occasions the conversation in the earliest stages would deal with shared direct insights into the processes and sensibilities that each was going through, but then the topic of the possibility of death being a transition to something greater would always come up.

Nearing the later stages of an individual's life, the topics would always be the same, such as how one can tell when it is time, how it must be when it does begin to happen and has anyone seen another go consciously or were they all asleep when it happened? The questions themselves indicated the actual stage or degree to which one was at in the dying processes and, in a short while, a few of us had become very good at determining how long one would have just by their particular stage of thinking.

For example, when we found one of us beginning to isolate themselves in conversation and begin 'the stare', as we called it then, we knew that little time was left. The individual in isolation had to live with the remaining conclusions on life that they had come to and much of what was contained in this process related to self-suggestions like, 'I'll never do that again' or 'It doesn't matter any more.'

I realize that I am only giving a few details of a larger picture, though it is a true fact that one goes through a psychological process that eventually comes to a limiting projection of visions and desires where the individual sees the whole world as going on without them. Usually this kind of thinking is its own quality of consciousness and often it was this very thinking that we all understood which aided us in realizing just how far from understanding the truth of life itself that our families, friends, loved ones and visitors had been unable to comprehend.

It was a certain reality for us all that when someone would come into the room, we would all go silent. Once the individual had left, we would all talk about what we saw behind the appearance and what we felt was being hidden behind the words. I realized that even though these individuals had no specific training as observers, they were clearly able to identify the overall psychological condition of another thinking individual for the first time in their lives.

We often spoke of how we knew this and the conclusions were always the same as we felt that we touched upon a reality that forced us to look at ourselves in a truer light. In other words, because we had given into to thinking about leaving the world, we were able to see that others had never done this themselves, and that such was left until the time that one found out nearing the very moment of death itself.

We all agreed that if we had thought this way at any time during our lives, and had prepared ourselves for the inevitable much sooner, our appreciation for reality and life would have been greatly enhanced. We also agreed that we were at something of a loss in our thinking without having done this before as well. It was this thinking lifestyle that was adopted according to the inevitable reality of death that gave way to clear insights into others; this very ability to have gained such insights so soon before death that intrigued me the most then and I took it upon myself to study these associations with greater interest.

Within a short period of time, I was writing out my findings nightly and passing them on to certain nurses I had come to know and some of these were making their way to the doctors who were on my ward daily. Eventually, I found that there was quite an interest being developed by many of these professionals, even to the point that I was asked to help a graduate student in social studies who was put in touch with me then. The psychological insights that were explained in detail over a two-month period eventually made their way into the general studies of others in the hospice and palliative care wards.

Over this same period I had a few occasions to believe that I was still not out of harm's way and had come very close to dying again. During such times, I found that having already passed through the afterlife drama unique to myself, and then having survived to see and come to know others on a very intimate level, I was experiencing a very unique insight into the world and humanity at large.

I noted that while there were as many as 50,000 deaths daily and even more births during this same period, very little was known and little or no information was available to those who were proceeding into these processes. On many occasions, an article or book would find its way into our ward and it was immediately digested by many a thirsty mind. I thought of writing about this in the future which I eventually did, though it was to be many years before these insights were finally published.

Though I am quite aware of the overall situation that goes on daily for humanity, I have found that there is a general fear and suspicion that prevents much valuable information from ever reaching those who literally starve for such data.

I found this a strange thing at first, as one would think naturally that it would be in the best interests of these individuals that such material be brought to the general public attention, though I have come to realize more today that death is still a remorseful, despondent and uncertain experience that the masses are not yet ready to consider while in good health.

In some circles it is even mistaken as a morbid effort

to concentrate on such things even though it is the least understood experience that we all must pass through in our lifetime. Even in the case of family, I found that there was tremendous fear and concern over the fact that one should not speak to the dying directly about the inevitable, as it would be most disturbing to them, and I also discovered that denial on the part of the living is much of what prevents the experience of death from being elevated to the very unique and special event of a lifetime.

I also found also that priests, ministers and clergy were not well received by many a faithful individual preceding death as many intentionally avoid sharing potential concepts on the subject. In fact, I have witnessed many who asked direct questions of their spiritual mentors only to find greater disappointment overall. In short, I felt there was much that could be done to aid an individual in such cases.

In my own situation, being unable to speak aloud, I did write on many occasions about the actual moments prior to death and this information generated many newer conversations that seemed to give a more rational approach to inspired thinking for the many at hand. Even to find out that a feeling of dizziness and a slight change of temperature preceding the actual event were some of the indicators of death's nearness was warmly received by those with whom I did manage to communicate, as I found that any information was helpful as well as desired most seriously.

As for the conversations shared nightly regarding the potential to survive after departing the body, I found that many had the same kinds of dreams and, once exposed, there was a greater tendency on the part of others to begin serious efforts at meditation in a most natural way.

What I mean to say is that meditation had not been spoken of though I found that all were doing it in the later stages of their life.

As for myself, I found that the soul behind the scenes in each case was managing the actual processes, and that when the individual had reached a specific capacity to deal with the inevitability of their desires coming to an end, death was immediate. I came to see how many personalities who remained troubled and did not find mental calmness, even though there was plenty of time, always had greater difficulty in leaving their body.

Eventually, I came to see the hidden process of the many from my vantage point and I was able to observe how greater difficulty in release from the body existed only for those who were continuing to make accusations and who mostly regretted their life's choices. In each case I also noted that the less selfish individuals had the greatest experiences of all. These types always left with a smile and a determination to love beyond their death and, likewise, the family members were most moved spiritually at these times. I have also been privileged to see love renewed only days before the death of many and I found that the greatest heartache came from their feeling that they were not loved, or not able to love as much as they then sensed they should have.

In every scenario, I noted the attempt of the waiting soul to engage the personality in contemplation which would lead to the resolving of the conscience ahead of time and this seemed to be of primary import to the soul itself. Having already passed through the entire experience first hand, I was able to see how beneficial it was for the personality to take up the unresolved matters of life and then to have a restored vitality for a greater revelation of love, family and humanity.

When I came upon those who had felt resolved to their conscience I witnessed tremendous humour, good cheer, the ability to deal with the grieved most easily, an ability to assure and to define love as the greatest gift of life overall. The love that these people felt for the whole of humanity before their death was astounding.

In conclusion, I found that when one came to real terms with their life, the soul was enabled to establish a form of communication through inspired visions and dawnings which opened the heart to mysteries and insights never before sensed or touched upon. It was as if the dying were coming to life in their death, as I noted how similar the death process for those who had time was to my own afterlife experiences. I knew then that much of the afterlife process could be conducted before the event of actual death and many of the insights gained were intended to aid the individual in coming to terms with their new life as a birth into eternity from the womb of incarnation.

Over the two-year period that I stayed in hospital I came to experience at first hand the death of more than fifty individuals and had also been able to identify more about what and why the conditions in the afterlife were so uniquely tuned to the events of the incarnate life. I was also able to identify more of the specific objectives that the advanced souls in the afterlife who still continue to aid humanity in their passage out of this world have as a skill in action.

In other words, I became much more familiar with a group of souls and entities whose primary objective was to aid humanity directly into and out of this world of incarnation as well as the other groups of souls and advanced masters whose objective it is to influence current events most immanently in our little system. Through these insights and continued contact I was able to distinguish the differences existing between or from one group of souls and the many others whether in or out of incarnation.

New Life, New Voice

I   Leaving hospital

It wasn't until some time in the early part of February of the following year that I was beginning to prepare to leave the hospital altogether. Apart from a few surgical procedures to correct the damage to my larynx, I was getting ready for my return to the world at large, which for me meant a new experience in solitude and independence within my own home for the first time.

After spending more than a year in hospitalized care, I had become accustomed to the company of the many nurses, doctors and administration staff, as well as patients. On many occasions, I was involved personally and intimately with patients after their stay in the same ward as myself, and many of my visitors had become these new friends who continued to offer me solace and hope for my own recovery.

It was as if a new life had begun for me with new friends and that the friends of the past had diminished completely apart from just one specific couple who had been friends from my teen years. I had decided during this time to go forward into my own uncertain future, though most willingly since I had great determination to succeed in overcoming all of the obstacles of health and finances and for a short period I was moved to my home town and stayed with my friends of the past for a time.

I remember how grateful I was to have survived much of the trauma-associated illness and, even though the doctors felt that I only had perhaps one or two years left to live, I felt quite certain that intervention would continue as I had come to depend on it; and, likewise, my spiritual development had skyrocketed well beyond any measure imaginable.

II   Readjustment

When I moved into my friends' home I had no wardrobe, no money, no income and even though I had started a lawsuit against the individual who ran me over twice on that particular evening one year earlier, the prospects of financial restoration were greatly diminished when he died in a fatal car accident only eight months later.

At that point it appeared that there was no chance of compensation as the death of the driver prevented a full hearing and discovery regarding the events of that evening. Further, my lawyer suggested that the opposing insurance company felt they had no responsibility to me as their client was using his car in a crime scene for which they were not legally bound to cover him.

I should state here that at this very same time, my health was still poor and I was still unable to walk more than a few feet without running out of breath. Not only had the damage to my lungs limited the flow of blood oxygen but the internal scarring of my lung also restricted the normal expansion and contraction of the lung itself. Having to learn to breathe again in ways where I was able to force air into a limited lung and to expel that same air was quite an undertaking. Added to this problem, my larynx was limiting the flow of oxygen into the lung, so I was now having to live with the reality of a full-time trachea.

Having about 30 per cent of the normal breathing capacity at my disposal limited my ability to climb even a few stairs into my new home and often I would find myself having to sit down wherever and whenever to regain my overall chemical balances. There simply was not enough energy or oxygen to help in the redevelopment of new muscle tone - and exercise was simply out of the question - so I also had to deal with the problem of having little mobility. Furthermore, I was continuing to suffer severe pain due to the pancreatic fistula that persisted in spite of the seriousness of the bacterial remedies and antibiotics being administered, while headaches from shortened ligaments in the neck and back area only added to the fatigue.

Even though I was limited as such, my friends made it possible for me to aid my own recovery by daily leaving me a list of household chores to attend to. On the average day, I would attempt to vacuum the living room and, on alternate days, I would vacuum my room and the main hallway which certainly tested me throughout the period of my three-month stay.

During this time, I was able to visit my daughter though our communications were limited, and I also managed to get out with my friends to others' homes. The infrequent occasions where I was able to go out publicly were most difficult and testing at best; however, I did assume an even greater degree of independence over the time spent in their home.

III   Victoria

Within these three months I had come to realize that my

future needs would require some financial support and I was able to obtain a loan which would allow me to move from Windsor to Victoria, British Columbia where my son was.

Though I had had the opportunity to communicate with some people, I knew that once I moved I would then have to face the greater truth of my independence and those limitations which eventually proved most frustrating yet educational. After saying my goodbyes, I was driven to the airport for my trip to Vancouver. Within five hours I had arrived in Victoria with 35 dollars to my name and a suitcase that I was unable to lift.

By the time this decision was made, even though I knew there was more surgery required in the near future, I had come to develop a definite skill for seeing things as they were in spite of what others had perceived. It was on these results that my meditative study continued which gave me more to ponder daily than I had expected. I had taken up a specific study regarding my own self-talk and mental reflection by then and was anxious to continue in this study by the time I had arrived in Victoria.

I had managed to talk to a porter at the hotel in Victoria and he was able to aid me in storing my luggage. I then headed directly by taxi to the school where I would be able to contact my son. I waited outside the school and when I saw him coming out I stood and made an attempt to capture his attention by flagging my hands.

We were both very happy and taken by this moment and within a few minutes I was invited into his home for a visit.

I had let his mother know that I was coming so she was very open and receptive to my appearance by then and I was struck to find that she had been planning to get married that very next weekend. The unusual part for me was that when I was introduced to her husband to be I recalled an impression from the afterlife regarding the home and this man himself.

I spoke as best as I could and wrote out what I had experienced while suggesting I had kept a record of everything in a book that was in my luggage. I went on to describe a man who was not her fiancé and whom I thought I had seen in her home on the night of the accident. As I did so she named this man. (She confirmed later that this was true as she had been called later the next day by my mother to let her know what condition I was in then, and she recalled being with this specific man that night.)

Soon afterwards, I told her what I saw in my son's room and was invited in to see it for myself. The room was exactly as I had seen it and the pictures, cars and furniture were exactly the same. For a brief time, I felt as if I was in two time fields at once: that I was in the afterlife drama then as I had experienced it and that I was somehow identifying my own presence at that very moment.

I suspected this was a trick on my own mind rationally and that I was just putting two events together at the same time though the outcome was verifiably true. It was just as I had seen it. We then began to discuss what the conversation was between her and the man whom I had witnessed in the afterlife was about. I said that I thought it was about the relationship she was having with this man.

She hesitated for a moment, laughing as her fiancé wondered what I might have meant, and then revealed that she had been in a relationship with this other man (whom I had witnessed) but that she had decided to become serious with the man who was now her fiancé and who was now in our presence. After having to explain herself she commented on how I was still able to effectively interfere in her private life even in my own death.

After about two hours had passed, I was feeling quite weak and asked to lay on her couch but was offered my son's bed. When I awoke, I found that she had contacted her neighbour friend and said I was looking for a place to live. The negotiations for rent were swift and within the hour I was living in a home only ten minutes away from my son and had the privacy of a room to myself.

IV   Regaining speech

Little more than a week had passed and I found myself unable to stop the pain in my abdomen from subsiding. I was certain I had to return to the hospital in London, Ontario - and did so the following day. Once there, I was scolded by my doctors for not having come back for surgery when I had been scheduled to do so though the surgery did go ahead and it was in the first week of recovery from having my gall bladder removed that I was introduced to a specialist who had begun to take a much deeper look at my vocal situation.

Though the doctors were unable to reach the pancreas during surgery due to the immense internal scarring and even though it appeared that the bottom half of my pancreas had become petrified in this mass of scar tissue, my new specialist still thought he could go ahead with a very unique procedure.

Apparently, there was a small chance that a bone transplant directly into the larynx might enable me to have the trachea removed and aid in my breathing needs; it might then be possible to inject Teflon directly into the muscle above the larynx which might aid in my ability to communicate. I was very excited to hear this and even though this form of surgery had never been done on a human, I felt there was direct intervention that I could rely upon and in the end I chose to go ahead with this surgical procedure.

I was told before surgery that if the result of the bone transplant proved unsuccessful, they would have to remove the larynx immediately and I would then lose the cosmetic value of appearing normal. In the worst-case scenario, I would lose the appearance of the frontal portion of my throat and would definitely be tied to a trachea for life thereafter. In my own mind, the option to speak aloud again warranted all that the percentages inferred as a loss. With this being clear to my specialist, he chose to go ahead and after another sixteen-week stint in the hospital, I was taken back to surgery one more time to remove the stint placed in the core of my larynx.

The very first day that the wires and plug were removed, I was breathing about 50 per cent better and sensed success in the procedure. Over the next two weeks I was given injections directly into the musculature above the larynx while awake during these minor surgical periods, and I had recovered a muffled yet audible sound. I was on my way to being able to speak again though I knew that it would take several months if not years to perfect this small gruff range of sounds.

Indeed the procedure was a full success and I able through continued therapy to speak aloud even though the sound of my new voice was muffled, gruff and whispery.

V   New voice, new life

I had been given a chance of chances to re-establish my character and personality back into a world that had for some time appeared to be silent.

Until these first moments, even the nursing staff who had come to know me were overwhelmingly surprised to find that I was also reasonably intelligent. Over the last two weeks of my stay in the hospital and with a small but obvious ability to be understood now, many were alarmed to find they had misunderstood or misinterpreted me simply from not having heard me speak directly.

I knew and concluded that much of what I believed to be true was in fact illuminated and that without the ability to express my own feelings through words previously, this limitation had led to a complete misinterpretation of myself as an individual. Only now could I begin to live my life again, and to the fullest measure that I could utilize my voice, I vowed then to do so without hesitation.

I believe that I understood the plight of many who were unable to be heard or understood thereafter as I came to see that our individual sensory perceptions were the most responsible agents of change in our world. I had studied my own innate voice, and capacity for self-imagery and their linkage over the long period of hospitalization, and had made several new conclusions that were not even recognized by psychological research.

These conclusions became the foundation of a new science that was to be eventually completed in the years ahead and it was due to the limiting sphere of communication, or to the overall incident itself, that I was now in a position to propose new insights into human behaviour.

I was so grateful to have been able to experience the actual trauma and period of restoration which gave me this new life and felt as if I were living a completely new life though in an older and familiar body from which I was able to complete my own soul's objective in full manifestation and with total clarity. It was a gratefulness that I cannot express in words alone, and that I even now feel is rare and precious indeed.

Sharing the Vision

I Confirmation

I returned to Victoria shortly afterwards and within a month I had managed to make a claim for disability income from a pension plan I had bought into from the government. I could now look forward to at least being able to pay my rent and cover some of the basics. As for the medicine and other equipment I was using then, according to the medical plan it was free for all Canadians.

I had come to trust the intervening realities of my spiritual life and - as had always been the case - my needs had swiftly been met, though never beyond the necessities. Within a month I had found another apartment and had advertised for a room mate, and that is when I first began to speak openly about my afterlife experiences at length.

My room mate's name was Michael, though many of his friends including myself called him Mikey which suited him better. Mikey drove a limousine for a living and had recently become separated from his wife and daughter at their request which made for some common themes and lifestyle conversations as we developed a very healthy relationship together in the first months that passed. Since neither of us were in the position to afford much, we tended to watch television and movies most nights, and that is how the later conversations led me eventually to allow him to look at the book of notes that I had written over the past year.

I had come to learn to be careful when speaking about my personal experiences regarding the afterlife as I found differing results previously though I felt Mikey had come to know me well enough in our time together for me to begin to speak more openly to him about such things. I waited one evening for him to read a portion of the notes before beginning a full conversation and, even though I felt he was a bit apprehensive, I intended to go further as an exploratory venture to discover how others might feel about this same information.

He appeared somewhat awed as he enquired further that evening but the more I revealed to him the less comfortable he seemed about the conversation. I noticed that he had begun to question himself about his own beliefs and it was when he suggested that he didn't know how he would handle it if it were true, I went further.

At one point, he asked me if I had been able to see him in my future and if there was anything written about him in these notes. When I said yes, he quickly became excited though not in an objective way. I watched him as I pointed out the notes where I had found myself speaking to a stranger about his shoes, which I hadn't thought much about in general in relation to my afterlife experiences, and I'd had no significant interpretation of this incident.

It was then that he became a little frightened. Only a week earlier, unbeknown to me, he had gone into my room and stolen 120 dollars to buy a new pair of shoes as his had holes in the bottom. He was obviously ashamed and explained that he would pay me back but his embarrassment led to something more which I found out later.

Mikey had construed in his own mind that I must have known about the money and had showed him my notes to verify these facts and didn't quite know what he should do about it. Even though I had told him I had not given any thought to it and that I did not know he had taken money from me, he began to think that I might know something else that I was not saying. That is when he began to ask me how much of the future I had come to see or know about and he wondered what it meant overall. One of his questions was a query as to whether the world would eventually blow itself up or not, and I realized then that I was into a more responsible situation now and that I had better help him to adjust to what he had learned.

Over the few months that passed after our initial conversations Michael had come to trust me, and had come to the conclusion that such things might be true, though he always feared I could see right through him after that. In fact, on several occasions he would bring some of his other friends over to spend time watching a movie or for just getting together where he would take the opportunity to ask me specific questions that were about these very friends.

Within a short time I came to learn that a certain fear of exposure became evident among those I had chosen to share my private information with. It seemed that they all sensed I could see through them, and that I had some special ability to help them out of a problem they were attending to. Either way, I felt I was being used at the best of times and that I should stop speaking about my findings directly to anyone.

II Preparing for expansion

Having decided to keep the matter to myself, I came to meet and become friends with a large number of people in Victoria and in spite of not having mentioned anything about my afterlife experiences to them, I found that I was being asked for my view more than I had ever previously been accustomed to. For good reason, I suspected that my own language was changing from my own gains and insights, and it seemed that my responses had certain effects on those whom I had come to know.

I became very good friends over a matter of six months with one particular individual named Marcus who trusted me explicitly and after many conversations on relationships and about people in general, he commented to me one day that everyone wondered how I knew so much and how I got to be so informed, and was wondering if I had studied along these lines without having said so.

I began then to see how in fact I had indeed changed and how my language and responses had likewise changed to the point that others felt I was a credible advisor. I found myself considering this at length and then realized that I did have the ability to explain the obvious to those who seemed unable to see the cumulative situations of another and that even though I had learned this from the afterlife experiences, I need not mention this and might even begin to consider doing a series of seminars on specific subjects.

Within a year, I had begun to consider certain strategies and how I might create certain topics of interest which were directly related to my own findings. By the spring of 1984 I was ready to begin my career of educational seminars and had contemplated producing specific programs that could be taped and used by students who were studying human behaviour.

This was the first time I had come to realize that my health was sufficient to go ahead and consolidate my findings and to apply them in educational formats from which I could develop a suitable income upon which to survive.

In December 1984, five years after the accident, I was able to speak sufficiently and had managed to deal with my continued health problems mostly through alternative health processes and meditation. Much of what I began to bring to my public seminars was directly related to alternative health care and meditation itself, and it was upon these subjects that I produced over 800 taped programmes and some 200 seminars.

My most successful seminars were those that led to longer courses about self-resolve, self-analysis and bereavement, though I had begun to give greater focus to alternative health maintenance and meditation programmes alone.

By that same December I was ready to enter into the work I had intended to proceed towards and which was purely related to my relationship with my host guide. Behind the scenes, and in spite of all outer appearances of health or preoccupation, only a few trusted friends were ever privileged to become acquainted with my most intimate and serious efforts in meditative work that had come to a moment of synthesis. It was almost six years since the accident and quietly yet very actively my most serious spiritual work and continued contact with my host guide had brought about a major event in my life. It was during the Christmas season that I had chosen to spend some time alone before making certain decisions about goals which would require all my strength and ambition to attain thereafter.

For the four years I had spent in Victoria along the ocean's edge, where I often sought solitude, healing and inspiration, I had lived up to the challenge to integrate my afterlife experiences into my daily life, and my vision of the world, humanity and the progressive aspiration of my own soul had finally merged into a unified consciousness.

No longer was I subject to the previous misinterpretations of myself and others or of the limitations previously characterized by habits of sense perceptions born of earlier conditioning. By this time, I was free from the fault-finding tendencies of brain consciousness and of the duality that most often proves for many such a hindrance to clear objectivity. My personal studies had provided a sufficient foundation for me to be able to identify, articulate and demonstrate my discoveries as scientific facts.

The expansion of consciousness experienced in the later phases of the afterlife drama had now come to bear on my overall consciousness in form, and I was then able to utilize these gains to bring about a unified experience in brain, personality and soul consciousness. By January 1985 I was able to utilize the same consciousness in my given day, as I had done in the afterlife. The world then appeared within my sight, as I had come to see it spiritually, as a series of greater moments of triumph over illusion and self-ignorance. With the passage of every new day, I observed the conscience of humanity coming to the fore.

I had been given a very special opportunity during these years to enter into a specific study brought to my attention by my host guide in my deepest moments of meditation and, through our combined rhythm at these times, I was able to draw upon the inspired vision of my host until such time as I could draw upon this source of Divine sight for myself. It was in January 1985 that I had earned the right and privilege of continued access, and it was further expected of me by my guide then that I was to pursue an even greater personal goal of integration and expansion in the years ahead as I focused my efforts on service to humanity.

While this particular spiritual event was culminating and a newer cycle was beginning, I chose to enter into a deeply intimate period of silent meditation which lasted for seven weeks in all. Other than taking time out for necessary activities such as cleaning, washing and eating, I remained in solitary isolation until the process had come to its ends.

The Habit of Accusation

During this period I was drawn to review the past six years of my life following the accident and passed through many situations on spiritual levels which enabled me to identify my longer term goals.

In the end, I found that I had attained a sufficient capacity to gain the necessary authority to begin to intervene, heal and influence others in lifestyle and health-related transitions which were spiritually based realities. My new goal then was to establish a credible educational programme which would then aid others in the alternative health care arenas, and to open a lifestyle spa where healing, meditation, rejuvenation, restoration and revitalization could occur along with educational studies in the therapeutic arts.

Apart from the spa, I had decided to bring about the new sciences of sentiency, impressionism and esoteric psychologies which would provide the foundation for these same therapeutic arts and lifestyle programmes, as well as any other potential opportunity for direct service to humanity. My own commitment was to maintain the intent to inspire self and others wherever and whenever possible.

As I came to assume a much more responsible relationship with those individuals who participated in seminars, workshops and classes, I likewise came to discover the greater difficulties that the average untrained observer would find in their attempts to deal with relevant information arising from their meditations.

I was most surprised to find that those who had begun to work their way through the many layers of self-conditioning in an attempt to discover and overcome negative tendencies were faced with serious decisions regarding change. For many it was a foregone conclusion that overcoming negative tendencies was a very rewarding experience and that overcoming specific shortcomings was worthy of the effort and ambition that need be brought forward in such work.

In many other cases, however, I found that as much as one knew the truth that their negative criticisms, complaints and punishing tendencies were unwanted habits, the choice to rid oneself of these specific characteristics and undesirable behavioural habits which followed was too difficult to maintain.

One clear example was that I would aid the individual to investigate themselves through meditation, to discover how the tone of one's private self-talk could impair one's ability to overcome irrational self-accusation and self-punishment.

By this method, one was able to see clearly that unintentional or discarded and ignored conversation with oneself and the conclusions drawn at such times were often the root of a behavioural condition. Further, by suggesting that one attempt to change the very tone by which one chose quietly and privately to speak to oneself, a greater and more objective interpretation would follow in daily self-expression.

Through these practices, it was intended that the individual come to realize much about others who engage in self-talk daily - to the tune of more than 100,000 conversations, in fact - and that by attempting to become more aware of these many conversations, a basic foundation for clarity of one's conduct and direct insight into others' conditioning would enhance the study of one's own nature.

When it came to recognizing and then verifying the fact that this was true, many of the thinkers would not follow through on the work of overcoming negative tones when it came to criticism of others; or of complaint which they still wanted to keep as a part of their personality expression; or of punishment when it came to feeling insulted, criticized or punished themselves.

I found that there was a very difficult period in the work where those who chose to complete it knew that negative self-talk and the desire for negative response were hindering their success and that, without diminishing the negative tones during self-talk, one continued to be limited to the habits and conditioning which they often did not favour.

After a time of dealing with this condition in study, I came to realize just how much suffering, grief, heartache and self-sorrow along with denial was hindering more than half of those who had begun the study. Certainly there were great advantages to the study and anyone who completed the course found themselves free from those conditions that had been preventing the fruition of their basic ambitions and aspirations. Even those who remained critical, complaining and punishing had gained the advantage of understanding others in much broader and more insightful ways, though I could see for myself that it was inevitable that a life of continued anxiety, stress, sorrow and pain was predictable for those who refused for one reason or another to ignore these specific tendencies.

Having the advantage of understanding the basic processes and development of a thinker, and knowing the objective for each of these souls, I continued to work all the more to bring greater clarity and example to those who studied with me; however, on many nights I meditated upon the plight of humanity and for many years found myself feeling quite exhausted to find that a dreamy form of consciousness was the norm for so many, and that humanity had come to suffer in denial as a means of dealing with what they believed was the futility of life.

Finding fault was much more prevalent than I had first perceived and accusation followed by condemnation and punishment was the preferred condition that the masses were bound to through conditioning and lifestyle habits.

I often alluded to the fact that it was due to the brain that a thinker was a more negative than objective fault-finder and that the habit of accusation was the greatest secret weapon a thinker could use upon themselves or others.

In these moments, I often attempted to demonstrate the fact that freedom from accusation itself, through education and through attempts seriously to understand one's own nature in this regard, was the quickest remedy for ill health, and the loss of the satisfaction of life. While this was understood clearly, and though it was verified by many who had undertaken to do just that, accusation and negative criticism of the unenlightened remained the most basic and yet greatest hindrance for all who chose to ignore it or for those who had yet not known this simple yet complex fact.

On many more serious occasions, I had taken the opportunity to gather together with those whom I had come to consciously communicate with spiritually, and this same fact came to be verified yet little could be done to raise the consciousness of those who were imprisoned by their own accusational conditioning.

As I stated earlier, I was simply overcome at times and I quietly continued in this affliction for many years to follow as I perceived this most harmful and limiting condition of accusation to be so overwhelmingly encompassing and imprisoning. I remember the many moments of triumph as well, as those who found their way out of the illusion of benefit to accusational tendencies had themselves tasted of the rejuvenating and life-restoring liberty of consciousness thereafter. It was due to the success of the minority though that I persisted in making the point that the greatest and most disabling quality of human character was that of self-justified negative accusation.

In the later years I found that an even greater and more lengthy course on this subject alone had become most popular and within one year of studying the facts about accusation alone, more and more individuals had become liberated thereby to proceed into the future of an objective and fulfilling life.

Though it was true that accusation had been born out of the instinctive attributes of the human brain, it had become a characteristic of the personality, so much so that in the opening evening of my later seminars on this subject, a great ease would come about for the participants as they realized just how often they spoke to themselves daily in this manner. With the success of this seminar in the following years, I chose to focus upon this subject most intensely and had managed to raise sufficient funds that by summer 1994, I was able to build the first stages of a small resort and spa.

Awakening to Our Potential

I The evolution of consciousness

By February 1993 I had completed yet another phase of my own personal development and was afforded another expansion of consciousness which brought an even greater focus and ability to reach more of the public. At this same time, I also made a decision to prepare myself for another series of workshops and seminars that would be the final goal for this life to complete.

Behind the scenes once again, and separate from my usual work, I had come to develop fully the ability to see into the spiritual life of a soul in incarnation and had privately come to observe and carefully watch certain personalities on the stage of world leadership. This was most rewarding and proved to be great entertainment as well over the years as I kept a close eye on current events.

By 1994 I had chosen a small but significant group

of individual therapists and earlier students to participate in developing these same sentient skills and our
most enjoyable moments surrounded the outcome and
investigation of the world's most influential leaders,
their priorities, policies, choices and personality tendencies.

I had first learned to assimilate the rhythm of another individual through circumstance as I had experienced
the naturalness of this same attribute of the soul in the
afterlife. A few years later I was able to utilize the sensory equipment of my brain and body to aid in the con-
tinuation of this developing skill and within seven years I
was able to begin to instruct others in this same science.

Having carefully chosen only specific individuals
whom I had come to regard as capable of such a skill in
this lifetime period, I undertook to aid these same
friends in understanding all the attributes of the sentient
soul that were capable of manifestation in human form.
By 1994 I was finally enjoying the company of others
who had come to verify the existence and nature of their
own soul, and it was quite normal to gather together at
times to enhance and sharpen these skills of intervention.

My first goal had been achieved and there was sufficient evidence now to verify these findings and the fact
of the soul as a reality in our world was coming very
close to being exposed most directly. It was for the future
events that we all knew and expected that our study
together had continued and with each year the evidence
of a transition and an expansion of consciousness for
humanity at large was becoming most evident.

With the expectation that the progressing souls of
humanity were on the verge of a great transition and initiation into the revealed world of the soul itself, I

watched ever closer daily as the events began to unfold and it was as if my connection to world leaders and current events through CNN was as frequent as my relationship with my own host guide over the years.

A series of amazing revelations and transitions began to unfold in the last phase of a 52-year cycle, as has been noted in this last decade of the century and of the millennium, and while freedom from old ideologies and the Church itself gave humanity their first clue of global change, the transitions ahead will prove to be even more significant and testing.

It is the challenge of the masses to maintain their conscious and emotional balances daily as the greater challenges and tests of conscience among world leaders in this final decade prove to usher in a newer revelation of such integrity and truth that the world will become changed in conduct and appearance unlike anything imagined today and yet all of these transitions will soon occur in a relatively short period of time.

One of the greatest revelations that I came to experience in the afterlife was the fact that evolution, to those most graciously placed in the authoritative leadership of the universe, is the evolution of consciousness itself! To this fact I would add that the challenges and struggles of daily living, in the absence of knowing that evolution is about conscious development alone, leave people feeling uncertain and fearful about the usual happenings and current events that surround us all daily. In my own case, I enjoy more the fact that there is so much truth indicated in every event of every day and that we truly have nothing to fear at all. Knowing that we are all bound to become wise through the continued challenge to deal with impressions that come our way each day, it becomes much easier to put one's life into perspective.

On many an occasion I have suggested to those I work with that from the moment we awaken in the morning, we could tell ourselves that today is about passing the tests of character and conscience that will pass, which if followed for a time would prove the fact. For someone who knows this, the day is about impressions alone and our resolve daily is what we are up against as a test.

Are we at peace with our conscience today? Are we resolved to issues that truly are about keeping peace with our sense of conscience daily? Were we so accusational today that we feel confused and disoriented? Are we so free from accusation that we sleep well and live well daily. It is the combination of these two aspects of our human nature that allow one to begin to see that life is merely about our awakening to our potential which is to see things in an objective way and to fall away from the greatest problem in the world today which is accusation itself. The second worst thing an individual can do in their life is trouble themselves daily by continuing to be accusational instead of learning to be objective.

Many a time, while communicating with my host guide or those who work directly with humanity, this subject recurs and we rest upon the conviction that we know that the people or souls in incarnation are not aware of the great liberation that could take place for each one if they only began to overcome their accusational nature which of itself is only the animal instinct in the incarnate form. This duality which we all must struggle through in form became very interesting when identifying the condition of a nation or of an individual over the years and, when applied daily, one begins to gain the insights that few have enough experience to see.

The real sight in spiritual terms is the ability to see the truth of another individual's condition as they progress along the path of the evolution of their own consciousness. That is to say that when a soul looks upon you they will see the fact that you are first Divine in nature and then they will note to what degree you realize this yourself.

Quickly following this, the third element of discovery is to know to what degree we can be influenced to understand that we continue to suffer in the absence of knowing that we need be less accusational to begin to see each other more clearly. It is a guarantee that we are never accused of anything by those who spiritually partake of our lives, and that the main task of all highly developed spiritual beings is to assist in the awakening of our true consciousness as we so choose ourselves.

We need only attempt to avoid the trap of believing in our own accusations or attempt to identify the fact that being less accusational affords greater reception with each other. Instead of learning how to maintain appearances in front of those whom we choose to draw close to, we would need only be free from accusation to gather all the affection and love that can possibly be managed.

The following is an excerpt from an invocation to humanity which I once wrote and gave to a friend who was seeking to understand why the average thinker would not deal with their accusational nature:

If only they knew what it was like to see the authority of the universe touching them every moment in every conversation, in everything they do, and how perfectly nurtured to illuminative being all things are that exist. If only they knew the true law and the true justice of being understood completely by everyone every time they spoke, Of not being judged!

If only they knew that the universe has never accused them of being more enlightened than they are. If only they knew that no one dies and how important it is to overcome the accusational nature that suppresses the day of liberty at hand. If only they knew that their unenlightenment has preserved them in the necessary light where their true Divinity can come to the fore in their maturity. If only they knew that it was all up to them to choose to be unafraid or to hinder themselves by going against their own best judgement. If only they knew that in the end, no matter what they thought, they would be welcomed beyond expectation into the eternal worlds of their own right of inheritances. If only they knew that their children were souls who have returned to awaken to the objective view of each other and to then invent out of their own potential, the future glory of all who shall pass through this way. If only they knew that they were perceived to be Masters in the making!

Inevitably, we will all one day realize that our habits of accusational mind use, and of self-talk, are the secreted and less visible sorrows of our internal lives. The fact that each of us as adults in the world suffer - this is evident yet only when the children are seen in the greater light as visitors from Divine heights shall we come to the responsible day of asserting and espousing the truth that accusation is the illusive pain of the masses. That objectivity is the key to the door of the kingdom of eternity.

In 1994 I wrote a manuscript that was partially a journal. It was the story about myself and a dear friend with whom I worked over a five-month period as he was suffering with pancreatic cancer at the young age of 32. He was a father of two children who were ten and three years of age. My reason for writing the book was to bring attention to those who were suffering cancer, that others were likewise experiencing similar experiences and also to shed some light upon the subject of personal resolve prior to the inevitable moment ahead. I had noticed something quite significant about people in such situations, and had decided to find a way of saying as much through conversations that were taped during the five-month period that this individual was given to live.

In as much as I have mentioned the accuser in people's lives, and matters of conscience being a requisite, I chose to expose more along these lines in the attempt to aid in the speeding up of the process of personal resolve itself. I feel that it is important enough to make a point of it here as similar revelations have aided so many others since.

It was when Joseph was trying to tell me he could not overcome feelings of distaste for some of his former friends and family that I was able to make a specific point that changed the way he had looked at those he was unsettled with beforehand. I suggested he look into his memory and find as many instances as possible where he had the occasion of making a friend and then losing that same friend over time. He was also instructed to seek out memories that verified that he had once liked certain individuals and in later months that followed, he may have changed his mind about these same individuals.

Having done so, he brought up about thirty individual cases. We started with his former boss to begin with. I asked him then to recall how he first felt about his boss and he suggested then that right off, when he had begun to work for this man, that he had already been fond of him as he seemed fair, honest and genuine. When I asked him to recall the exact moment when he felt his feelings had changed towards his boss he recalled a memory about another co-worker who was treated much differently than the others by this same boss.

In fact, his boss had gone out of his way to make this employee's life most miserable and had begun to show favouritism to certain employees over others. He also commented that the fellow that his boss was mistreating was well loved by everyone with whom he worked and that the boss was just being a jerk.

Looking at other situations in the same way, I was able to demonstrate a pattern to Joseph at the time. I suggested to him that there must have been something significant which he was perhaps less aware of now that was cause for the change of heart in every case. With this in mind I then asked him to identify the reason for the end of other relationships. In some cases he said that former friends turned out to be selfish, ignorant, mistrusting or that he generally learned to dislike them for the way they talked about others.

In this way, Joseph was describing an unconscious attribute on his part that was at work in each case. I then asked him if he thought that his boss lacked conscience and his reply was a certain yes! In the other cases when I asked the same question of conscience, he responded in kind. Yes indeed, Joseph had discovered and chosen to disapprove of those whom he perceived to be lacking conscience, morals, ethics or principle.

The fact that remained was that he had numerous reasons for disliking these former friends though he had never seen it as a matter of conscience. In conclusion,

Joseph began to realize that he was seeing the truth about people but did not know enough consciously to see it clearly as a simple matter of conscience. Much later, Joseph pondered the conclusions that he had indeed stumbled upon a secret attribute. An ability to see the truth clearly. A level of insight unbeknown to him previously.

This was what I was depending on his discovery of, and the result was that he found that he had always had that same innate ability to see himself and others in the same light, though he had never known beforehand that such was the case. Understanding that he might have other innate talents of insight, we went further until the time came when he was finally free from the unresolved past. Point in case, Joseph was able to see that he could identify the relationship another individual has and has had over time with their own conscience. With that in mind, his resolve came quickly, followed by an expansion of sentient skills and consciousness.

Is it possible that when one suggests they dislike another that they may have unconsciously identified the fact that such an individual lacks conscience? In many cases the answer is yes. To Joseph, it was of great import. He considered it a gift of insight at the time and he tried to tell his friends about it prior to his death. It was true that Joseph had called his older acquaintances to tell them that he had been too judgemental in the past, having realized that they only lacked conscience at certain moments in their life. I was also privileged to see the results of these conversations and what the outcome was.

Joseph realized that he had a great insight now but he further realized the responsibility he now had for making certain that he was not too quick to judge, criticize or punish those whom he had accused of being tasteless.

My main point here is that we are all capable of see-ing why we have chosen to dislike others beyond our present conclusions and it is likewise true that we may note that this ability to see the effects of conscience upon the face and countenance of others in the world can be very liberating. If we were to note the reasons why others do not like us today, I am sure there would be many reasons spoken aloud though each could be seen clearly to be correct when we look closely to see whether we were acting unlike our conscientious nature when we found ourselves being disliked. It is true that it is appar-ent to those who give a more serious effort towards see-ing these facts in our lives that we may lack conscience at times, but it may not be so clear that we have discovered the primary function of the soul in each other.

Our ability to recognize that others lack conscience instead of claiming them to be liars, cheats, morons, idiots, manipulators or traitors etc. gives a less negative accusational tone to our statements and conclusions and can afford us the opportunity to understand the short-comings of others who are less enlightened personally regarding their own nature. Though it is true that we are quick to accuse, long before we are willing to perceive others in a more objective light, it remains a possibility that we can gain resolve most quickly in life by realizing that we can account for the very conditions noticed in others before we reach out to oppose or punish them, or remove them from our lives.

We may also gain the ability to verify the fact of the soul in our lives much more rapidly if we were to under-take to understand our need to make conscientious con-clusions in lieu of the usual conditioned responsive habits of repulsion and intolerance. We need not fear those who lack conscience likewise since it is they who suffer the loss of an objective consciousness. It is only important that one learn to be true to themselves and to others when the truth of accusation as a slayer of our attributes becomes noticeable or recognizable.

For many who have read the manuscript mentioned earlier, I have come to hear that it was as if they thought themselves to have found a pot of gold in reference to the notion of conscience and accusational tendencies before their departure from our world. Others, even though they may have been less sensitive to the material, have likewise suggested that it was very revealing, though I understand that what was so revealing was the fact that they came face to face with the identical dilemma in their own lives.

We can love those whom we have let go of in our lives to date and we can have better relationships in the remaining time we all have left if we were to make a point of maintaining our resolve daily while keeping our conscience in mind. Likewise, we can continue to suffer the uncertainty of our nature and our decisions in life by simply ignoring this.

II The 26 essential truths

Before ending this section of the book I would like to make a list of those essential truths that I have come to realize from my afterlife experiences and the ongoing communion with my spiritual hosts thereafter as they relate to the individual members of humanity in general. It is my hope that some of what may be mentioned hereafter may find its way into the consciousness of those who seek to be inspired and to inspire. I cannot claim these truths to be more than my own and it is in this spirit that I ask you to consider these statements for yourself as is deemed sufficient, reasonable or otherwise.

I believe the statements to follow to be truths that suggest the innocence of each, and to be most reasonable associations by which the individual soul could be perceived with a greater spirit of compassion and understanding.

A   That we are all born into this world without a
    sense of history or understanding of what has
    transpired in our world.
B   That we are not given an early education regard
    ing our attributes of mind, senses, dreams, body,
    instincts and emotions.
C   That it is up to ourselves ultimately to make
    sense of the information and impressions that
    we absorb daily, regardless of our parents, peers
    or educators.
D   That we ultimately teach ourselves, from child
    hood onwards, whatever had been suggested by
    our guardians.
E   That we are not conscious enough in childhood   or
    able to distinguish the differences between
    the truth or a lie.
F   That we are most likely to find fault before beauty
    as we get older.
G   That we have the ability to assimilate a condition or
    an   experience   noticed   in   others   within   our
    environment.
H   That what we assimilate, we are apt to demonstrate
    or emulate.
I   That we talk to ourselves several hundreds of
    times daily though we are not certain what we
    have talked to ourselves about.

J   That we talk ourselves into and out of most of
     our personal expressions and beliefs whether
     true or not.

K   That we visualize, dream, imagine and premeditate
     without understanding the mind to a large degree.

L   That we long to be loved and to love.

M   That we suffer the uncertainty daily of not knowing
     what is true about ourselves and our identity.

N   That we learn to act and to keep up false appearances
     to avoid punishment, exposure or remedy, in favour
     of gaining what we most desire.

O   That our desire nature in adulthood basically
     rules most of our decision-making.

P   That we are more concerned with ourselves to a
     larger degree than with others.

Q   That peace of mind comes only to those who
     maintain resolve of their own innate sense of
     conscience.

R   That our conscience is our guide though we
     rarely use it to premeditate or forecast impending
     goals.

S   That we are unable to account for our mind use
     in many cases daily.

T   That we rarely take a break between our own
     self-conversations.

U   That we tend to accuse, complain, criticize or
     punish those whom we do not love or of whom
     we cannot make use.

V   That we tend to make use of others to our own ends.

W   That our enlightenment and lifestyle really are
     our own choice.

X   That unless we begin to understand the nature
     of our own body, mind and soul, we suffer the

illusion of self-accountability.

Y That we are generally unconscious to our own truths.

Z That our goal is to become wiser each day whether we know it or not. That we are worthy whether we know it or not. That we are Divine in nature whether we know it or not. That the universe that surrounds us is a living and intelligent being.

It would appear that the odds are against our becoming enlightened sufficiently so as not to have to return to this world of incarnation. However, it is through having raised oneself through the futility and trial of our innate character and attributes that we finally stand triumphant over ignorance and uncertainty ever more, in the continued life of immortality and imperishability to come.

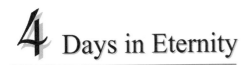

4 Days in Eternity

Part V
Imperishability and
the last life

The Ramifications of Our Immortality

I decided to dedicate Part V of this book to the ramifications of our implied imperishability as souls, in a process of conscious development through time and space, and in my first considerations I came to realize that even if one was to have experienced the afterlife as I had, and had then returned to daily lifeas a human, even knowing these truths might not bring about a change of perspective on behalf of the thinker.

I further realized from most accounts that I have read or heard about that few have been able to speak of a sustained adventure beyond a few moments in the afterlife as is usual in near-death reports. In such cases, it was reported that a direct change in the way one saw and then lived their lives had come about. Certainly a change of lifestyle is evident in many cases, though I have never before heard of anyone who had an out-of-body experience or near-death experience where the very perception of the individual was overturned in favour of the truth regarding our imperishability.

For these reasons I have decided to focus upon those points which, if true, would certainly raise new questions in the minds of the curious, and the more specialized thinker who seeks greater insights into the sciences that may help to provide a clearer impression of these facts overall.

It would appear - and I have experienced such enquiries at length - that if people actually did enjoy the revelation of a truth that revealed mortality as an illusion and imperishability of the soul as a fact, they would or might be struck with an awesome assortment of ramifications from which the test of their former perceptions might then lead to some period of time in confusion, or at least a momentary period of disorientation as they came to adjust to these truths overall.

In other words, I would expect that following such a revelation, the one who actually experienced the afterlife - even if only for a brief period - would then have the extra added weight of proving the experience as factual to themselves first and then, after acknowledging these experiences to be true - they would then have to get used to thinking, dreaming, imagining and speaking as one who actually had come upon a newer perception of the reality surrounding themselves at the least.

Over the years, I have come to study these probabilities if only to identify whether or not certain individuals indeed had a genuine experience in and of the afterlife and it was through observing such individuals in interviews that were eventually broadcast in documentary form that some light was shed on the subject at hand.

For the many, a common sensibility was what seemed to have brought about change in their lives even though their experience was minor in duration. This sensibility suggested that they had gone through a softening of their character, a renewing of their emotional body, a gaining of insight into the plight of others or some supersensible sensitivity towards those who suffered.

Beyond the implications of a newly charged sensitivity which I suspected to be reasonably true, I suspected that there was a very difficult period of adjustment that was most likely continuing to trigger questions about life that were still unanswered by themselves. My reason for suspecting this was because it takes time for the brain, body and emotional status of an individual to bring about new change.

For instance, one may have gained a new inspiration regarding themselves or others which is quite usual for many in our inventive and highly creative world today. In doing so it has been proven many times that an adjustment in one's belief system generally comes under scrutiny and a challenge by the rational mind ensues where challenges to the newer or changing perceptions require greater evidence through education, concentration and actualized lifestyle changes themselves.

In short, this means that one must pass through a period of concentrated effort in thinking when old perceptions are weighed against newer ones. In order to be successful, one must prove the new perception to be most correct and, at the same time, one must also prove the older perception to have been flawed or less true factually. This normally requires one to be able to gather information in such a way that concepts can be drawn upon which may add weight in either direction, and then one must first understand what their actual perception was to begin with.

In my studies of human nature over the last two decades, I discovered that the majority of the masses today, that is over 80 per cent, are generally unable to account for the actual perceptions they do have in any moment. When asked what one's intention or ulterior motive for an action is, most thinkers are likely to give a superficial answer and only a few thinkers have ever delved deeply enough into their psychology to discover the actual root motives for anything they do.

This means that even if one was certain they had experienced the afterlife, they would also be able to confirm that adjusting to a new perception would not necessarily have been easy. I would expect a minimum statement of confusion that identifies some need for further reconsideration or at least a statement where the individual admits being at a bit of a loss for some time as they attempted to grasp the larger ramifications of such a truth.

In my own case, I found it very difficult for a long period of time to get used to the fact that we were imperishable and that death was an illusion. Having to adjust to these facts was not so easy as my own rational thinking and belief system before the incident, where the revelation of a continuum beyond death was experienced, were very negligent. I can honestly say that I had less information or memory regarding such a revelation than I had then about the merits of brushing my teeth. I simply had not given myself to actually begin to think of myself as eternal, imperishable or the like to any degree before the actual moment and experience.

In much the same way that those who are told they are going to die in a short period of time often feel rushed, confused and troubled as to how they might start or begin to think about the possibilities of an afterlife, it would only be normal not to adjust to these facts as quickly as we experience them.

Even though a woman is told she is pregnant, there is often a period of adjustment where it takes time to sink in that the couple are already parents even though the child is within the womb, or even when people know they have won a lottery, it takes time to adjust to the ramifications. In almost every case where a new dawning, inspiration, sudden good fortune or even bad news has entered the consciousness of an individual, the greater time in dealing with ramifications ensues.

The following passage from the New Testament may very well parallel the situation we all face when standing in the light of a greater revelation:

And I went unto the angel, and said unto him, Give me the little book. And he said unto me, Take it, and eat it up; and it shall make thy belly bitter, but it shall be in thy mouth sweet as honey.
(Revelation, 10: 9)

It may be great news to hear we do not die but when the ramifications are understood it may well be that it is a bitter lot to have to make the adjustment to the ramifications. I decided to use this passage as I want to attempt to bring a greater light upon the fact that not only is one capable of gaining a new insight or a great revelation, but if it is true, they may not want to expand on the ramifications as it requires dedication, serious effort, ceaseless concentration and eventually eliminating one's ability to act in contradiction to the newly acquired knowledge.

I have long suspected that many thinkers have experienced a momentary illumination within their lifetime though I also believe that many, once they realize the price they must pay to have the advantage of clarity by dealing with the ramifications in total, may just decide to store the experience in memory rather than to pay that stated price.

So as I consider those who have had brief excursions into the afterlife words, I am likewise reminded of a very heavy price that goes with such experiences. Perhaps there are many who have had similar experiences who had not been sufficiently prepared to equate or mentally deal with the ramifications for one reason or another, but I can assure you of one truth, and that is that if they did experience the fact of the continuum, they would have been spending serious time and energy afterwards attempting to prepare themselves in an effort to become ready for the inevitable, long before it was to come about again.

In my case, I cherished the experiences and chose not to lose track of what had occurred for me then, and in the ensuing years I had to work very hard to maintain these inspired revelations in order to come to grips with the full ramifications. It took me almost nine full years eventually to bring the requisite stage of concentration and continued study to completion. These nine years were spent seriously studying, meditating and concentrating upon a wide variety of sciences, which brought me to a height of educational attainment previously unsuspected. Still, I can understand how easily people might overlook the ramifications of a great inspiration or revelation, having no desire on their part to educate themselves further. I suspect that for educational reasons many have lost out on what was intended to be a helping hand in their life overall.

It is not that I do not believe others when they say they have had afterlife experiences even though they still appear quite ignorant and uneducated, or that they don't seem to have been moved by it, though I do expect that if one truly did and that if they were to have attempted to deal with it properly, then they will tell you themselves that they are now prepared to leave our world at any time. I am also certain that if people did have a true afterlife experience, they would admit some confusion but would be continuing to this day to put it all into perspective. The perspective that they would be targeting today would be akin to dealing with the fact that they and everyone else in this world, without question or doubt, is imperishable.

How would one begin? How would one look at others, complete strangers, or friends of the past? How would they begin to deal with the new view that their worst enemies live forever as well? What do we say to ourselves when we believe we are imperishable and yet we expect others to be fully accountable who do not share our perception? Would we be speaking to ourselves about the usual kinds of things? Would we be entertaining thoughts that would now be considered delusional, glamorous and untrue? What about other issues?

I would suggest that there are more questions than one might imagine when it comes to finding out that they are imperishable beings. It is even more difficult to rearrange one's perceptions without knowing what goes into making a perception itself. This requires a unique understanding of the workings of one's own mind, brain, central nervous system and so much more.

Some of the evidence to back up what I am now suggesting regarding a period of adjustment, and the time to deal with ramifications as a normal circumstance, may be discovered with a little help and a lot of pondering upon the subject of information processing itself.

Human Beings as Information Processors

Consider that at this very moment your body and brain are very busy processing information. Within the passage of an hour, trillions of bits of information will have been processed and a variety of decisions and conclusions, some conscious and more unconscious will have also occurred.

While our body and brain are busy maintaining chemical balances, even the most minute molecule is busy at the task of sharing information with other molecules and cells. For instance, our immune system may presently be fighting off a virus or cold that has found entry into our body, and trillions of white blood cells may have just received the signal to search out and destroy the impending virus attack. While a small army of individual and intelligent lives called cells are at work attending to the identification of the differences between what remains and what gets destroyed, a few of these cells rush back to the immune centre and spell out the sound and vibration of the attacking virus in an attempt to send out prepared soldier cells to attack and destroy the virus with this new information.

In this example - and we could go on for hours - there is a system of intelligent lives being collectively articulated and action has come about akin to the strategic aspects of an army general with his troops in the field confronting an unknown enemy. In this way, we can identify the fact that information is flowing to each and every aspect or part of our entire body many times per second.

It might be obvious that the main functioning aspect of each of these cells is to negate the attacking virus; however, I suspect that there is an even greater function less appreciated by most investigators to suggest that information is being processed. What could the brain or body do

without having this single attribute of information processing being a fundamental function of each of its parts?

It becomes more obvious as we look at our present-day
technologies which naturally seem to replicate the human
sensory aspects to provide us with ears in the sky, eyes on
the world and a network of information akin to the functions of the human brain and body. To begin to observe the
fact that every living thing has a foundational skill for
receiving and processing information, one might suspect
eventually that there is a form of direct communication
occurring everywhere in the universe at this very moment.

It is a fact that each and every single life form, whether
it be a quark, a particle, a cell, an organism or even a substantial being, has the ability to gather and to process information that can then be passed on through processing such
information to inform other beings likewise. With this in
mind, one can begin to look at their body to see that every
atom in their finger is actively participating in processing
information on behalf of the overall being and itself.
Further investigation would reveal that every other part of
the human body is presently doing likewise and that taken
to a larger degree, we may find that the primary function of
time and space itself is dependent on the attribute of communication through information processing itself.

We could enter into the sciences of chemistry and biol-
ogy and begin to identify the many processes and transitions that occur between things as being directly a result of
processing information with the unsuspected environment
of a set of laws called physics within our local universe of
time and space. Further yet, we could take all of our known
sciences and apply this same practical premise, and we would
in no time see that such was a fact.

We could even go back to the essential beginning of our

space/time world and universe, where it is suspected that all that we see today was once reduced to a small mass the size of a grain of sand, and then we might also suspect that then and there, before the Big Bang, there was a collective intelligence that intended to produce an effect that depended upon the primary function of retention and information processing as a requisite for all that should follow.

In fact, we could go further and suggest that it may be true that by following in the theory that all things are capable of identifying differences and processing information, our present universe is still processing the information following the Big Bang to some specific ends. It is also possible to suspect that our very senses, such as hearing and the organized human ear, were an intended outcome by which other forms of information could be processed which would further infer that everything in our universe had a function based on the premise that information is and must be processed!

With this 'must' we could go further to imply a theory that everything in appearance must be able to process information and the things that are not visible must themselves be able to process information though on some supersensible level. In the end, we could say that there must be a reason why all the information of every moment and everywhere must be happening.

Of course we must not forget, when taking this information into consideration, that we are processing information as an information processor first-hand, and that our body of appearances may well be taken to be seen as a highly sophisticated data probe. Of course we should also bear in mind that while we talk about individualized life, it is a scientific fact that there is no medium known by which two things actually ever touch.

This little bit of information will likely lead to a response from the average thinker where he/she may feel it is necessary to qualify the ramifications at length. To what length one goes will determine the actual value of the experience itself. In this same way, I feel that our universe of time and space is bound and determined to eventuate a predetermined value gained form experience itself.

Some may now ask for what purpose would the universe have come about with all the events being likened to information processing and my answer is: for the outcome to have occurred. I believe that the outcome of education, experience and learning is greater wisdom in regard to individuality.

I further believe that individuality is the great gift that we have come to call spirit. The outcome of my own experiences has been a greater ability to enhance and eventually manifest those attributes that lay beneath the surface of my soul, which of themselves provide a wider and greater expression of influence.

When taking this to a greater length, I am aware of a fact experienced in the afterlife that demonstrated how we are all eventually to come to a point of conscious evolution where our overall countenance becomes likened to the very intelligence of the collective universe itself. We are like children in a universe of well-advanced parents whose very being was established long before time and space were eventuated and where the gift of personal existence has been brought about.

I once watched a documentary where a journalist was seeking to discover what might be in store for the world regarding the technologies and computerization of our world. In this documentary a leading scientist suggested that one day they would be able to download the information necessary to create a cyberspace continuum.

When I heard that I realized just how close we were to discovering that our universe is much like that which he described as a cyberspace with the function of educating the individual. In many ways, our inventiveness today is paralleling the activity and purpose of our own universe and it will not be long before we are able to accelerate our learning processes connected directly to experiences which will lay a foundation for a super-race of souls without the need for the dense forms once utilized.

It was this kind of information that I was privileged to consider and to have learned on my journey throughout our local universe while living in the afterlife worlds, and it was having learned about their processes which gave me direct insight into the matter of information processing on substantial and yet less visible levels.

From the recognition of this theory in the afterlife, I was eventually able to understand how our future materials needed for space travel as well as for our inhabited worlds could be drawn from the very ocean we have shouldering our small yet significant continents. Eventually we will discover how consciousness itself is the active agent in generating sound, light and substance.

In the same way that I have utilized the discovery of information processing and retention to be aspects of our functional lives, I have also gone into great detail in understanding how information processed in youth comes to be identified in the language of an adult each time they speak aloud. For example, people may often find themselves saying something along the lines of 'When I was younger I used to think that parents were like God and then as I got older I realized they were just like anyone else. There was nothing special about them but nowadays, I think of us all as being like children in adult clothing.'

From learning to listen very carefully, one may find that the actual statement covers a period of history for the individual where conclusions were once made, updated later and then considered at length much later so that what they say about today is an expression of a series of processes regarding original impressions. How people change tone or utilize their emotions is also another way of identifying just how resolved they may be with regard to the material stated aloud, and can also give a trained listener much information regarding the condition and limitations as well as creative talents of the individuals themselves.

It is possible, with a little bit of serious effort towards study, that a listener could see, know and understand how a particular form of therapy could be of assistance to another who has had problems processing information. Further, it can be known from a direct study of one's sight, imagination, mind use and sense perceptions, while coming to realize more about information processing, what one's actual condition and status as a soul in progress could be.

In fact, it is a requisite that a soul in incarnation come eventually to know what and how the actual make-up of their very essential equipment, such as our human body, when understood along the lines of information processing, has to do with consciousness itself. I call this study of the equipment and tools of the human body sentiency.

Though it is not necessary to master this science of self-existence as a thinker in our incarnate world, in order to proceed into the greater life and lifestyles of the most advanced, free from the need to return to our dense sphere of temporal life, we need only begin to ponder and gather more information about our given nature daily. Eventually, there comes a time when experience and knowledge come together figuratively speaking to perform a small yet inevitably seeming miracle: the miracle of an expansion of consciousness.

This event is one of the primary assets and evidence that the soul and the personality are indeed imperishable entities, while still remaining in this world. As more and more individuals pass through this stage and eventuate this exacting experience for the first time, the symptoms, transitions, changes and the outcome will eventually be brought to light for public consumption.

It is for the future that I have come to write these statements today so that when such incidents of an expansion of consciousness have occurred beyond the expectations of our present professional medical and psychological schools of thought, some consideration may come about which may ease the minds of those who will undoubtedly feel at a loss to explain it for themselves.

I have come to learn from my afterlife experiences, and those moments of continued contact thereafter, that just such a day is coming. I expect that before we reach the midway point of the coming century, the expansion of consciousness mentioned will have occurred for the majority of individuals in incarnation at that time.

We are at the last moments of a long and painful journey of evolution where human ignorance continues today to limit the opportunity for the event of an expansion of consciousness to take place globally, yet there will be much more experience in the next decade alone to cause the eventual condition of a planetary initiation to take place.

Returning to those who have survived an afterlife experience and to what degree change in their particular personality, perception and even consciousness could be determined, bearing in mind that information processing is a fact of life, one can expect to see gradual change over time as these individuals come to peace with themselves over the initial ordeal.

As for how many, or what percentage, of these reports are likely to be true, I would guess that many would be true fleeting experiences yet only in the case where a greater measure of time had been taken up dealing with the ramifications of being imperishable would there be more evidence to back up such a claim. In any case, the sooner one begins to process information upon the possibility and probability, the sooner one will begin to process valid experience about oneself and one's true nature, which is the goal of the soul itself.

Sensitivity, Passion and the Rhythm of the Soul

I Rhythm

When I had first entered into the afterlife, I had begun to feel a certain rhythm or sound as I called it then, that has remained with me to this day. Over the years I came to know what it was to live as a soul in my body, and I learned how feelings, moods and emotions were a direct result of the connection between information processing and consciousness.

I found that we all have the ability to identify and name certain feelings, emotions and moods, and that behind this seeming instant ability lies the fact that what we truly feel overall is exactly what our soul is feeling, though in a brilliant and inclusive way. When I was out of body, the manner in which information was being processed was similar, except that the answers to questions came without words.

The manner in which these impressions arrived upon

my consciousness and the manner in which I was able to understand in what appeared to be an instant was due to the fact that I was feeling the rhythm of the soul. This rhythm is the combined total of each and every probable and possible feeling and sensitivity within our potential nature that we can communicate and process information universally through. It is more the fact that we are a unified totality of potential sensitivity, and how we feel in human form at any time is only what we are aware of in human form.

Our human form truly shrouds the senses of the soul and if people could only experience a momentary release from their body, they would then see what I mean when I say that our sensitivity is then enhanced thousands of times. Only those feelings and sensitivities that manage to make it to the surface of our body through emotions are the ones we have named and understand to a degree. Yet there are many more sensitivities yet to be experienced mostly because we have not learned to bring about the experience so that they can be known.

I could suggest that we have passions and drives that are virtually identified as the primary motivations of our life, though it would take some personal investigation to discover that it is our passions through which we long to feel fulfilled. Once we begin to quench the thirst of our underlying passions, we find attributes that tend to replace the former dull feelings that we have during our incarnation.

These attributes are akin to basic passions such as compassion, which in turn becomes benevolence and bliss. What I am attempting to bring to light here is that our feelings are a form of communication and they also have the ability to identify the states and conditions of others more than we may think at first glance. It takes very little work through meditative concentration to begin to unfold the feeling of the soul within the form and to this end I have continued to influence many to do just that.

The more we understand how our consciousness works, the more we will see that our ability to know without thinking is related to our sentient body which of itself gives birth to the general senses and feelings discovered in the human form. Truly, the sensibility of understanding is ours though it lies just beneath the surface and the obvious method of approach to illuminate this is through repetitive efforts at striving to uncover our basic attributes and emotional motives.

Because we have long processed information along certain lines that are mostly habitual like driving a car, holding hands, communicating with strangers, or contemplating utopia, we have out of our own given curiosity limited our range of sensitivities.

II Repetition

It takes more than a hundred sensitive feelings before a single feeling can be named, and then it takes another hundred times thinking about feelings before we comprehend emotions, followed by another hundred emotional experiences before we understand moods, followed by another hundred evaluations about moods before states can be understood and named. Finally, after concentrating more than a hundred times about states, we are able to identify the repetitive methodology which then begins to register the truth as we enter into the door of sentient emanations.

I realize that this sounds like a simple model for repetitive thinking and feeling; however, it is the brain consciousness that needs to capture the essential experiences without having to wait for them to arrive in one's lifetime, if they ever do. I used to give a model of the repetitive methodology which matched the neurological requisites for reaching specific levels of attainment and they were similar as I suggested that sensitivity as a child leads to the development of a thought and that by thinking long enough, an idea becomes born.

Following an idea, we need to think about the birth of the idea until we have another hundred ideas, at which point we would have acquired the ability to be conceptual. After we take our concepts and think them out at length many times each, we find that we have now arrived at the ability to become perceptual. Following in this pattern, we can become then realized, enlightened and finally, illuminated.

It is no great secret that repetition develops skill and if applied to our own conclusions we may find ourselves becoming inspired very quickly as our consciousness begins to expand accordingly. It is only a matter of determination in following such a method whereby it is eventually possible for an individual to identify themselves as an imperishable being. The only hindrance to our natural process of evolution through repetitive patterns of experience is that of denial, which of itself is a closed mind and a deaf ear. For some, it may be difficult to give up certain habits once it is discovered that such habits are regressive or unhealthy, though if one applies oneself sincerely, it is very possible to rediscover one's true nature simply by targeting such an objective.

Of all that I have ever come to know and experience spiritually, I would add that the most important thing that a thinker can do is to set out to actually get to know themselves intentionally. It seems that while many keep tabs on themselves daily it can be assuring to realize that such a habit of self-accountability need only become consciously driven. Doing it just because it is healthy will suffice to awaken even the least suspecting thinker.

In this same manner of repetitious experience, in a universe of pure originality it is possible for a thinker to identify their potential sensitivities. Practising feeling certain states and moods or trying to identify the word that goes with certain momentary feelings, one could eventually master the art.

The unified sensibility

More important than the mastery as a fact is the fact that without having to practise our sensitivities to awaken them we can know that every moment, even now, is known to us by the feeling sensitivities behind thoughts and consciousness itself. This body of sensitivity gives us the ability to feel a full range of sensitive vibration belonging to other organs and cells throughout the form, and further enhances our ability to communicate on less conscious levels with our own environment.

Certainly the body is busy every moment communicating with the outer impressionable beings of our world and it can be consciously registered and eventually manifested to our personal gains by simply seeking to discover this.

Have you ever been able to tell what mood someone else was in by just being in their presence? We can feel the wind on our face and the disposition change in a clear moment of sunshine as we walk into the sunset, can't we? When we give in to the feeling of our entire nature for long moments, we can feel a system of communication that is in fact quite miraculous. It was this unified sensibility that remained with me, that I came to use to gather direct insight in the afterlife and which I had previously taken for granted. I was grateful, though I had not a single idea then that our sensitivities are and do produce our form, our bodies and our presence.

Whenever we attempt to be true, these sensitivities come to the surface and through repetitious attempts to be true to ourselves, there eventuates an ability to see, feel, hear and know the truth at the heart of every soul and every person we meet, that has already been developed historically for us by the indwelling presence of our soul. It is our calling card in the afterlife.

Without this ability to communicate through a unified heart, we could not be. It is the soul in us. Once we know our feelings and have taken up the task of rooting up the older repetitious virus of accusation, negativity, complaint, criticism and the tendency towards punishment of self and others, healing can begin and the sensitivity of the soul can manifest unto a point which would initiate formal contact with the truth in everyone else.

Our intelligent universe has seen fit that an awakening of our sensitivity and of our consciousness takes place in a graduating series of lives through varied shapes and forms until the moment when the truth becomes apparent. Thereafter, our universe has seen fit that each individuality seek by sensitive aspiration to go about the business of discovering their imperishability and infinity according to their sensitive uniqueness and originality. The place and foundation for the birthing of the offspring of our universe is of a range of sensitive sounds that are unified in a triune sound responsible for the very root of life itself.

It was the presence of the one great life whose host rhythm or personal sound we adapted to. It is also into the future that our greatest passions strive to have us identify and assimilate this very first primary sound through which evolution and the very foundations of time and space bend to aid us in our determined outcome of uniqueness of individuality.

Imagine for a moment that in the moments preceding the Big Bang, there was a unified sound to what was about to be released outwardly into the making of time and space. Assume for a moment that this first sound eventually gave way to every other sound and vibration within the universe as a whole. Now imagine that our human form is able to pick up on certain of these spectra of sounds while also limiting our ability to come into contact sensitively with the remaining sounds.

Such is the case in every life great or small as the sense relationship of communication becomes limited to a smaller range of sounds that in turn gives one the sense of self itself as well as identifying the fact that other forms of communication exist beyond our range of detection. The body of the soul is much more capable of identifying all the more than the human body does now, and much later our formless relationship with spirit itself will open up another range of sensitivities that will enable us further to discover the nature of the one life responsible for our own.

IV Beingness

When in the afterlife, I experienced the presence of a Feminine Principality, I had made contact with a pure being from spiritual spheres. It was in the first moments of this rapport with this angelic feminine presence that I came to be advised as to my own shortcomings. In her presence, I found potential within myself to assimilate her rhythm, and I sensed then that I had a long journey before I would be able to match and thereby have formal contact with her again.

Thereafter, I have occasioned the opportunity for rapport with her and others who live and emanate such purity and each time in their presence I come to realize more of what I need do to acquire a similar rhythm for myself. I call this identification and following revelation the methodology itself of beingness.

For example, if one were to sit quietly and repeat the word honesty to themselves until such time as they felt as honest as they could possibly arrive at in time, it would then be possible to take note of a simple fact that suggests we have the ability to forecast our own betterment and being.

By seeing a more honest self in the future and by feeling what it would take to become that very way, we are unconsciously tapping into our soul's ability to identify what lies ahead for us all. At the best of times, I might catch several comments in a given day by those I meet where this is evidenced as they suggest aloud to me that they wish they could be nicer at times, or if only they were kinder themselves.

These type of comments about our wish for being more true comes from the very fact that we can feel the perfection of our soul within ourselves and make comparisons between that body of sensitivity and our own present condition and status. This attribute works in many other ways though few have ever taken notice in their attempts to make it through the day. We may be preoccupied so much that we may always overlook the most basic notions of our nature, though it is a fact that in little time we can come to know our soul's attributes and begin to make use of these in the given day to succeed at all that we aspire to.

You have to have enough interest in yourself just to be able to know about yourself! The more interest, the more information. The more information, the more experience at knowing more. Knowing more makes a difference. Each time you look and talk to yourself about yourself at length, you will feel differently about yourself. According to the law of originality, you will never feel the same way about yourself overall, and that itself evolves.

Imagine that through information processing you could manage your accusational nature to a point where it no longer exists, and then you would know what it is like to be free from those forms of limiting impressions that imprison you normally. Knowing that difference makes an even bigger difference. When you know yourself well enough you can make yourself come to life all the more by becoming more objective every day until you hear the sound of attainment ringing in your consciousness, singing in your ear, touching you with grace and accepting your Divinity. Information comes by way of repetitious experiences such as when you seek to discover your truths and to adhere to them expecting a day of attainment.

Initiation

I Planetary initiation: the great cycles

An experience can be had which confirms that we are truly imperishable beings in a process of unfolding our potential. I have coined certain words to describe this event such as initiation. In using this word I am implying that the universe has a plan and that this plan is guaranteed. That the outcome will occur as it was intended to in spite of all seeming doubt, concern or imagined differences. Further, the word initiation refers to the moment and to the individual who meets that specific moment where events that are predetermined actually take place as planned. An initiate is one who seeks to attain initiation into a higher level of life and being.

Having said as much, I would like to recall certain moments in the afterlife experience I had in 1979 where I was shown the future. I would not want you to think that the future is exactly as I saw it though I would like to expand on what I actually discovered, regarding the definite events of the future instead.

I was shown how our Sun, having its own orbit, takes approximately 36,000 Earth years for every one of its own years. During the cycle of time that it takes for our Sun to travel this distance throughout our local system, I was shown how three major events were determined to come about with regard to the evolution of certain races of souls during this single period.

In the first division of 12,000 years, those in incarnate form from the standpoint of evolution are given to experience a range of sensitivities which bring about the ability for one to become self-conscious. Other divisions of time within this first cycle of 12,000 years were shown to me and I took note of how, step by step, the faculties of the human brain are awakened where dreams begin to unfold as the mind itself becomes an attribute and a tool of the evolving being.

In the final stages of this first cycle, a fully awakened mind and a keen sense of individuality comes to the surface and humanity is then on the brink of an initiation. An event where those who have been prepared sufficiently then experience an acceleration, or a moment of transition and expansion, which causes self-consciousness to come into being.

This event marks the first of several initiations and in the second cycle of 12,000 years the inventive qualities of mind and consciousness come to fruition and humanity comes to engage in unified communities which eventuate the cities and populations and inventive systems of justice and economy.

At the ending of this second cycle, an integration of the

developed personality and of the soul itself takes place which raises the level of consciousness in man to that of the soul. It is then in the remaining cycle of 12,000 years that our greatest accomplishments personally, and of our inventions outwardly, come to a fruitful moment of triumph and humanity is then liberated from the limiting worlds of sensitive development ever more. When this cycle closes, the remaining individualities of the world choose to remain or leave in order to complete even greater goals that are then evident. It is also at this time that humanity has passed through another series of initiation where the populous has become enlightened and then illuminated.

Following these three great cycles of the solar system, a new group of souls arrive to undertake the identical process as those who have left. It should be understood here though that each time the final cycle has ended and a new one begins, the greater societies begin to fall and the world becomes rediscovered some 24,000 years later.

The level of attainment and inventiveness of humanity becomes even greater at the height of each new cycle. For instance, in our world we have arrived at the last cycle of 12,000 years and our present technologies will take us further than before as we will now enter space and eventuate contact for the first time in our own personal history. What will be accomplished within the next 48,000 years remains unknown although the heights to which humanity gains become ever greater and the ends of uncertainty and ignorance eventually disappear completely.

I only know of one fact regarding our planet and it is that in the next round and cycle following the next and remaining cycle of 12,000 years to date, there will no longer be a need for souls to inhabit the dense forms that we do today. I suspect that we will have completed sufficient development that in the next round our planet will establish itself and will not be visible to the limited senses of the human form we are adjusting to today. Earth will most likely be an evolved planet by then, and will most likely be home to advanced souls in the kingdom of souls where our cyclic pattern around our present Sun will change.

There are many cycles not only of suns and planets but of individuals. It may be that it is the time for certain groups of souls to take an initiation that will occur on their behalf at a specific period of time. In such a case, an individual may or may not be aware of the impending fact and regardless of how they live or what they have chosen, when that time comes, they will have gained the initiation and will undergo an expansion of consciousness.

Suppose that in the year 2049 you were initiated and entered into your inheritance of the soul, and you no longer needed to take up a form in our system again, thereby being free to choose your future goals. Now let's say that today you are a criminally minded individual with terrible habits of violence and selfishness. This would suggest that you can expect to experience more intentional impacts upon your life than you would normally.

What this means is that you cannot change the outcome, though between cycles you have the opportunity to prevent yourself and even to cause limitations to be put upon you until you finally recognize and overcome those habits. It might well mean that you will die very soon and then take another life very quickly where it is possible for you to overcome the former ignorances and then after another death in early adulthood you may then return again to the final life that has been determined for you. It is still possible to give up on your own opportunity but your soul will then make it with or without you.

Certainly this is very difficult to explain but the basic rule is that events that are guaranteed will occur, like it or not. These events may not be within your present consciousness and at any time soon it may be difficult to tell if it is so but those who are in contact with their soul certainly know when the determined moments of initiation will occur for them and they wait upon these moments daily.

In the case of one who does not know but is going to enter into an initiation by surprise, such as one that will occur in the near future for many, a growing interest in things spiritual yet not religious, a certain longing for that which cannot be seen or contacted, an overall sense that there is more that one has to do but that they just can't put their finger on it, will occur prior to that moment.

When that moment does arrive, a new experience with the greater sensibility of the soul begins and from that moment on, we enter into a new world of fearless and highly creative living.

In other words, the masses begin to sense the opportunity that is approaching and changes in attitude, demeanour, character and lifestyle often prove to be symptomatic of such impending outcomes. When it does come to pass, we begin to see with the eye of the soul behind the scenes and into the revealed facts of an already populated and intelligent universe.

II   Initiation and conscience

Now at another level, I would like to explain something about one's seeming elusive sense of conscience. When it becomes apparent that things are going wrong for you, look to your conscience, especially these days. I say this because the conscience of humanity is the first-stage development of the initiation principle. In other words, our conscience begins to turn up the volume and we begin to identify our shortcomings much sooner than ever before. As the greater population enters into an initiation cycle, and since the outcome is determined already, there is less opportunity by the hour to prevent yourself from the outcome. Only those who would continue to oppose their own conscience under the duress of a great moment will be making a big mistake.

The first signs of an initiation is that everything seems to come to a head while one feels they have never been so much in touch beforehand. It feels as if you are being observed, watched and advised whenever you tend to go against your own best judgement. The feeling that one need settle down and take all things into account backed up by dreams of a period of life coming to a close are most common.

The sense that you were intended to achieve something that is not within your view yet seems to keep at you. All of these instances are indications of an impending initiation, but when the sense that your heart or forehead is coming under duress even in the most calm of moments, these are more evident. Eventually, a sensibility to one's crown upon the top of the head, and a greater sensibility to the area upon the forehead just between the eyebrow begins to awaken.

It is in the moments when one is most true that the obvious comes to be known and that inspiration begins to flood the mind. One day it is very inspirational and then for a few days nothing happens, then again another day or two of inspired thinking occurs and ends again. When inspiration begins to happen suddenly and frequently, that is the time to remain calm and peaceful as this facilitates the transitions one will pass through over a period of about three years as they are initiated into another level and skill of consciousness.

In more ancient times, one would go through a series of painful renunciations and practices to bring an initiation about though in our day it is the whole of the masses that will pass through the next phase and expansion of consciousness regarding the planet itself. Though we will pass through just such an initiation in our present generation and though the world will change dramatically for the better, it is still possible that some will experience an even higher initiation at this time.

There are a small yet growing number of serious individuals who have dedicated their lives in youth to attaining such initiations through their own methodologies and in their own time, and it is for these that the possibility of an even greater initiation is possible. In such cases, one could expect to achieve full contact and acceptance into the hierarchy of servants and masters who reside within our world already while for many it will be a greater form of consciousness overall that will be called enlightenment in the years that follow. Whatever level of initiation you do undertake will always be to the next greater one yet to be achieved so it is quite normal to expect to see yourself in a better situation thereafter.

I did not make these last point just to impress the individual reader and to allow them insight into an event that will likely occur for them long before they actually leave our world, but there was another point which I would like to make now. It is apparent to me that there is a lot of free play and time in between incarnations and initiation; however, these planetary initiations happen only after long intervals of time and one needs to be in the right place at the right time if they are going to take advantage of a great event that is final proof for the many who were unsettled as to their true identity previously.

Proof is always the best method of maintaining one's sanity at the best of times and it is for the final evidence and proof that many wait for these days, not being aware of how to take an initiation of their own and in their own time. It is evident that there are already many thousands of individuals who claim to have taken initiations and I am just one of these. However, it was the evidence of the fact that just such an event occurs that moved me the most following my own afterlife experiences.

Since the accident, I have experienced three initiations which for many is nearly impossible to attain in just one lifetime. I have experienced these initiations within my own body and have a direct awareness of what transpires and has transpired in between these events. I am likewise looking forward to the last two initiations that will take place in a short time for me; however, it is most important that the reader learns to recognize the potential within themselves to bring about just such an event.

III   Methods of initiation

There are two direct methods of approach and the one which is the easiest of all is called devotion. In this methodology, we can learn to meditate upon the love aspect within our nature while focusing upon the heart and ambitiously yet seriously awaiting a momentary inspiration from the indwelling presence of our own soul. In this method we attempt simply to remain devoted to loving humanity and being true to ourselves while pledging ourselves to the task of initiation where we can contact our own soul.

The other method is much like the first, though it requires us to manage our mind use and come to the centre of our heart and consciousness where a period of silence accompanied with the expectation of contact can begin. We must remain receptive to the innate sense of conscience in this case, and we then strive to remove the hindrances to a pure heart such as negative accusation, which happens to speed up the process immensely.

By dealing with our conditioning habits of behaviour and of the connective psychology, and by holding true to our conscience daily, a period of increased inspiration will begin to make itself felt appropriately by the soul itself. The bottom line is to remain receptive to inspiration, and to wait on inspiration following a serious question with patience and until a response comes.

Once we have become accustomed to inspiration in daily life, old habits are overcome steadily thereafter. It is the desire to inspire and the intent to be inspired that we should keep in mind, regardless of the methodology, when attempting to confirm the fact of the soul as a presence within ourselves.

This fact has been proven by thousands to date, yet it is only in the actualization of a methodology of approach to purity that we gain pure evidence ourselves. This fact that verifies an actual event that can be confirmed by the thinker following an initiation is what the whole world waits upon, and when many tend to present these facts on a more frequent basis, the masses will then see that Divinity is a fact for themselves as well. Once it is proven that we are all of Divine origin, the world will finally come to be free from the ignorance of the past ever more.

IV   The last life

In my own language, I would add this final statement of fact that suggests it is only our turn right now. Others have come and more have passed, yet a little love for every soul is what we have to offer. We are not the first to have come to an initiation or to a moment of transition in the greater scheme of universal life, and we are not the last, but it is possible to see that though we have lived before in the incarnate worlds, we need not make this individual life just one more time.

This can be the last life you decide to accept as the first one to never forget. Only in the last life do we begin to appreciate the fact that this is the first time we have chosen to make it our last, and the last time we will choose to make it the first one that we salvage.

Such is the goal as we all stand at the midway point of evolution in our universe. Now is the time to choose to never forget yourself again, and to do so you must attempt as best as you can to understand your own nature as a soul in incarnation.

The Appearance of the Soul

I A shape-shifting body of light

At this point, I would like to introduce another experience that I had during the four-day afterlife drama which followed me into this restored lifetime. I have left these unique and unusual experiences until now, as I felt a bit of information on the soul as it relates to our psychology was necessary preparation to begin to understand the implications and ramifications to some degree before going on.

Almost from the very first moment in the afterlife I had begun to notice how everyone in these spheres was alight. It seemed at first to me that the bodies we occupy by magnetic resonance, which allows us to maintain the similar appearances that we were accustomed to as humans, was indeed made of light.

Only later did I come to see that the substantial conscious forms, which made up the light body itself, were made out of the elements recognized in our present-day sciences as particles. The flowing, colourful, and energetic outward forms were tied to one's sensibility so that, as one thought, so too did they appear to take shape. As one's mood changed, so too would their overall colour and brilliance.

On closer inspection I also found a direct connection between the vibratory tones and these colourful particles. What amazed me the most in the earliest stages was how mobile, or seemingly unattached, these particles were from the general appearance that we are most accustomed to. It appeared to me that the particles were moving as single units while remaining connected to the body of light that was emulating the consciousness of the individual.

In other words, while the former face, height, weight and strength, along with specific characteristics like eye colouring and hair colour were almost identical to the appearance of the body left behind, streams of light flowing about the soul rarely conformed to these characteristics. I supposed then that this was because they were not generally of the body but of the thought of the individual.

Much later, I came to converse with a group of souls who were making sentient applications to their sciences in a nearby system, when it was exposed to me that the manner in which communication occurred for us all could be seen in the aura of the individual. Within the aura of a soul, there are three points of light focus, just like three small but very dynamic particles. This reminded me of my lessons on the atomic worlds.

The three primary lights of a soul are permanent atoms. These three make up the combined potential, aspects, attributes, skills and powers of the soul itself. In much the same way that we are able to identify an individual according to their will nature, their emotional nature and their intelligent nature, these three primary points and their responsive lights are the representation in beingness of a whole unit of life.

In other words, the entire soul was the size of three atoms of energy that gave off a hue of energy colour. If one were to isolate three particle waves, it is likely that it would be impossible to notice them as they are below the threshold of our sensible range of sight. It is no falsity that one can put a hundred thousand souls on the point of a pen. When these three points of lights take an appearance in the formless worlds, or in the afterlife spheres, they can separate from their unified triangle and size to generate their own appearance in any size or magnification that the soul chooses to.

In this way, our soul can be understood to be a shape changer or a shape shifter. Having the ability to reproduce any characteristic of their own former experiences, a soul could appear as a grain of sand, as a great white whale or as an ant. It makes no difference what shape or appearance a soul takes as size, dimension or mass make no difference and have no effect upon the soul that produces appearance by willed desire alone.

II Generating and transmitting thought forms

I also learned that through these three primary points of light many fluctuations and conditions could be represented by the soul other than those attained or noticed by sight. In other words, a soul has the ability to reflect light as if it were a million cut diamonds with various light shades and colours to introduce a message effectively.

In much the same way that we might imply or pass on special information without having to say anything aloud, and as much as the average thinker can identify or read these inferences, the soul communicates through the production of these shapes of light. In these ways, a soul passes thoughts and impressions to others. If one can see the frustration indicated by a certain look or appearance in this world, then in the life afterwards they will be able to identify the same condition but through light relationships.

Our sensory body that I have called 'sentient' is better explained as a sensitivity characteristic which allows for forms of thoughts and impressions to become manifest. Not only does a soul talk in these ways, but a soul also knows that when these light forms are produced before releasing them to another soul, they have their own substantial life of independence for a time. Another interesting fact is that when a thought form is produced, the energetic aspect of that form continues intelligently to attempt to make contact with the individual in mind at the time of creation.

It was in the first moments of the afterlife that I took notice of these points of light, and the forms, as I came to know them later, were then seen as messages. It was a fact that the appearances of colourful lights in one's magnetic aura were attractive and intelligent messages left for the receiving soul to capture and unfold any time they chose to. Much like email, and similar to the way we broadcast information itself, thought forms are very real life forms.

Most of our messages from advanced souls and spiritual entities, not excluding human thinkers at times, are akin to spiritual mail draped in indigo, gold and more frequently white. When these messages are from humans, though, there is always a variation and a weakness to the message itself as it is often precipitated under less energetic methods. In other words, humans tend not to concentrate upon their thoughts long enough for them to be released properly and to survive the day.

Learning to precipitate thoughts in history was once considered an art known only to certain white masters of the esoteric sciences, or to the angelic hosts of the heavens. Such a capacity to send informing messages and inspirational intervening impressions to another thinker in our world was long held to be probable though not possible. Even in the hermetic schools of thought, it was taught that thought forms were of the stuff of Divinity and only the most advanced priest king pharaohs were able to demonstrate the art effectively.

I suppose that most readers today have had the occasional moment in their life where they wonder if they can concentrate sufficiently to send an impression to a loved one at some distance from them, and in this same manner of curious circumstances over historic time, certain fears, suspicions and superstitions were developed. In fact, if you tell someone today that you are able to communicate with your loved ones through concentrated efforts and mind use alone, they will certainly suspect there is something wrong with you, or that you have taken up with the wrong people. Regardless, such has been proven a fact by science. Research into kinetic energy and the ability of a thinker to influence objects beyond the reach of their own body is rapidly verifying these stated sentient facts.

Getting back to the idea that messages are living things, I had come to recognize on my return to form how these same particles remained within my sensory range of consciousness. It struck me in or around the first week of consciousness in the hospital that I was seeing into people's private business though it was only in the human form again that I had not taken this for granted any longer.

I remember quite well how in the afterlife I had simply taken it for granted that I did not have to make use of my own mind as was the case in human form, and on return I was most amazed to find that communication with my own guide had produced these same forms which were now visible.

I used to sit and look at my hands or watch one area of my body while awaiting the moment when a receptive impression would appear. Shortly thereafter, I began to concentrate in an effort to capture the inspiration which would then flow into my own thinking and unfold a series of impressions thereafter. I learned in a very short time when and how these thought forms worked and set out to produce the same quality of impression myself.

It wasn't until much later that I had mastered the art of concentrating and producing an impression that I could pass on though some of these practices would often occur among friends in the hospital who had no idea of what I was up to. At first, I started with words and would try to get someone to say the word out loud as I continued to concentrate. Later, when I found that it worked only under silent and calm conditions did I begin to succeed.

The ability to precipitate thoughts is not only one of the easiest skills to learn, it is also happening hundreds of times a day though rarely does one recognize the fact.

At other times, while sitting quietly at home, I was able to capture someone's impressions as they were thinking most seriously about myself. I was reminded then of the many times I would think about someone and was glad that they didn't know. It was only much later, when I started to observe individuals who were strangers, that I had found I could see these particle impressions coming into another thinker's field of light.

In some instances I could tell that they were being attacked and other times when they were being concentrated on because of something they had done wrong. I learned then how, through fear, one remains open to suggestion and further reveals their guilt even then among the untrained thinkers so easily. I was always amazed at how children could pick up on someone's private thinking or how usually uneducated and dreamy people could do so likewise. It was the ability to remain very calm and to maintain a quiet mind which gave way to the ability to recognize the subtler and sometimes obvious impressions that would enter into and out of another thinker's form.

I learned to utilize this skill in order to aid someone in a healing process, or for therapeutic reasons, though rarely did I make use of the skill to entertain myself or to enter into someone's privacy. As the years passed, and the skill expanded to other more valuable work, I came to understand how it was that the state and condition of a thinker in regard to their conscience was one of the aspects or interests the brain had maintained a constant vigil over.

In short, our brain through subtle spiritual work, has gone beyond the expected practices of surviving and defending the thinker from harm that is not within the psyche's ability to effect, and the consciousness of the brain now includes the ability to identify the true condition and status of anyone and everyone we meet with regards to their relationship with conscience.

In fact, I used to instruct individuals to try a test of this to see for themselves. I would suggest one go to a mall where there would be plenty of strangers for the experiment. They would then find a place to sit and observe the many strangers as they passed by. Their task then was to say to themselves as a command, 'I want my brain to allow impressions to enter into my mind which indicate the relationship that these people have with their conscience.'

The results were astounding. It was obvious to many that the ability to do so was within their grasp, though to what extent and to what degree of predictive success one could reach as evidence remained an unknown. For those who studied as suggested, though along more serious lines of investigation, it was very evident that it was within their capacity to question and then see whatever they chose to regarding the conscience.

In as much as the brain works along elocutionary lines of adaptation, where information on the environment is then passed on to the generations thereafter, our soul works to provide information to our brain where adaptation to insights and inspiration is also passed on. Perception is also another form of evolutionary law that finds its way into the generations not yet born. In these ways, our present humanity has many avenues of approach to a series of impressions that remain within the genetic core of our cellular life within the brain and body. It is the thoughts of one life that manifest in the next.

III   The sentient form and brain-conscious information

Getting back to the idea that I was able to see the particle life messages surrounding or within a soul's aura, I was very excited when it was revealed that these messages eventually become adaptable insights which follow us into new lives ahead and well into eternity. The name for this body of light impressions is the sentient form.

Through a greater study of this body within us all, and within the blueprint of the universe itself, I came to see that the predetermined universe was itself a thought form of the one great eventuating life. In this way, I have come to value the dreams of life, as the impressions that generate the future itself.

Every thought that becomes a permanent impression does indeed find its way into the soul and eventually such thoughts allow the evolving consciousness of the individual to transcend the limitations of the human brain and form altogether.

There are also thoughts that are unfinished, unresolved, incomplete, agitated, anxious, separate or uncontrollable and negative, as compared to their opposites as they act upon the consciousness of the individual; such thoughts will aid or hinder the goal of attainment and liberation from illusion overall.

It should be carefully considered and eventually understood that one's very thoughts do have an effect on one's present health and consciousness. Imagine for a moment that your physical form captures your every thought within its magnetic body. These thoughts would appear as minute sparks of light that move about the entire outer skin of the body itself, and up to a distance of 20 feet away from the physical body itself. Like a cloud of light surrounding our body, these thoughts, ideas and concepts remain active while attempting and awaiting to be processed by the human brain and brought into waking consciousness.

As a matter of curiosity, one could ponder these inferences and they might come to understand how the priority of placing new information into one's consciousness comes first through acquisition, or at least acquiring the data which is a process in itself, and then secondly by awaiting the moment when the brain is receptive to the awaiting or incoming information.

The human brain comes to a moment of receptivity in

many ways, though the most obvious may be understood to take place when you simply wonders what is on your mind or what priorities you have to remember today. In each case, where a moment of enquiry comes about, pertaining to what remains unfinished in your mind, the thought forms that wait to be recognized and processed have an opening.

Once you have begun to ponder or think at length about your unfinished business, or whenever you reconsider past conversations or past events, those unfinished thought forms enter into the mind and are eventually collected by the neurons within the brain for storage and eventual use. In this case, we call the outcome brain-conscious information.

The prioritization of certain events and information then undergoes another process where categorization of the information is conducted, thereby enabling you to speak freely about your experiences in the most natural of ways. Without having to rediscover what information is locked within the memory of your cellular body, your brain simply allows for the digestion and organization of the material to be at the instant disposal of the thinker.

While this occurs many times within the passage of a single day, we need also consider that certain information that enters our brain and eventually our overall conscious-ness does so because of previous efforts by the thinker to establish criteria of their own. In such cases, the brain is driven by suggestion alone to remind or to hold on to infor-mation that is important to the thinker.

We may see examples of this as we find ourselves con-centrating or daydreaming when suddenly we are remind-ed of an event that we have to get to on time or in other cases where we find ourselves looking about our environ-ment while being unaware of just what it is we are seeking to find. Another example that demonstrates this fact happens when we look into a crowd of people and our focus appears to be upon blondes, brunettes, shapes etc.

When a young man tells himself that he would like to meet a blonde, he may not realize that afterwards his brain when contacting such desired objectives tends to point out every blonde in his environment. Many an accident has occurred when one's concentration is evoked or interfered with by former self conditioning and likewise many a new discovery has occurred by this method of targeting itself.

We could intentionally seek to discover what our conscience has to do with our usual thinking and, by the end of the day, another category of information will have been actively gathering information along these lines. It is only when we speak to ourselves unintentionally that the most harmful and the most confusing situations occur for the individual, the causes for which may later be very hard to discover.

IV   Negative impressions

Going further, with regards to the particle thought forms that surround us and remain locked into our magnetic field of impression at all times, it can be revealed through meditation that negative impressions enter our brain and consciousness and have yet another effect upon our overall health. In the case of negative accusation or criticism, one is bound to store the thoughts along these lines in the exact condition that they were in when thought of first.

Later, when people are reminded of something that made them feel bad, they begin to re-experience the physical, emotional and conscious condition once again. It is as if our thoughts when pondered upon repetitively are shown to have the ability to transform our appearance and inner condition which of itself then has an effect on our physiological chemistry. When a bad mood is remembered, one simply ends up in that bad mood again. When sad love songs are remembered, the state we were in the first times we heard the song returns and manages to condition us so that in the end, we are in the same state once more.

So many times we tend to repeat mood states and attitudes that were previously experienced in the original incident that, as an adult, it becomes very hard to escape from such conditioning regardless of our desire for change.

Thoughts that for one reason or another seem to go unfinished tend to return to the fore of our mind in an effort to complete the process that the brain itself has in design. In such cases, we find ourselves suddenly reminded that we had begun to consider some one thing yet it was never completed and the brain tends to generate a subtle pressure on us to complete these thoughts. When these same thoughts are dismissed frequently, or remain unfinished intentionally, stress tends to be felt. It is a true fact that unfinished business is the greatest and most responsible cause of stress overall.

When we feel stressed we should ask ourselves what unfinished business needs be tended to which would alleviate the stress itself. In such situations it can be proven that attending to our unfinished thoughts is exactly the way we reduce stress and renew our health without the use of chemicals or medical attention.

One can imagine how much stress there is in the world when thinkers are unable to arrive at solutions or outcomes, or resolve themselves personally. Our brain requires of us that we tend to our own thinking and our brain also tends to prevent ill health by these methods. In short, the brain attempts to preserve its own integrity and health by processing information as its main priority. One could easily imagine that if the brain allowed for unfinished business to be negated or ignored in order to preserve its integrity and health, the evolution of consciousness itself would be impaired greatly. In essence, the brain is intended to participate in the salvaging of pertinent information in order to best serve the original intent of the universe itself.

V The final synthesis

When one come to their final days of life in the incarnate world, the thought forms of a lifetime that have managed to be properly and efficiently processed are collected within the central nervous system and find their way into three major areas of the human body.

In the head, our impressions are gathered near the pineal and pituitary glands, and in the heart region, the whole life information is gathered in an area nearest the thymus gland. These three locations are the main areas of activity for the soul and there are threadlike connections from and to the central nervous system where the connection is made which makes it possible for life to continue.

When one of these threads is destroyed, broken, cut or damaged, the individual may remain alive though the remaining primary threads within the head or heart are then responsible for doing the work of the original three. This can be observed in the case of those who are and remain in coma.

Continuing on, when the information at the time of death or departure from the form is being released, a synthesis of the data occurs and within this process, a preparation for the actual departure begins. In similar ways, the soul sounds a specific note when the developed foetus is prepared for the transition of birth. Certain glands are responsive in these moments and the activities of the body are then under the complete guidance of the soul.

Once the thread in the head is removed from the pineal gland area, the entire central nervous system then flares up, and the data is salvaged within the causal body. This body of continuity is the same as the sensitive body of the soul when I previously referred to the sentient form. This body is built over a series of several lives, and only when it is sufficient and able to survive the destruction of the human body itself does one leave through the aperture in the head known as the crown.

Until that time, one leaves through an opening in the solar plexus, as has been the case for the majority over the past few thousand years. In this case, the magnetic resonance of the physical body itself is utilized by the soul to salvage the individual for a longer duration preceding release back to the waiting soul, or in a few cases - where the soul then enters into a transformation itself - the individual then takes on a body of appearance for the duration thereafter. In either case, the difference is length of time spent in the afterlife preceding incarnation, or release overall from the wheel of rebirth.

For many, there will be a time period of a few days to a number of weeks before the process is complete in the afterlife and then the individual gains what was formerly theirs. The soul then releases the information gathered throughout the history of incarnate lives, and the individual stands for the first time in the light of triumph where a synthesis of attribute, skills and powers are then given over for the individual to use on command.

In cases where individuals have gathered sufficient information to aid themselves ultimately in the evolutionary cycles of conscious development, and where some unfinished or negative data remains, a new process begins. In that process of elimination, which tends to occur in the first stages of the afterlife experience, unfinished business becomes finished and negative tendencies and attributes are looked upon at length and eventually overcome by seeing in the light of pure objectivity. In either case, the result is the same: namely, the restoration of one's experiential data.

In the case of an individual who suffers a greater measure of personality negativity and tends to habituate their own conditioning by will and even those who tend toward darkness, the elimination process may not suffice to resolve the condition and though the soul is preserved along with all the other information from previous lives, only those forms that were completed remain. In the ensuing drama, a personality may be lost or not sufficiently developed; its gains are salvaged though the thought of the personality is lost.

Historically speaking, many of us today have lost vast amounts of experiential data simply by being unable to capture them through immaturity or underdevelopment. In such instances, one is considered as a soul in progress that is not yet ready for the bridging and completion of a final personality.

This negativity is reshaped and reinvested into the individual's lot and life ahead: the soul of one personality may take several incarnations to correct the hindrances and conditions developed in any one life.

In some instances, it is also probable and very possible that they may not effect the necessary condition for release from form before the cycles of incarnation are passed. In these cases, the soul is aided to find another opportunity for development in other systems. In total, one should consider how very important every moment in thinking is to oneself. The great habits of unintentional mind use and excessive daydreaming are largely responsible for hindering the soul in its efforts to sustain the opportunity on behalf of the individuality or personality and a life is thus often near the portal of release though unable to complete the objective.

Where there is a need for one last life, or nearing the evidence of such a gain, it is not an awful thing that we need return and start all over since much of our basic tendencies are already able to reproduce the same given character and personality conditions where it is very possible to complete the said objectives of the soul.

I used to think upon my return to body, that I have yet to succeed in the afterlife more than I succeeded in the incarnate life, though now it is evident that we are all attempting in our present generation to complete the objectives of our soul, and more than 120 million souls will do so in the very near future. To defeat the need for restoration and resolve before the time of death is ever the great goal of all souls.

The Dark Ones

There is one more point of interest that I should mention as I bring this section to an end and it is in reference to the dark ones.

Those who have attained a greater intellect for the sciences and are able to understand the misuse of our scientific powers run a risk of arrogance and alienation which in turn can bring grave harm to our world and to the populace at this time. The individuals who use their intellect to distort the truth, to accuse falsely, to destroy life and to bring harm to the world intentionally and knowingly, will find themselves in a most difficult situation in their afterlife.

I should remind you that there is no accusation of such an individual who has yet to attain the expansion of consciousness called enlightenment, and there is no real punishment of the soul. However, there is a condition upon release from form where it is still possible, even then, for an individual to oppose the restoration process itself.

In certain circumstances which are rare indeed, a dark one can interfere with the process and find their way back into incarnation by being aware of the fundamental laws of the universe, though at the end of a cycle they will find no more opportunity to repeat their resistance. In those cases, and only in the very end, will they find themselves lost to the opportunity for release from the system that we live in.

As for the fears, concerns, superstitions, and mortal fright of many a thinker, I should suggest that the devil, as depicted by most religious institutions, is largely made up of the overall consciousness of the masses as they strive towards selfish intents and harm. One might imagine that there are fields of thought forms that are produced by those very advanced souls within our sphere that are there for the plucking when one is receptive to information beyond their own aura, and that these thought forms tend to counter the negative and ignorant inventions of the population overall. In certain cases, one might imagine a dark individual being able to concentrate upon another individual where their health becomes impaired, or confusion and paranoia have found their way into the aura of the unsuspecting thinker. This is possible, though the effects always return to the sender as is the case where concentrated efforts in objective ways such as prayer or meditation can bring about healing.

Our system is designed and founded upon specific universal laws which prevents the long-term abuse of any individual upon the many and certainly, beyond our world of incarnation, there are no dark entities that have power over anyone. The story of the devil throughout the millennia has its origins in the original testament of truth, though the devil was depicted then as the 'Great Accuser'.

The accuser is made up of those thoughts that have been referred to as negative accusation, complaint, criticism and punishing tendencies. It is always the way of the dark ones first to conspire to accuse, then humiliate, deceive, complain, criticize and then seek to punish the often innocent victim of their desire.

It is the intent of the accuser in all of us to harm those who most represent the truth itself. Once one is given to eliminate the habit of negative accusation itself, the sooner one is released from the conditions which follow in the afterlife which are often the cause of one's return to incarnate life.

By remaining aware of the fact that our very thoughts determine much of our future, it remains possible for us to attain to the objective perception of life overall. In the end, the objective thinker gains the reward of release from illusion, pain, futility and confusion, while entering into the spheres of the eternal servants of Divinity.

Negative accusation and objective understanding stand as a reminder to us all of a Divine law of limitation and liberation. We must no longer attack ourselves spiritually. Accusation that is personalized is an attack and a threat to punish the unenlightened in an attempt to destroy what is true and beautiful.

This is what need be eventually uprooted from the consciousness of humanity. Such is the spiritual goal for each and every free-thinking individual within humanity. Choose the path of pure objectivity just as those who now seek to serve us all daily have done since their last days as incarnate thinkers themselves.

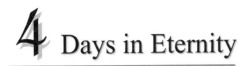
4 Days in Eternity

Part VI
From A Distance

The Law of Non-Imposition

I   No judgement

I have suggested a great deal so far about the many varied and unique lifestyles with regards to the souls and spiritual entities who live beyond the limitation of our human incarnate forms, though now I would like to express my own opinions of the perspectives shared by these same hosts as they tend to reach out and serve the younger advancing souls of the material universe itself.

In earlier statements, I mentioned my own guide who shared his rhythm with me while involved in the afterlife drama, and who still communicates with me throughout my days. It has been due to this continued contact with my host guide that I have come to understand not only myself, and what my particular relationship is, in relation to the universal, but also the relationship the universal has with us all.

Though I have mentioned the fact that certain hindrances and obstacles remain upon humanity in general, and that these impediments need be intentionally qualified and eventually eliminated preceding the event of an expansion of consciousness, I would also suggest that at no time is one ever identified, qualified or assessed by the servants of humanity in the manner that they are by the less experienced members of humanity themselves.

There are no judgements, accusations, charges or opinions made at any time whatsoever by those who have already passed beyond the limitations of the incarnate cycles of time and space. Regardless of what an individual does in ignorance or despair, confusion or uncertainty, the view of these individuals is always the same in the end as it is for those who are moral, reserved in faith, pledged, or vowed, conscientious and even enlightened.

The view of an individual within the cyclic circumstances of our world remains the same so long as an individual remains within the educational stages of development throughout time and space.

We are all seen as souls in a process who, through the cycles of incarnation, are given the necessary tools and guidance that will eventuate that particular stage of consciousness and realization of our human nature and condition. It is known that in time, and through the evolution of consciousness in particular, we will all one day come to know our true nature as Divine offspring of the universal Life.

It is also realized that the shortcomings of any one or more of the members of humanity is no more than a demonstrative need for greater wisdom, and that eventually humanity at large will come to remove the basic hindrances to their further development through the acquisition by experience of such wisdom itself.

In these ways, the perspective of our very host and guides throughout the necessary foundational stages of conscious development identify us all as Divine beings in a process of self-mastery. In short, we are seen as eventuating Divine beings who are struggling to reach beyond our limitations of consciousness, while remaining subject to a great forgetfulness at birth, and while under the influences of the illusion of mortality.

The compassion and enlightenment of advanced souls allow for tremendous patience and protection of the Divine rights of all incarnate souls, regardless of their condition at any one moment. In other words, we all have the inherent right to seek out the truth and to become like that truth, as well as refusing to seek out the truth according to our free-willed conscience. This means that you can do anything you like and, regardless of your choices, you have the right to continue in your aspirations, good or bad, until the moment of choice arrives when one has actually attained the awakened consciousness as a requisite to entry into the Divine spheres.

This, however, does not mean that there is no price to pay for ignorance and intentional avarice towards others. What is implied here alone is that it is the right of the individual to pay attention to or ignore the truth personally. This does not give one the right to impose their ignorance upon another soul in incarnation at any time, but rather simply suggests you can do what you will to yourself alone.

There is a given law in the universe and lacking the ability myself to explain this law through language alone, I can suggest it is a law of non-imposition. The justice of the universe is pure and swift indeed, though it is never less than perfect, as much as one may think not. The law itself is tied to the very moment of our given thought, and acts through the physiological and chemical aspects of our human form so that when one has acted out of ignorance, such is noted and has an immediate effect upon one's whole being.

The thinker cannot escape the inferred impression that comes into being at such moments. For example, one may choose intentionally to humiliate, lie and abuse others through violence, which in its turn starts certain chemical responses in the human brain and body which initiates conditions and habits of a type that causes a loss of consciousness in some, a sense of the loss of satisfaction with life for others, eventual stress and illness, and the inability to arrive at a true sense and peace of mind.

These are only a few of the many psychological conditions that eventually lead to changes in brain function and shape, as well as a host of mental and emotional conditions that therapists struggle to deal with every day. There is always a condition that follows an intentionally ignorant thought and action, and only the objective thinker has the necessary freedom and health to pursue the goal of attainment with vital interest.

The negative habits of despondency, anger, frustrations, disappointment, control, manipulation and many many more of these conditioning situations in any one individual's life stand as reminders to such thinkers of the action of the past, and if these are not taken up properly and dealt with properly, then the individual comes to be subject to an increased magnification of the law.

Only those who refuse to accept the truth and wish not to be bothered by their conscience can escape the natural response of the universal law for a time and this is not a healthy idea as an entire life of intentional ignorance can lead to the concretization and eventual shattering of the personality life thereafter.

Those who sense the negative ramifications of their behaviour, and who likewise sense there is a need to restore themselves, the experiences in their day tend to allow them to recognize the root problem, and to begin to deal with the elimination of such habits while attending to a more objective lifestyle. However, if they cannot see themselves turning around, then the most vital root problem will tend to appear in their experiences repeatedly until the thinker becomes aware of such. In each case of intentional ignorance, they become subject only to the experiences which will afford to expose the root problem.

That is the way it works at school where it is obvious that, if students have not prepared for a course and fail, they have to repeat their course or semester.

We truly are in a school where human nature is the primary subject, and when our behaviour and thinking conditions are understood, we become free from the need to repeat the same experiences. As it is intended that we pass through our courses with the assistance of a trained teacher, so too is it similar for a soul who has the objective of attaining their degree in the end.

So it is, that the watching and waiting host guide supports the unaware soul through many experiences, and intervenes through moments of inspiration in the educational life while awaiting the day that the teacher is recognized. The sense of imposition that we all have within us stands to be a reminder to us of an innate sense of justice at times and serves to aid the young soul in making adjustments in behaviour to suit the universal law itself.

When we refrain from humiliating or forcing our opinion upon others, exposing the private affairs of another or acting with violence, then we have met the basic requisite for maturity as a soul and can then undertake to understand true justice thereafter. It is intended that our lessons as souls in our world demonstrate how we are to allow and accept the shortcomings of others upon themselves, while understanding the condition one has which impels them to act otherwise.

We are also intended to understand how it is that we may influence the world at large through our invention and expressions, though without causing harm to any in the doing. This is an essential requisite as it is a fact that our powers as Divine beings are not liberated until the sufficient requisite of control over these same attribute powers has been firmly established. In other words, when we can be trusted to act or express ourselves freely and with power, only then shall we find our day of liberation from the limiting spheres of our present world condition.

When we perceive ourselves to be harmless, caring, accepting and understanding individuals, we are then on the brink of discovering the greater truths of universal justice where the law stands immutable and immovable.

When we impose on others, make use of them as a means to our own ends without concern, violate their rights to prosper as souls, or prevent others from their goals intentionally through negative acts, we are giving in unconsciously to even worse habits that can cause great limitations upon ourselves. When we live by the sword of imposition we are apt to become subject to the identical hindrance and limitation in our own life.

Fortunately, most thinkers today are keenly aware of when they have gone too far, or have wronged another, and tend to hold themselves responsible for such behaviour which serves as a quick and speedy measure towards recovery, and through having made our mistakes early we are then free to understand the shortcomings of others.

It is certain that we will impose on others in youth and perhaps as adults, but the very habit of imposing without agreement stands to be the main problem and also the main requisite for entry into the spheres of existence beyond our own.

While I was living through the drama of the afterlife, I noted how through imposition many a soul has prevented the day of liberation from ignorance and at the same time I saw how only those who knew this law could come graciously to live the spontaneous moment in eternity.

II No punishment

Imagine that you are awakened to find you have passed over to the soul's kingdom and that there is one individual there who thinks you deserve to be punished for crimes against humanity. This scenario is not possible. Even if it were true, the individual is seen as being subject to negative tendencies which means an unenlightened status.

Unenlightenment is the primary cause of all forms of ignorance in the incarnate worlds. There is no punishment for unenlightenment. The individual simply returns to the world at a later date and pays the debt of further education until the negative tendencies are overcome altogether. Reform in heaven is education.

I realize that many who have suffered under the influence of the mentally ill, or unenlightened, wish for vengeance, or at least for punishment of the individual, though if they knew there was a full accounting and a restoration period decreed for the individual after their incarnate lives, and that the personality of the individual is lost thereafter in favour of the soul, it might be of some consequence.

However, there is no death as is wished for here in our

incarnate world by most for high crimes and, rather, there is a reformation period that suffices the law. Even though this may be difficult to digest for many, such is the truth and we can all be grateful that we have not had to pay the price of being unenlightened.

Being unenlightened is the most natural of perspectives regarding the resident population of our world today. Treating others as if they were unenlightened requires great understanding, tremendous patience, the acquisition of wisdom and the attainment of enlightenment by the soul itself. However, I believe that if one knew that the majority of the masses were not mentally stable as is the case of the unenlightened, then we may begin to understand how it is that we should not expect these types to be truly accountable at all. We make a severe mistake when we accuse and punish individuals today by thinking them to be sufficiently accountable and conscious of their true nature.

The man who kills out of instinct, ignorance or passion is truly unenlightened and the only recourse is to aid that individual to understand the make-up of his given nature and its shortcomings. We may incarcerate dangerous criminals though we should understand that they are not enlightened or consciously responsible for their acts and they should be treated as mental patients accordingly.

Such is the method of approach by the universe to the unenlightened of our world. We are given our existence and right to exist, though under the limitations of our sentiency while in form, and are given an education every day as to the facts of our nature. Eventually, we find ourselves on mortal parole and later our day of liberation from the imprisoning human form comes to an end, resulting in our triumph over ignorance and evil. I should state here that not all incarnate lives are here to repair or restore the past and not all are on mortal parole here; however, we are subject to the conditions of our present states of consciousness collectively.

The facts regarding the direct insights that an advanced soul has with regards the average thinker in our world today may best be understood when we consider that no one soul is ever pronounced to be consciously guilty. No soul in our world is guilty of anything they do as unenlightened thinkers, and there is never an accusation that can be identified as correct. There is no punishment of the individual who suffers human ignorance ever.

For those who serve the masses from their high spiritual status and position within the ranks of the hierarchy itself, there is never a second thought given to the matter as all souls are perceived in our world as being simply unaware as yet with regards to the truth of themselves or the universe itself. It would serve an individual thinker to understand how we are all seen as students involved in a process where misadventure, and misperception, along with delusion and fault-finding, are the common sufferings of the many.

We need not wonder how we will be seen by those who are much wiser than ourselves when our time comes to leave this world and we can complete our lives in a more objective and pleasurable way by allowing others to outgrow their ignorance naturally while knowing that the universe has already taken the matter to its ends, and every moment is filled with the merciful protective and comforting assurance of perfection.

As much as we can depend on the world appearing before our eyes in the morning to follow, surely we are perceived as guiltless souls in a very demanding process of self-realization through educational experiences in shapes and forms.

It is not easy for the average thinker to accept the fact that we are all seen as mischievous students who will ultimately mature to the day of utter triumph over ignorance ever more, even if it takes a thinker another hundred lives to do just that, as many today would prefer to judge and punish an individual for the remainder of their lives.

It is the obvious problem of our desire to accuse quickly and then punish out of ignorance, and not as a result of wisdom or law itself, that stands to be the major hurdle for humanity at present. However, even those who wish for swift justice would do well if they would only consider that justice in the universe is not aloof, and that we are all subject to this law daily. It comes down to a disagreement with the law of the universe by the unenlightened alone as many are given to believe that there is no justice beyond the determination of man alone.

While one thinker would like to see someone suffer a death sentence, it may not seem fair even to them that they are liberating a soul through such sentencing, and not effectively producing any true sense of justice outside of their own false sense of emotional satisfaction at all. I am sure that the ones who have brought death to the innocent, and even to those who seemed to be consciously responsible though unenlightened, will have nothing to suffer except the need for greater education preceding their appearance in the spiritual spheres beforehand, as their ignorance is understood likewise.

The point is that there is no gain to vengeance, no gain to murder, no gain to punishment and no gain whatsoever in believing that one is justified in the taking of life. The illusion of benefit is the main foundational problem that continues to be misinterpreted even today as the majority seek to punish anyone they believe is a sinner.

It is not an old idea that we should punish the ignorant and mistreat those who appear to be less given to moral expression, since it has been evident over the last two thousand years that some in authority, particularly in religious institutions, prefer to punish the less godly types. It is a large mistake however to pass such hypocritical information on to our children or to even subject our children to such dark doctrines of behaviour.

Who in their right mind, would ever advise the masses to accuse and quickly punish the unenlightened? Why should anyone be punished for their own beliefs? Why should anyone be punished for a mistake along the path to enlightenment? Only in the minds of men over the centuries has it been accepted and brought to our day as a social reality, that mistakes are a punishable offence to the greater mass society?

How quickly we tend to accuse and punish without ever questioning the reasoning for such misadventure. How terribly unenlightened must we be to not see that a mistake is just a mistake along the way. Only when we are imposed upon by others directly do we have the right or need to fight for our freedom and then only to regain the inherent rights to continue as the universe has decreed. Those that impose may need to be given an opportunity for greater education and perhaps incarceration, though the idea of punishment should find its way out of the consciousness of the masses as quickly as possible.

Rather, we should seek to understand what is not yet understood by those who do impose to find our solutions to such problems and there should never be the aspiration to punish. Only our untamed animal instincts call upon us all to seek vengeance or to kill, and it is this appetite for harsh justice that surfaces as the illusionary condition or drive to punish so as to repair.

We gain nothing by punishing another. There is no real benefit to anyone by believing and acting in such ways, and when the day arrives that we discover our opposing concepts regarding such issues on spiritual levels, we will see the wisdom of non-accusation of the unenlightened.

The basic fear of being punished has come to be a serious agent of illusionary self-conditioning over time, and the very behaviour of our children today who suffer this illusion produces the negative reactions of withdrawal, deception and lying, because they believe they will be punished if they tell the truth. If we told our children, and lived up to it, that they would not suffer or be punished for mistakes or for telling the truth, then perhaps they could begin to believe in a greater wisdom which does not expect so much so soon from those with little experience in living.

Thus it is in heaven where we are free of accusation and the soul of an individual is weighed in the light of what need be done to aid the individual in acquiring the requisite status for the eventual appearance upon the spiritual spheres of existence.

My experience in the afterlife has given me every evidence of this fact, and it is so that the authorities and servants to humanity in general have this shared perspective. One is seen only in the light of what need be accomplished as yet. This means that we are looked upon and it becomes evident that we have not yet completed our task and in that light a new life opportunity rises where certain conditions are brought about to aid the advancing soul in attaining such.

We are involved in a process where it can be known that our true judges seek only to aid and to assist us in actually attaining our triumphant release from the world of suffering and ignorance. They are all on our side. They never see us through opinionated lenses. We are free to regain ourselves. Naught prevents anyone from the attainment of the ages. We are all intended to be aided until the last moment of attainment.

The perception of the authorities that reside above the workers and servants of the hierarchy itself is that humanity has to attain such a degree by a certain time and all that the workers and servants need to make certain of is that this outcome does manifest. The highest authority in our local system continually focuses upon the outcome in which we are all together in unison, having passed through the day of illumination. There is never a moment where any members of our humanity are perceived as guilty of anything.

It is more apparent that the view from on high is that the masses are not yet conscious of their true nature and that the eventual expansion of consciousness that will aid them in the future is now being acted upon. Once again, there has never been a moment where anyone who has lived within our world is perceived as unworthy.

III   No hell

Only in the churches and institutions of this world, and only in the minds of men, has there ever been an event or judgement that one need fear in advance. The false creation of hell and the similar negative influences of accusation and punishment are man-made only. One need seek the kingdom of liberation and of truth and beauty within themselves first if only to prove that the advice of such institutions is without merit at best.

In some thinkers' minds we are perceived as humans who must do the will of God or suffer eternal death in hell. This makes their god a less perfected being who presupposed we should be born in ignorance and serve blindly or else suffer forever! I truly believe that such ideas may have worked well when the uneducated masses tended to do the will of those who stood in front of them with arms bared, claiming to know the will of God.

Today, however, we have no threat of punishment, banishment or of eternal death, and our free access to education allows for us all to overcome the social mores of the past, and to reinvent the objective future without hesitation.

Some of the other perceptions of the universe in regard to humanity at present can be considered for digestion when thinkers have begun to weigh their lot in life. When they wonder what their life has added up to, they need only seek to understand their own answers to themselves.

What is often overlooked is the actual effect that their seemingly elusive sense of conscience plays out in their lifetime of thinking. When asking ourselves what we have added up to thus far in life, we may notice that the assessment is determined by the amount of peace we have with our former experiences, how much regret remains which supports the view that unfinished matters of work need be done, and how much true determination there actually is within us at that moment which will determine the overall issue.

In the end, we may sense that we have done reasonably well in spite of some few regrets and feelings of guilt that remain though we may also infer that we truly need to become more ambitious in our life if we are to feel completely satisfied with ourselves overall. Or we may find that we are greatly satisfied that we have lived up to all the guiding of our conscience and have no problems while feeling completely satisfied with ourselves.

In either or more cases, the point I am attempting to bring to light here is that we can depend upon a source of innate wisdom that answers our every question regarding ourselves at lightning speeds, and without error. It is our conscience that best serves to guide us through our lives though few recognize the portal of wisdom from which we derive such wisdom with such perfect accuracy.

Conscience: the Great Guide

We need only look to our conscience to see that we do indeed have the semblance of a perfected guide and, when studied at length through meditation, we can discern for ourselves that it is through this particular supersensible faculty that our guide does speak with inspiration at the speed of light itself.

When we finally arrive on our journey as souls into the unknown and unsuspected world of light, one of the first lessons will be that of the elusive sense of conscience and how our guides have always worked though this medium to communicate with us effectively without being personally involved. A perfect impersonal source of light wisdom comes to be known in the afterlife as the earlier sense of conscience, and it is through the continued status of this Divine attribute for justice itself that the views and per-spectives of the most advanced are unveiled.

Perhaps you need to confirm what has been stated thus far for yourself by enquiring of your own innate sense of conscience whether such statements are true or not. Ask yourself if what you believe you have added up to today can suffice to cause you to feel you are on the path of decency or not. If not, then ask yourself what you must do to become more decent as an individual soul in the process of evolu-tion that you are involved in presently. Our conscience is the best source of advice and if anyone outside yourself were to advise you, they might suggest that you seek advice from your conscience as the better source.

When you think about your conscience, you may not realize that it is the only unchanging aspect of your life. It has never been less wise, or more wise. It has always been a perfect interpreter. It has never steered anyone wrong. It is like God himself - they are very similar if not identical. To consider the differences between one's conscience and their own idea of God would be a good exercise, if only to verify the simple fact that one part of our life has never changed. There is that something very special and wise that we can depend on in the worst and best of times for guidance that always points to the truth itself when applied correctly.

When I speak of the initiation in the spiritual spheres which are above the kingdom of the souls, I refer to the illuminative light of these principal beings, which in effect is the quiet sense of conscience in our incarnate lives. This light of truth is our evolved consciousness, in all its brilliance and capacity for rapport with the host of hosts within our manifest universe of intelligent lives.

Even in the world beyond human limitation, our innate sense of conscience serves as a medium for rapport and advice between the most wise and ourselves and in that light, our perceptions of peoples, beings and events is brought to life. Our perceptions are the perceptions of the universe itself. The unenlightenment of the masses is just another stage in the overall drama of the evolving consciousness of the masses themselves. Enlightenment is our perceived goal and through the basic challenges of our intellect and spirit, we are ever moving towards greater understanding of each other.

Our friends in this life are our brothers and sisters in eternity to come, and our enemies of today may well be the guides of our future tomorrow. Regardless of how anyone treats you today, it is not impossible to realize that they will see you as a master in the making before too long. Regardless of how anyone perceives you, whether great or terrible, such views are of no account as only the view that the universe has of you counts. You are all masters in the making whether you know it or not. If that statement serves to aid the individual in building a reasonable perspective that tends to prove itself true over and over again, then it was worth making.

Our adventure though time and space is up to us. The events and experiences that take place are brought about by ourselves to a large degree and so it is that we have been given the very mysterious and miraculous gift of life itself, and now we need only make it worth our living.

You Are the Silent Presence behind Your Thoughts

From a distance, it appears that we are free to choose our way according to our basic passions and whims, which in time prove to become greater determinations. It is also evident that nothing can stop us but ourselves, and then only temporarily until we become wiser. It is further evident that the present generation has succeed in attaining the highest possible stage of development as thinkers, and that an expansion of consciousness on a worldwide level is about to take place.

In the very near future, we will all be subject to our own misgivings and we will inevitably change and turn towards the future with humanity in mind. We are gradually ridding ourselves of our older ancient animal instincts and, without these, so too will our emotional life become more realized, which will allow for a speeding up of our recovery and restoration into the light itself.

What has passed is generally taken for granted though billions of years of time and space experience have brought us to this very day, and when our true capacity to embrace the beauty and perfection of our evolving lives comes to the fore, so too will the many minds be relieved of the illusions, fears and uncertainties of the past altogether.

We are all masters in the making and there are many more billions of years of time and space to go before the ultimate closure of time and space occurs, so there is naught to worry or fret about excepting the salvaging of one's soul on this very day.

When we begin to experience understanding, we will then pass into another phase of development where we will come to understand experience itself. Upon that day, we will be free to live our lives as eternal entities, and our future will be that of our best hopes and dreams.

From a distance, you are seen as a soul that inhabits a purely computative vehicle of impression, meaning that your entire body is lent to you to identify the impressions of your environment, and that you are the one behind the senses or scenes in themselves. Your guide looks upon you as the consciousness on the mental plane of your entire body. Your body, at least to your guide, is merely a highly sophisticated computer that processes information through itself to you. When you close your eyes to the outer world, you are the one inside that listens and learns and then when you open your eyes you should see yourself as merely looking outside through the lenses of your human eyes.

It is more the fact that you are the silent presence behind your thoughts, mental activities, speech, and conduct. It is a truly silent self that need not persist in self-talk all day long, and you need not also use your visual mind unless you want to as well.

By quietly meditating on the real you behind the impressions and sensory data, it is possible that you will find yourself to be formless and that your presence is merely limited by your adherence to the activities of your body and its mechanisms. When your body is calmed, and your self-talk reduced to the concentrated effort of quieting the visions in the mind itself, then it is possible to see that you are within your brain hemisphere looking in and out.

One need not wait until release from form to discover the nature of the presence in you, and to realize that you are not the body but rather the intelligence using the body itself. This requires a necessary ambition and willingness to persevere in the method mentioned, until success has been had, though such is highly possible and can prove sufficiently that we are all souls.

As incarnate beings, we can begin to see ourselves as do the liberated souls of our world as the silent presence behind the scene, and perhaps it can be understood later that we truly are the continuing moment of silence and of action as are all Divine beings in or out of form expression. Our body is much like an astronaut's apparel and serves to aid us in contacting the denser impressions of matter in the universe.

Once taken off, our physiological sensory equipment works better and then later when the physical body is departed, our sensory equipment which is firmly established in our innate nature will continue to feel, contact and interpret less dense impressions of a higher order. Whichever way we see ourselves, the kingdom of advancing souls perceives us as light intelligence that is experimenting with shapes and forms to gather new information on our invisible nature.

One part of our soul's nature is absolutely silent and

remains silent forever. This would be called our central consciousness.

You are also the very feeling of life itself, so say the servants of humanity. In other words, you could quiet our feeling nature and realize that you can feel your whole life experience at once and then you can feel any other truth that you tend to single out or mingle with other feelings.

However, your first feeling is the originating sound of the universe itself and all other sounds and feelings produce a symphony of notes and scales. When you are silenced, you can feel your true rhythm unhampered by thought and feeling alone, and through meditation each and every other feeling can be named or identified. Only your host feeling is purest though few have silenced themselves enough to see the truth of what I am now suggesting.

You are the silent, intelligent, insightful, invisible presence of Divinity and you need only act accordingly to verify this respectfully as a fact.

Your goal as a soul was to feel stable and objective all the time while you experienced other feelings and other impressions, which were designed to act upon your attribute nature to entice you to look, see, understand and to know your hidden nature so that you could deal with being supremely silent in gracious glory as you live through the billions of manifest generations to come.

Your soul is the sound of grace, and the other feelings are merely illusory effects from life that you have not yet understood. You are the silence and the calm and so it is that when your breath is calm, so too is your mind, and heart. Your sight is the essence of the invisible truth, meaning that what you see in your mind today merely represents a greater truth and on the day you depart from this world, your sight will be your expressed realization.

All that you see then is the truth itself. Sight is how you come to know your consciousness. You have the ability to see your invisibility, to know the untouchable, and to perceive in vision that which you call existence. The more feelings one gains through experience in forms and shapes, the more sight and knowing that follows. The mind of the soul rests and sight alone takes up the former characteristics of mind when out of body. It is your advancing consciousness that draws all of the supersensible instruments and experiences together and eventuates the condition of consciousness called soul consciousness after death of the body and the unified experiences become a knowing and a sight of eternity itself.

Your spirit which gives life to your soul, is the final goal for all souls that transcend form, and when the day comes that the soul has mastered its sentient qualities and genius, the unified spirit is liberated from the world of impression altogether. You are the formless supreme light of eternity itself in the end though your present condition is governed by your ability to understand the basics of your overall nature.

Hence, the universe perceives us all as true offspring that are gradually returning to our birthing sphere at which time we will come to experience our lives as members of one or more dynastic families.

It is only because of free will that a soul can ignore itself or entertain itself, with whatever seems amusing until the day that the soul runs into itself altogether.

Every unwitting soul can create a dimness about itself, or a cloud of despair and uncertainty, a body of fright, a temperament of illness, a countenance of anger, a feeling of aloneness. The soul is a very highly creative sentient being that has the power to create moods, change temperament, reduce itself, enlarge itself, expand or become fixated.

More often it is what is unconsciously believed that produces these effects upon self and others, though it is also possible for the soul effectively to comfort and heal another being.

The soul can manifest its invention if one chooses to learn to concentrate, and the soul can also manifest form through speech and breath so as to share the vision of its own gains. There are few limitations upon the soul and most of the attributes and abilities of the soul can come to the surface for those who deliberately choose to study their own innate nature.

Through the hidden strength of inner silence, we can liberate ourselves from every shortcoming and protect ourselves from all harm, though it should be remembered that we are all imperishable and so there is no true justification, other than being subject to illusion, that anything can be lost.

You are the truth itself, regardless of how much you choose to downgrade yourself at times, and your word need only be true to make your speech true and your consciousness free.

Invocation

You also have the ability to invoke and command certain spiritual authorities in your life though it is best first to decide on the lifestyle you wish to live for the remaining years ahead.

You can declare yourself aloud by giving a true testament of yourself aloud to discover this truth. If you do, say no one thing that is not true about yourself and your life thus far - admit all, and go on at length to explain what you believe to be your present lot in life, while remaining fully receptive to your own sense of conscience in every word.

In the end, you might suggest that if you had some prior

notice or assistance in understanding the accusational nature of and within humanity overall, you feel you could gain some direct experience that may help to motivate you further.

I realize that many think of prayer as the same thing as an invocation. However, I believe that it is not necessary to denounce yourself, and that by accepting the fact that you have yet to attain an enlightened consciousness, you should be acceptable as I have so many times suggested.

Believe in yourself. It is true that you have no reason other than illusion to believe that you are truly accountable and in this way you may begin to silence the voices of accusation within yourself that only tend to create limitation.

Invocation is an act of self declaration, where one attempts to put their entire life into perspective and calls upon their host guides to assist in establishing a foundation by which one can discover and pass on to the greater path as so many have already done. Prayer as it is understood by most is a plea to the universe for intervention and it is often felt that one cannot do anything on their own as they have no true relationship with deity. Don't let yourself believe you need attend services or join a group to discover the innate truth of all that you enquire.

As suggested earlier, it is in our best interests to realize that we have a conscious life and a thought life. The thought life is usually the acceptable perception one has of oneself when thinking of one's nature; however, the conscious life is the silent self that lies behind all impressions and sounds.

We are perceived as not being able to identify our true nature today mostly due to our inability or disinterestedness towards silencing the many voices within. When we invoke the aid of the pure presence within our life and begin to silence our self-talk, the steps towards attainment come into view for the first time in our life, and it might help to understand here that when we choose to make this our last life, the work of realizing our nature becomes seriously sped up.

There is no time for illusion once the first moments of evidentiary inspiration have occurred, and the many expansions of consciousness each provide greater evidence until that final day when the sound of the soul and spirit uniting is heard throughout the entire conscious sphere within each of us.

The Gifts of the Universe

It is also true that we are perceived as able to forecast our own future by design. In other words, we are all capable of looking into the future a bit and seeing how we could be if we were to eliminate certain habits that prevent us from concentrating upon self-discovery of our nature. We can likewise quietly take an impression of someone we know and when we raise this picture into our mind and hold it still, we can begin to enquire as to the habits and conduct nature of such individuals. We also have the ability to see what is in the best interest of others through concentrated efforts as well.

It is further possible to assimilate and emulate the actual presence of another thinker or being and from this we can interpret each other most clearly. This is one of our abilities that seems to be ignored at best. Most of what we do automatically is taken for granted like seeing, touching, feeling, hearing, tasting and knowing, yet with a little investigation upon these stated practices, we can expand our potential abilities quite affordably and enable ourselves to capture the soul's ability to do so with great speed and efficiency as well as accuracy.

It is not so difficult to become someone else, or some-one else's experience for a time in meditative practice until the day comes when we can see through the person in front of us clearly, while understanding all of their apparent shortcomings and being able thereafter to provide specific information as to how they can liberate themselves from such limitations.

One of the greatest gifts and abilities of the soul that we can raise to the surface in our lifetime, and which has been coming to the surface for several centuries now, is the abil-ity to identify anyone in the first moments. It is our visa through alien worlds that comes to be a conscious skill whereby we can determine the truth of anyone more or less advantaged than ourselves.

How we are able to understand so easily in the afterlife is due to this primary recognition skill. One need only con-sider the ability they already have to determine what is true or false about the ones they meet daily. Our ability express-ly to experience another being's experience is one of the attributes of the One Great Life in our universe. In fact, all the skills and attributes of the soul and spirit are the true abilities of the universe itself which we are only now begin-ning to sense ever so dimly.

On the day that the connections between our outer body and our soul begins to unravel, we find that only the skills of the soul remain along with our own environmental impressions gained throughout our life. Then we pass into the very environment of what we know. We appear as small as an atom or as large as a planet, and an electric blue in colour. We are met then and in that moment we begin to bring about the automatic response of our impression of self and that is the first time that we appear in form when confronted directly.

Our impression then is what we felt we appeared as when in the body and, much later, we take on the hue of the environment surrounding ourselves until we breach the visual sphere and awaken to a renewed outer world of light. Then what we imagine will go on until we realize that we are a conscious being that lives on a conscious sphere of existence. Then we will gain our freedom from the habit of depending on a surface or a planet beneath our steps.

Then we will see all that we have ever understood to be true prior to our birth in our world, and will take on the unfinished impressions remaining in our consciousness of our last incarnation. Then our collective nature will appear as we truly are in a living expression that serves to indicate to all others the mystery of ourselves. Then we will see that worrying today is not going to change our nature in any way.

Once we begin to see that our actions and presence in this world that we live in today are connected to the future, it may dawn on many that there is no point in much that we do regarding the future itself. You may try to imagine yourself looking back at today though from a distance of about 2000 years. Would you be glad you read this book when you did? Would the argument you had last week have made a difference 2000 years from now? If not, then why be argumentative today?

Knowing that we will be alive well beyond our bodies have been separated, it becomes easier to realize the long-term ramifications of much of what we do today. In other words, I see no point in getting upset and arguing with anyone today, or of pretending or assuming false states of character or hiding what I believe to be true or of denying myself.

Getting used to the fact that we are eternal is perceived

by our host guides as the next major step in our evolution. What we learn then is how we could have lived while in incarnate form long ago if we had only sought to understand that we can discover the ultimate truth within ourselves through simply applying ourselves to the task today.

Become objective, become gracious. Learn these words well and apply them to your day as you discover more the evidence that you are truly objective and gracious beyond all that you have ever presumed. Seek out the manner in which you can see the world most objectively and never lose the sense of graciousness that is the foundational rhythm of every soul in our present world.

Try to understand that in the state of graciousness and objectivity there are no mistakes, no errors, no imperfection and all is accepted. In any other conditioned state or mood it should also become evident that the less objective are the less enlightened. Enlightenment comes by knowing the objective truth and seeing the less objective life lived beforehand. That is our evidence of one another and it is enough to say that cannot be denied upon inspection. Do something nice for others, and try to be good-natured most of your days and when the time comes, you will be glad that there is little to resolve and that the time spent in the after-life can be shortened.

Just be the decent individual that you truly are at the root of yourself, and become curious as to your inner nature. Again, you need to feel graciously objective to do even these small things. No other state or condition or thought-out impression will suffice other than the truly gracious personality of the soul. Stop attacking yourself and accusing yourself, and turn into your own accusation if it persists and fight the good fight. There is nothing you can accuse yourself of that can stand to be proven as a fact. We are all considered to be decent in the eyes of God, whether one wants to accept this notion or not. Objectively speaking, learn to see the world in the light of magnificence. Do what needs be done to discover all things anew.

Review every conclusion. Observe objects and discover the objective beauty of illimitable lives right before our eyes. See the living sea of life in which we live and move and have our being. Capture the essence of the objective truth that we are all being moved to the greater objective and revelation of pure objectivity. Put your every hour of thought to the objective test. What can there possibly be before your very eyes that is not more than you have already thought? The greatest gift aside from existence itself for me has been the direct sight into the shape, form, thing, and being that I have sensed, or made contact with. By keeping an objective eye, I have met the demand of the soul for pure objective sight. By keeping my heart and soul in the light of the rhythm called graciousness, I have been given the touch of the truth that proves and verifies and aids.

Turn your eye on the objective truth behind every seeming situation and there you will find the light of eternity in every case. It was through many years of maintaining my own spiritual rhythm that I was able to discover the word state that brings about illumination to the soul of a thinker. The gift of grace from our universe is poured out upon those who simply seem most interested in viewing things in a more objective light to begin with. It is with the eyes of objectivity that we are preserved from the cycle of rebirth and the afterlife is known for the wonder and magnificence it is.

Another great gift of the universe is the ability to create environments. It is following our enlightenment that we learn to create environments as such is the main function of our future quest as individualized beings. Our objective environment here on earth is the intended heaven on earth certainly, though it is already true that objectivity and enlightenment persist endlessly everywhere and it is more the fact that we use our enlightenment in the way we do as human thinkers that makes it so difficult to comprehend the facts. The gift of sight to see that we are creators of our will through the objective methodology has ever been the path of humanity.

For the Children

Just the experience of being a father and knowing with certainty what life has in mind for us all has allowed me to immerse myself totally into my son' life and to see what few parents have seen before.

Certainly, there have been billions of loving parents over the millennia and respectfully, there have been many who were bound to their own uncertainties who could not identify the varied needs and potentials of their own children. However, I must say that in all that I have come to experience and know, I continue to feel somewhat apprehensive and concerned for the children of our present generations.

Each day that I awaken to the circumstances of our world's choices, and while keeping my son in mind, I am unable to overcome the affliction as a result of seeing so many children mistreated, neglected, ignored, abused and defiled. At this date, there are approximately 35,000 children dying of starvation, abuse and murder every day! Four out of five children born today will face circumstances that may have long-term negative effects upon their consciousness before they are five years old.

It seems to me that the true humanity that I know to be

at the root of every heart in incarnation, remains somewhat dull and separative. Where are the true humanitarians? Certainly there are millions in the world today and they have done much to aid in the comforting and healing of the nations over time, though there are not enough yet to prevent the abuses and starvation of so many every day.

I am at times perplexed, even though I can see the solution and have evidence to suggest that this too will pass shortly in the next two generations. However, I am useless to say the least in my ability to reach out further than I already have to save even just one more child today.

There is no greater affliction in the heavens than at those moments when a child is suffering unnecessarily. Even though such children gain the lasting promise of survival in the spiritual spheres and worlds hereafter, they are still robbed of a lifetime of genuine invention and circumstance, where it could be their turn to salvage humanity through humanitarian measures and gestures.

The education of the parents of our world stands today to be the most immediate remedy to much of the needless abuse and harm that children suffer throughout childhood, though the education of the adult parent must not be depended upon solely.

I believe that if we are best to serve humanity and were to target the greatest problems apparent in our world today, the first choice would be to focus upon the education of the child at hand. I would further suggest that the education that would empower the family of the future where ignorance and abuse were eventually brought to an end would have to be wider and more precise than ever attempted in any other generation.

A new education that would provide direct insights into the instruments of perception, such as our senses and our working creative mind, along with instinctive/physical development programmes in early childhood, would go a long way to salvage our future generations, though this would require that a greater understanding of our sentient nature be developed and taught properly. It would have to be a new psychology and a new school of human preparedness as sentient beings.

Going further, I would say that over the last twenty years of being able to commune with my own spiritual hosts, and being able at will to leave my own body for long durations each night, I have found that the certain remedy for humanity in general, other than direct education, would begin with an immediate agreement between world leaders. If through the United Nations, they were to gather together to work out the problems facing our humanity in the new millennium, they might find that a great power rests in their hands that has been generally disregarded in the past.

It is possible that a few leaders, including the present superpowers, could agree to sign a new world agreement where it could be understood globally that an effort was being considered which would bring an end to the tyrannical past and an end to human rights abuses of the future. Would it be so difficult to ask every world leader to refrain from killing, abusing, deceiving and threatening their neighbours around the world? Is it possible that an agreement could be signed where on occasion, if an elected official were to be exposed with evidence, of being a killer, or of having supported the killing and murder of that nations citizens, they be ousted from power?

I think it practical and intelligent that if all the world's leaders were to sign such an agreement, and upon evidentiary conclusions they be ousted from office never to be allowed to run for office again, we will have begun to pluck the remaining elements of evil as an example from our lives forever.

If every leader of the world were forced to step down because of such high crimes against society and even against just one individual, how much more rapidly the world community would arrive at the greatest moment of triumph in history thus far. It would only take a single vote from those members presently occupying official seats within the United Nations as member states. I can imagine what it might be like for the world to awaken tomorrow to find that evil has been plucked from the forefront of our future at leadership levels worldwide.

So many times in the past I have given my every moment to confront the issues facing the children of our generation and humanity at large, and only now have I begun to understand how very possible it would be for us all, if we only made a pledge to make all of our present goals and successes over the next century to support the education of our youth.

As for my son Michael, I have found that since I chose to make his life the most important issue and premise for all that I should ever bring about in the remainder of my own lifetime, my own life has become full. On occasion I have made it a point to remind others that when we strive with all our might to manifest a proper foundation for our future generations, our present workload will no longer be considered a burden but rather a generous and vitally fulfilling lifestyle.

In cases where a single individual has given themselves to become wealthy and successful, though without a vision of what they will do with their gains, much failure has manifested for the majority of these. In those cases where an individual decides that all of their efforts will go to enhance the life of the next generation or of some one humanitarian organization, I have noted great success to the majority.

The difference is in psychology and in meeting the demands of our own innate sense of humanity. Those who work to further the gains of the next generation often have less stress about them and live more fulfilling lives since they are privileged to see their efforts begin to manifest within their own lifetime, and there is less the selfish aspect of the personality at work. Where there is no goal other than the self it is a rare thing that we find a successful and satisfied individual over the long run. It has always been evident to me that the more selfless one is about their gains, the more they are given to attain such outcomes, while the more selfish the intent, the harder the struggle and the rarer the success.

In short, our personal fulfilment comes by furnishing ourselves with the basic skills to further the generations yet to come, as can easily be identified through the efforts of those who first thought to bring about the constitution of the United States. Those parents who consider the future needs of their own grandchildren often find themselves living a very fruitful life while those who ignore the needs of their own children in the future will find themselves less satisfied with themselves.

I believe that it is within us all to reach inwards, to the very root of ourselves where our soul can be discovered and our Divinity aroused and upon which we can endeavour to transform the environment and the world we live in by giving our all to the children of the future.

In my earliest days of seminars, workshops and lectures, I trembled each time I went on stage, though it was the conviction of the truth within that held me up at my weakest moments and allowed me to pursue my first goal. From the moment I walked away from the hospital in deep financial despair and ill health, with only the thought of the children of the next generations upon my mind, I have managed to be aided and assisted in bringing about the present health spa and home that will one day be a school for therapists.

With that in mind, and continuing to desire even more for the humanitarians yet to come into the world, I am sure my son Michael will continue to glean wisdom enough to satisfy his days ahead.

I have often been questioned as to how I manage to keep up with all that we do and how we deal with the stress of it all, and my answer is always the truth. I have no stress when thinking of my present efforts as I see myself as an employee of those who have not yet arrived.

Though I do enjoy the grounds and home that I am living in temporarily, I do my best to keep it in good repair. I have no problem dealing with those matters that take up most of my day as the more it makes sense to others, the less hardship for those in the future. I feel that I have been surely blessed with a new voice to speak my mind and with which to live my life. I do not worry about money and if I find myself without food or shelter one day by remaining true to myself, then I shall be satisfied that my time has come.

These statements are not merely the results of positive thinking, or even of objective calculation. They are simply the truest answers I can give as I think in this way most naturally now. I have never been so satisfied as to feel responsible to those less advantaged than myself. I feel the same way about my son as I know that our future will merge and he will one day stand in the light and verify what I have come to see. When he sees that we are all true and that we need only live up to continuing to be true to ourselves, we will know a common condition and lifestyle that I am attempting to prepare him for today.

It was the testing and transitional opportunities of the last twenty years and having gained insight into the afterlife that has prepared me for the task of being as mature a father as I can be. For these experiences I am most grateful as I feel that for the first time I actually know how to love my son as a father.

I have spent many a day and hours daily over the last twenty years in an attempt to attain the greatest possible exposure and communion with the originating Divine parents of our Universe, and I have not been disappointed.

About the Author

Mr. Marentette is the founder and manager of
The Grail Springs Spa Resort, located in Bancroft, Ontario,
Canada. Along with his duties at the spa as a healer, consult-
ant, therapist and analyst, Wayne also does personal sessions,
workshops, seminars and lectures. He has also
produced over 2,000 hours of educational material
that is available to the public in
audio/video format.

Wayne can be emailed at: waynem@grailsprings.com
Visit www.grailsprings.com & www.4daysineternity.com